The Scientific Background to Modern Philosophy

Selected Readings

Second Edition

The Scientific Background to Modern Philosophy

Selected Readings

SECOND EDITION

Edited by
Michael R. Matthews

Hackett Publishing Company, Inc.
Indianapolis/Cambridge

For further information, please address
       Hackett Publishing Company, Inc.
       P.O. Box 44937
       Indianapolis, Indiana 46244-0937

       www.hackettpublishing.com

Composition by Aptara, Inc.

Library of Congress Control Number: 2022938401

ISBN-13: 978-1-64792-086-9 (pbk.)
ISBN-13: 978-1-64792-087-6 (PDF ebook)

The paper used in this publication meets the minimum requirements of American National Standard for Information Sciences—Permanence of Paper for Printed Library Materials, ANSI Z39.48–1984.

∞

CONTENTS

ACKNOWLEDGMENTS

The first edition of this anthology (1989) was compiled in response to an invitation by Jay Hullett, formerly in the philosophy department at Boston University and then publisher, now chair, of Hackett Publishing Company. Pleasingly over its thirty-year lifespan it has been well received and well used.

This second expanded and revised edition has been a response to the invitation of Deborah Wilkes, publisher of Hackett Publishing Company. The first edition took the dialogue of science and philosophy from Aristotle through to Newton. This edition adds eight chapters, taking the dialogue through the Enlightenment and up to Darwin. The conversation of science and philosophy continued in the works of Faraday, Maxwell, Mach, Planck, Einstein, Bohr, Heisenberg, Eddington, Jeans, and others, all of whose work bore upon the development of modern ontology, epistemology, and ethics. Can any of these fields even be thought about without reference to science?

The interconnection of science and philosophy has been a central part of my intellectual and career trajectory: science degree, science teaching, and degrees in philosophy, psychology, and in history and philosophy of science. Then several decades of research and writing in the domain of "History, Philosophy and Science Teaching" (Matthews 2021). I have had the great good fortune to have known and been taught by scholars who embodied the ideal of philosophy informed by science: Wallis Suchting (1931–1997), Marx Wartofsky (1928–1997), Abner Shimony (1928–2015), Michael Martin (1932–2015), Robert Cohen (1923–2017), and Mario Bunge (1919–2020).[1] Through thirty-five years of engagement with the International History, Philosophy and Science Teaching Group, and twenty-five years editorship of the Springer journal *Science & Education*, I had the good fortune to learn from many fine scholars who have productively brought together science, philosophy, and education.

The chapter introductions have benefitted considerably from the diligent and professional copyediting of two friends: Paul McColl, a retired physics teacher, and Michael Howard, a retired lecturer in political and social studies; and from the careful eye of Campbell Disbrow, the Hackett editor who astutely copyedited and provided valuable suggestions for the introductions.

---

1. Obituaries for Suchting, Shimony, Martin, Cohen, and Bunge can be read at: http://www.hpsst .com/obituary.html.

SOURCES

COPERNICUS   *The Commentariolus*; Dedication from *On the Revolutions of the Heavenly Spheres*. In *Three Copernican Treatises*, edited by Edward Rosen, 2nd ed. New York: Dover Publications, 1959.

BACON   *The New Organon*. In *Selected Philosophical Works*, edited by Rose-Mary Sargent. Indianapolis: Hackett Publishing Company, 1999.

GALILEO   *The Assayer*; *Dialogues Concerning the Two New Sciences*. In *The Essential Galileo*, edited and translated by Maurice A. Finocchiaro. Indianapolis: Hackett Publishing Company, 2008.

Dialogues Concerning the Two Chief World Systems. In *Galileo on the World Systems: A New Abridged Translation and Guide*, edited and translated by Maurice A. Finocchiaro. Berkeley: University of California Press, 1997.

Galileo's Inquisition's Sentence; *Galileo's Abjuration*. In *The Galileo Affair: A Documentary History*, edited and translated by Maurice A. Finocchiaro. Berkeley: University of California Press, 1989.

DESCARTES   *Discourse on Method*. In *Discourse on Method; Meditations on First Philosophy*, translated by Donald A. Cress, 4th ed. Indianapolis: Hackett Publishing Company, 1998.

Principles of Philosophy. In *Philosophical Essays and Correspondence*, edited by Roger Ariew. Indianapolis: Hackett Publishing Company, 2000.

BOYLE   *Of the Excellency and Grounds of the Corpuscular or Mechanical Philosophy*. In *Modern Philosophy: An Anthology of Primary Sources*, edited by Roger Ariew and Eric Watkins, 3rd ed. Indianapolis: Hackett Publishing Company, 2019.

HUYGENS   *Treatise on Light*. In *The Wave Theory of Light*, edited by Henry Crew. New York: American Book Company, 1900.

NEWTON   "Scholium" and "General Scholium," from *Principia*; "Query 31," from *Opticks*. In *Modern Philosophy: An Anthology of Primary Sources*, edited by Roger Ariew and Eric Watkins, 3rd ed. Indianapolis: Hackett Publishing Company, 2019.

D'ALEMBERT   *Preliminary Discourse to the* Encyclopédie *of Diderot*. Translated and edited by Richard N. Schwab. Chicago: University of Chicago Press, 1963.

DIDEROT   "Rationale for the *Encyclopédie*." In *Rameau's Nephew and Other Works*, translated by Jacques Barzun and Ralph H. Bowen. Indianapolis: Hackett Publishing Company, 2001.

DU CHÂTELET Preface to *Fundamentals of Physics*. In *Selected Philosophical and Scientific Writings*, edited and translated by Judith Zinsser. Chicago: University of Chicago Press, 2009.

"Hypothesis." In *Denis Diderot's* The Encyclopedia, *Selections*, edited by Stephen J. Gendzier. New York: Harper & Row, 1967.

ROUSSEAU "Letter to Voltaire on Optimism." In *Candide and Related Texts*, by Voltaire. Translated by David Wootton. Indianapolis: Hackett Publishing Company, 2000.

PRIESTLEY "Restoration of Air" from *Philosophical Transactions of the Royal Society*, 1772. With thanks to The Royal Society.

KANT *Metaphysical Foundations of Natural Science*. In *Philosophy of Material Nature*, translated by James W. Ellington. Indianapolis: Hackett Publishing Company, 1985.

What Is Enlightenment? In *Enlightenment Thought: An Anthology of Sources*, Margaret L. King. Indianapolis: Hackett Publishing Company, 2019.

LINNAEUS Introduction to *System of Nature*. In *Enlightenment Thought: An Anthology of Sources*, translated and edited by Margaret L. King. Indianapolis: Hackett Publishing Company, 2019.

"Observations on the Three Kingdoms of Nature." In *System of Nature*, translated by M.S.J. Engel-Ledeboer and H. Engel. 't Goy-Houten Utrecht, Netherlands: HES & De Graaf Publishers, 1964.

PALEY *Natural Theology*. In *God*, edited by Timothy A. Robinson. Indianapolis: Hackett Publishing Company, 2003.

DARWIN *The Origin of Species*; *Descent of Man*. In *On Evolution*, edited by Thomas F. Glick and David Kohn. Indianapolis: Hackett Publishing Company, 1996.

I thank the copyright holders listed above for permission to reproduce the materials in this collection.

INTRODUCTION

The history of philosophy and the history of science (or "natural philosophy" as it was known through to the mid-nineteenth century) are inexorably linked: they cannot be understood apart,[1] nor should they be taught or learned apart.[2] Their mutual impact goes back to the Athenian cradle of Western philosophy. The "science" (natural philosophy) of the classical and Hellenic materialists and atomists—Thales, Anaximander, Leucippus, Democritus, Epicurus, Anaxagoras, and others—was in constant struggle with the dualist, teleological, purposeful worldviews of Plato and Aristotle. The latter camp won, while for nearly two thousand years, the former was labeled the "pre-Socratics" and treated as the "rocky path" to the Athenian philosophical highway. Their achievements have received some small and belated recognition.

In one such reappraisal, a historian of Greek philosophy wrote:

> In their atomism, their theory of motion, their distinction between primary and secondary qualities, and most of all, in their insistence that explanation of natural processes shall be mechanical, the atomists anticipated much in the world view of modern science. (Allen 1966, 15)

For example, an early explanation of thunder held that it was emanations of heavenly Gods or spirits, but Anaximander's explanation was that the noise was produced by wind particles rubbing together. This well represents the division between materialist (or naturalist) explanatory systems and prescientific ones.

It must be remembered that the materialist program was hard to reconcile with people's observations of animal life and human experience. Whatever the strengths of the ancient (and modern) materialist program, the system and categories of Aristotle seemed much more appropriate and satisfying than the austere, "lifeless" program promoted by the materialists and atomists. Mortimer Adler, with good reason, called Aristotle "the philosopher of common sense" (Adler 1978).

There can be no adequate understanding of early modern philosophy and of the New Science of Galileo, Newton, and others featured in this collection without some comprehension of Aristotle's worldview, against which the new seventeenth-century worldview was forged. Central to all of Aristotle's thought is his essentialist, teleological concept of nature. Nature was not just matter moving as a result of random pushes

---

1. Some well-known scholars who have shunned building disciplinary silos are: Pierre Duhem (Ariew and Barker 1996), Alexandre Koyré (1968), Alistair Crombie (1994), and Maurice Clavelin (1974).
2. See Matthews (2015).

and pulls (ancient materialism), nor was it an unintelligible and imperfect shadow of some other perfect realm (Platonism). Aristotelian nature was differentiated into various species and objects, all of which had their own internal and essential dynamic for change, including growth and local motion. In contrast to unnatural or violent change, natural change was the progressive, teleological actualization of a preexisting potential, or "form," as it was known.

Everything in Aristotle's world, including, notably, human beings, had its own internal, preordained purpose or natural end and fulfillment. For example, the acorn, in natural circumstances, would develop through an internally generated process of change into an oak tree, not a gum tree. Science was primarily concerned with understanding these natural changes, rather than violent or accidental changes, as those did not reveal anything about an object's nature. What was the point of studying "accidental" features or incidents?

Aristotle was a great naturalist and observer; about a quarter of his extant work is devoted to investigations of the animal kingdom. He also wrote the first comprehensive treatise on scientific methodology, his *Posterior Analytics*. This work set the agenda for two thousand years of discussion in philosophy of science and framed a good deal of the discussion for the past five hundred years. Aristotle's book deals with what it is to explain something, the place of perception and observation in evaluating truth claims, and whether certainty and absolute truth are attainable in claims about the world (in science).

For Karl Popper, and many others, the Scientific Revolution was a "return to the past," a re-capturing of materialist ontology and non-teleological, mechanical, causal relations.[3] Australian philosopher Wallis Suchting well described these philosophical struggles in the Hellenic cradle of Western science and philosophy:

> Despite all the differences between Plato and Aristotle the latter carried on the work of the former in essential ways, like that of offering a metaphysical 'foundation' for the sciences and a teleological view of the world. Christianity took up elements of Platonic thought . . . but, its philosophical high-point, in Thomism, mainly appropriated Aristotle. Atomism carried on a basically marginal existence, . . . till it was recuperated by Galileo. (Suchting 1994, 45)

Scholastic Aristotelian philosophy was intimately connected with the Catholic Church. The fundamental Aristotelian doctrine of hylomorphism, which stated that all things were constituted by form and matter, gave a measure of, at least internal, intelligibility to the central Catholic doctrines of the soul, of transubstantiation in the celebration of the Mass, of the reality of angels, and much more. Fredrick Copleston

---

3. See Popper (1963, ch. 5) and Vitzthum (1995, ch. 2).

has rightly noted that Aquinas, the greatest of the Scholastics, "took over the Aristotelian analysis of substance" (Copleston 1955, 83) and further:

> According to Aquinas, therefore, every material thing or substance is composed of a substantial form and first matter. Neither principle is itself a thing or substance; the two together are the component principles of a substance. And it is only of the substance that we can properly say that it exists. "Matter cannot be said to be; it is the substance itself which exists." (Copleston 1955, 90)

This settled medieval philosophical-theological worldview was eventually unraveled by the New Science, which began with the publication in 1543 of Copernicus's astronomical work *On the Revolution of the Heavenly Spheres* (1543).[4] However, it was almost a century later that the unraveling took dramatic shape with the publication in 1633 of Galileo's *Dialogue Concerning the Two Chief World Systems* (1632) and, fifty-four years later, Newton's *Principia Mathematica* (1687/1713). These two books embodied the intellectual core of the Scientific Revolution; they constituted the Galilean-Newtonian Paradigm, a GNP far more consequential than any national GNP has ever been.[5]

In this new worldview, there was simply no place for the entities that Aristotelianism used to explain events in the world. Banished from the philosophical firmament were: hylomorphism, immaterial substances, unfolding natures and potentialities, substantial forms, teleological processes, and final causes. Much can be said about atomism and the New Science, but it suffices to repeat Craig Dilworth's observation that:

> The metaphysics underlying the Scientific Revolution was that of early Greek atomism. . . . It is with *atomism* that one obtains the notion of a *physical* reality underlying the phenomena, a reality in which *uniform causal* relations obtain. . . . What made the Scientific Revolution truly distinct, and Galileo . . . its father, was that for the first time this empirical methodology [of Archimedes] was given an ontological underpinning. (Dilworth [1996] 2006, 201)

The new science (natural philosophy) of Galileo, Descartes, Huygens, Boyle, and Newton caused a massive change not just in science but in European philosophy, one that had enduring repercussions for religion, ethics, politics, and culture. The early modern philosophers—Francis Bacon, Thomas Hobbes, John Locke, David Hume,

---

4. For the background, context, and impact of Copernicus, see references in Chapter 1.
5. An informative guide to the vast literature and debates about the Scientific Revolution is H. Floris Cohen (1994).

George Berkeley, René Descartes, and Gottfried Leibniz—were all engaged with and reacting to the discoveries, methods, and applications of early modern science.[6] So, of course, were the later philosophers of the French, English, German, and Scottish Enlightenments—Immanuel Kant, Denis Diderot, Jean le Rond d'Alembert, Émilie Du Châtelet, Adam Smith, Dugal Stewart, John Stuart Mill, and others. Some of these luminaries are discussed in later chapters.

The seventeenth-century Scientific Revolution was the seed that bore eighteenth- and nineteenth-century philosophical, cultural, and social fruit. A century later, the Darwinian Revolution elicited a comparable philosophical reckoning.[7] Select major figures in this long narrative, up to and including Charles Darwin, are discussed in separate chapters. Fifty years after Darwin, another philosophical reckoning, to understate the matter, was occasioned by the scientific work of Albert Einstein and Max Planck.[8]

This anthology is an attempt to help bridge the gap between the history of science and the history of philosophy. It soon becomes apparent that the very distinction between scientists and philosophers is almost impossible to draw during the seventeenth through nineteenth centuries. Histories of philosophy standardly omit or minimize the philosophical contributions and impacts of the famous "scientists"; conversely, histories of science and science teachers routinely gloss over or ignore the philosophical framework of the theories being taught and discussed. Such egregious separation is to the detriment of both humanistic and scientific education.

The hope is that this anthology's selections will, in the first place, generate further interest in the primary sources. The writings of Bacon, Galileo, Boyle, Huygens, Newton, Priestley, d'Alembert, Du Châtelet, Paley, Darwin, and the others are a joy to read. At times there is some pain, but there is always intellectual gain. Once there is familiarity with the primary sources, then the secondary sources can be informative. But to substitute the latter for the former is to repeat the mistake of Galileo's opponents who read textbooks about the moon instead of looking at it through the telescope. Texts, of course, do not speak for themselves; they have to be understood, and crucially, first understood in their own terms. Here, teachers, annotations, and secondary sources are all invaluable and indeed necessary.

Short introductions to each chapter are provided. These are meant to situate the selection in the context of the work as a whole and to indicate in neutral terms (or nearly so) the philosophical debate to which the selection contributed. An effort has been made, as they say in cricket, to play with a straight bat. Interpretative arguments rage over Bacon, Galileo, Newton, Kant, Darwin, and the others. Here the objective

---

6. A classic discussion is Dijksterhuis (1961/1986). On the wider impact of the Galilean-Newtonian method, see references in Chapter 3, Galileo and Chapter 7, Newton.

7. See references in Chapter 16, Darwin.

8. See at least Cushing and McMullin (1989), Kragh (1999), d'Espagnat (2006), and Krips (1987).

is for students to read something of the original sources, to appreciate the intellectual achievements of the authors, and to begin making their own assessments of the philosophical worth of the material.

For each chapter, a modicum of pertinent literature is cited. Web-based *Wikipedia* and the *Stanford Guide for Philosophy*, especially the latter, are good beginning guides for each chapter. Beyond these there are the *Encyclopedia of Philosophy* (Macmillan) and the *Dictionary of Scientific Biography* (Scribners).

REFERENCES

Adler, Mortimer J. 1978. *Aristotle for Everybody*. New York: Macmillan.

Allen, Reginald E., ed. 1966. *Greek Philosophy: Thales to Aristotle*. New York: The Free Press.

Ariew, Roger, and Peter Barker, eds. 1996. *Pierre Duhem: Essays in the History and Philosophy of Science*. Indianapolis, IN: Hackett Publishing Company.

Clavelin, Maurice. 1974. *The Natural Philosophy of Galileo: Essay on the Origin and Formation of Classical Mechanics*. Cambridge, MA: MIT Press.

Cohen, H. Floris. 1994. *The Scientific Revolution: A Historiographical Inquiry*. Chicago: University of Chicago Press.

Copernicus, Nicolas. (1543) 1952. *On the Revolutions of the Heavenly Spheres*. Translated by C. G. Wallis. Chicago: Encyclopaedia Britannica.

Copleston, Fredrick C. 1955. *Aquinas*. Harmondsworth: Penguin Books.

Crombie, Alistair C. 1994. *Styles of Scientific Thinking in the European Tradition*. 3 vols. London: Duckworth.

Cushing, James T., and Ernan McMullin, eds. 1989. *Philosophical Consequences of Quantum Theory*. Notre Dame, IN: University of Notre Dame Press.

D'Espagnat, Bernard. 2006. *On Physics and Philosophy*. Princeton, NJ: Princeton University Press.

Dijksterhuis, Eduard J. (1961) 1986. *The Mechanization of the World Picture*. Princeton, NJ: Princeton University Press.

Dilworth, Craig. (1996) 2006. *The Metaphysics of Science: An Account of Modern Science in Terms of Principles, Laws and Theories*. 2nd ed. Dordrecht: Kluwer Academic Publishers.

Galileo [Galileo Galilei]. (1633) 1953. *Dialogue Concerning the Two Chief World Systems*. Translated by S. Drake. Berkeley: University of California Press.

Koyré, Alexandre. 1968. *Metaphysics and Measurement*. Cambridge, MA: Harvard University Press.

Kragh, Helge. 1999. *Quantum Generations: A History of Physics in the Twentieth Century*. Princeton, NJ: Princeton University Press.

Krips, Henry. 1987. *The Metaphysics of Quantum Theory*. Oxford: Oxford University Press.

Matthews, Michael R. 2015. *Science Teaching: The Contribution of History and Philosophy of Science, 20th Anniversary Revised and Enlarged Edition*. New York: Routledge.

Newton, Isaac. (1687/1713) 1934. *Principia Mathematica*. 2nd ed. Translated by Florian Cajori. Berkeley: University of California Press.

Popper, Karl R. 1963. *Conjectures and Refutations: The Growth of Scientific Knowledge*. London: Routledge & Kegan Paul.

Suchting, Wallis A. 1994. "Notes on the Cultural Significance of the Sciences." *Science & Education* 3, no. 1: 1–56.

Vitzthum, Richard C. 1995. *Materialism: An Affirmative History and Definition*. Amherst, NY: Prometheus.

COPERNICUS

NICOLAUS COPERNICUS (1473–1543) was born in Poland to German parents in 1473, twenty years after the Turkish capture of Constantinople precipitated the migration of Eastern scholars and libraries into Europe. He studied law, medicine, theology, Greek, and Latin in Italy. There he became engaged by the rediscovered Greek learning, particularly Plato. In 1512 he began his career as a canon at Frauenburg Cathedral. In the same year, he circulated the first draft, *The Commentariolus* (*The Little Commentary*), of his epochal heliocentric theory of the solar system (selection below). The final version, *Six Books Concerning the Revolutions of the Heavenly Spheres*, was published in 1543, the year of his death (Dedication below).

His heliocentric, rotating-earth theory of the solar system was put forward in opposition to the long-established earth-centered theory proposed by Ptolemy in 150 CE. Both were answers to an astronomical task purportedly enunciated by Plato. In the words of Simplicius:

> Plato lays down the principle that the heavenly bodies' motion is circular, uniform, and constantly regular. Thereupon he sets the mathematicians the following problem: What circular motions, uniform and perfectly regular, are to be admitted as hypotheses so that it might be possible to save the appearances presented by the planets? (Duhem [1908] 1969, 5)

By Copernicus's time, a mass of information had been accumulated concerning planetary appearances: times of the rising and setting of planets, periodic reversals (retrograde motions) in their constant easterly paths, their changing brightness, the relative position of planets against the stars, and so on. Plato's question effectively illustrates the interconnection of philosophy, physics, and mathematics so characteristic of the astronomical and, more generally, the scientific tradition. Philosophy dictated that there was an order to be found behind the planets' chaotic appearances and, further, that their movements would be constant and regular. The assumption of cosmic and terrestrial order was a prerequisite for the conduct of natural philosophy or science. Mathematics told philosophers that the most perfect movements were circular. Given these constraints, the astronomers had to produce a model of regular, circular movements that resulted in the apparent movements of the planets. Then, as today, the business of science was to construct a model that gives order to sense impressions; and development of science meant alteration and refinement of the model.

The Aristotelian tradition, following Eudoxus, proposed a realist, mechanistic model, whereby the planets were embedded in moving homocentric crystalline spheres, the outermost one, moved by the Prime Mover, relaying its movement to the inner spheres. This satisfied religion and the need for a causal mechanism, but it only imperfectly saved the appearances. Ptolemy launched an antirealist, instrumentalist tradition in astronomy with his model of circular deferents, epicycles, and eccentrics. It was a complicated model, but it was consistent with common sense, philosophy, physics, and the Christian religion. Ptolemy was prepared to put aside the question of the actual mechanism for planetary motion and instead concentrate on perfecting his epicyclic model so as better to save the appearances. For mathematical astronomy, how the planets actually move was of little concern, provided the model agreed with how they appeared to move. Correct prediction of astronomical phenomena was the overriding concern of the Ptolemaic tradition.

Copernicus maintained all the classic metaphysics concerning the necessity for planetary motion to be circular and regular. He understood the relativity of perception—whether subjects or objects move, appearances stay the same. In answering Plato's question, he simply changed the reference point of the solar system: everything went in circles about the sun (or almost about the sun). In the "Little Commentary" sketch, the sun was at the center; in *On the Revolutions of Heavenly Spheres*, Copernicus had the sun slightly displaced from the center of his model. This was done to explain the apparent speeding up and slowing down of the planets. In *On the Revolutions of Heavenly Spheres*, the center of the model was the center of the earth's orbit, and the sun was slightly off this point. Thus his system is more correctly called heliostatic rather than heliocentric.

Copernicus ought to be regarded as the last great medieval astronomer rather than the first modern one; by suitable adjustments in astronomy, he preserved the medieval, Aristotle-anchored worldview.

However, if the Copernican system simplified celestial physics, it greatly complicated terrestrial physics. A spinning, revolving earth had all manner of counterintuitive and counter-experiential consequences: there should be a constant wind from the east, bodies ought to fly off the earth, dropped objects ought not to land beneath the points where they are released, and so on. Copernicus did not provide a new physics to support his new astronomy: he saved celestial appearances but lost terrestrial ones. Nor did he provide a new metaphysics and epistemology, nor a new theological interpretation of the oft-quoted scriptural texts against a moving earth.

The founders of Protestantism, Martin Luther (1483–1546) and John Calvin (1509–1564), both denounced Copernicus's heliocentric model. Conflicts with literal readings of the Psalms and other Old Testament verses were too obvious. Famously, Joshua asked God to make the sun stand still in the sky so the children of Israel would have enough light to continue their winning battle with the Amorites (Joshua 10: 12–13). The sun "stood still in the midst of heaven and did not go down about a whole day." It requires some sophistication to reconcile that story with Copernicus's stationary sun.

Such sophistication did not come quickly. Seventy years after publication of *On the Revolutions of the Heavenly Spheres*, Galileo in his 1615 letter to Grand Duchess Christina would get the ball rolling on this hermeneutical task. Further, heliocentrism meant moving our earth out of the center and into the periphery of the cosmos; it was a downgrading that did not sit well with the overall Judeo-Christian story about humans as the children of God and so deserving of a central place in the Creation.

To placate such opposition, the Protestant scholar Andreas Osiander (1498–1552), who had been entrusted with the manuscript's publication, inserted an unsigned preface into the *Revolutions* (this is not Copernicus's own Dedication to Pope Paul III which follows) extolling an instrumentalist view of science and saying that its heliocentric model was in the tradition of mathematical astronomy, where truth was of little account compared to the calculatory function of the model. This deflected religious criticism, but it did not represent the mind of Copernicus. He thought that his system was the actual system of the world: it was truth, not an algorithm.

Although Copernicus was convinced of the reality of his system, of the truth of the heliocentric worldview, few others were. One estimate holds that in 1600, nearly sixty years after publication of *On the Revolutions of Heavenly Spheres*, only ten natural philosophers in all of Europe endorsed a realist interpretation of the Copernican theory (Westman 2011). These included Galileo, Bruno, Stevin, Digges, Harriot, and Kepler. Heliocentrism did not become the accepted view in Germany until 1760; even later in Eastern Orthodox countries where, in 1804, a teacher in Greece was condemned for teaching it. It was not until 1758 that Pope Benedict XIV removed the book from the Roman Catholic Index of Prohibited Works. Within 150 years, the efforts of Kepler, Galileo, Newton, and others would sweep away the old circles and, to varying degrees, the old philosophy and theology and provide a new physics of inertial motion and force. This constituted the Copernican Revolution, a revolutionary movement in which science and philosophy were inseparable.

REFERENCES

Blumenberg, Hans. 1987. *The Genesis of the Copernican World.* Cambridge, MA: MIT Press.

Duhem, Pierre. (1908) 1969. *To Save the Phenomena: An Essay on the Idea of Physical Theory from Plato to Galileo.* Chicago: University of Chicago Press.

Gingerich, Owen, ed. 1975. *The Nature of Scientific Discovery: A Symposium Commemorating the 500th Anniversary of the Birth of Nicolaus Copernicus.* Washington, DC: Smithsonian Institution Press.

Gingerich, Owen. 2016. *Copernicus: A Very Short Introduction.* New York: Oxford University Press.

Sobel, Dava. 2011. *A More Perfect Heaven: How Copernicus Revolutionized the Cosmos.* New York: Walker & Company.

Westman, Robert. 2011, *The Copernican Question: Prognostication, Skepticism, and Celestial Order.* Los Angeles: University of California Press.

The Commentariolus (1512)
Sketch of His Hypotheses for the Heavenly Motions

Our ancestors assumed, I observe, a large number of celestial spheres for this reason especially, to explain the apparent motion of the planets by the principle of regularity. For they thought it altogether absurd that a heavenly body, which is a perfect sphere, should not always move uniformly. They saw that by connecting and combining regular motions in various ways they could make any body appear to move to any position.

Callippus and Eudoxus, who endeavored to solve the problem by the use of concentric spheres, were unable to account for all the planetary movements; they had to explain not merely the apparent revolutions of the planets but also the fact that these bodies appear to us sometimes to mount higher in the heavens, sometimes to descend; and this fact is incompatible with the principle of concentricity. Therefore it seemed better to employ eccentrics and epicycles, a system which most scholars finally accepted.

Yet the planetary theories of Ptolemy and most other astronomers, although consistent with the numerical data, seemed likewise to present no small difficulty. For these theories were not adequate unless certain equants were also conceived; it then appeared that a planet moved with uniform velocity neither on its deferent nor about the center of its epicycle. Hence a system of this sort seemed neither sufficiently absolute nor sufficiently pleasing to the mind.

Having become aware of these defects, I often considered whether there could perhaps be found a more reasonable arrangement of circles, from which every apparent inequality would be derived and in which everything would move uniformly about its proper center, as the rule of absolute motion requires. After I had addressed myself to this very difficult and almost insoluble problem, the suggestion at length came to me how it could be solved with fewer and much simpler constructions than were formerly used, if some assumptions (which are called axioms) were granted me. They follow in this order.

Assumptions

1. There is no one center of all the celestial circles or spheres.

2. The center of the earth is not the center of the universe, but only of gravity and of the lunar sphere.

3. All the spheres revolve about the sun as their mid-point, and therefore the sun is the center of the universe.

4. The ratio of the earth's distance from the sun to the height of the firmament is so much smaller than the ratio of the earth's radius to its distance from the sun that the distance from the earth to the sun is imperceptible in comparison with the height of the firmament.

5. Whatever motion appears in the firmament arises not from any motion of the firmament, but from the earth's motion. The earth together with its circumjacent elements performs a complete rotation on its fixed poles in a daily motion, while the firmament and highest heaven abide unchanged.

6. What appear to us as motions of the sun arise not from its motion but from the motion of the earth and our sphere, with which we revolve about the sun like any other planet. The earth has, then, more than one motion.

7. The apparent retrograde and direct motion of the planets arises not from their motion but from the earth's. The motion of the earth alone, therefore, suffices to explain so many apparent inequalities in the heavens.

Having set forth these assumptions, I shall endeavor briefly to show how uniformity of the motions can be saved in a systematic way. However, I have thought it well, for the sake of brevity, to omit from this sketch mathematical demonstrations, reserving these for my larger work. But in the explanation of the circles I shall set down here the lengths of the radii; and from these the reader who is not unacquainted with mathematics will readily perceive how closely this arrangement of circles agrees with the numerical data and observations.

Accordingly, let no one suppose that I have gratuitously asserted, with the Pythagoreans, the motion of the earth; strong proof will be found in my exposition of the circles. For the principal arguments by which the natural philosophers attempt to establish the immobility of the earth rest for the most part on the appearances; it is particularly such arguments that collapse here, since I treat the earth's immobility as due to an appearance.

The Order of the Spheres

The celestial spheres are arranged in the following order. The highest is the immovable sphere of the fixed stars, which contains and gives position to all things. Beneath it is Saturn, which Jupiter follows, then Mars. Below Mars is the sphere on which we revolve; then Venus; last is Mercury. The lunar sphere revolves about the center of the earth and moves with the earth like an epicycle. In the same order also, one planet surpasses another in speed of revolution, according as they trace greater or smaller circles. Thus Saturn completes its revolution in thirty years, Jupiter in twelve, Mars in two and one-half, and the earth in one year; Venus in nine months, Mercury in three.

The Apparent Motions of the Sun

The earth has three motions. First, it revolves annually in a great circle about the sun in the order of the signs, always describing equal arcs in equal times; the distance from the center of the circle to the center of the sun is 1/25 of the radius of the circle. The radius is assumed to have a length imperceptible in comparison with the height of the firmament; consequently the sun appears to revolve with this motion, as if the earth lay in the center of the universe. However, this appearance is caused by the motion not of the sun but of the earth, so that, for example, when the earth is in the sign of Capricorn, the sun is seen diametrically opposite in Cancer, and so on. On account of the previously mentioned distance of the sun from the center of the circle, this apparent motion of the sun is not uniform, the maximum inequality being $2\frac{1}{6}°$. The line drawn from the sun through the center of the circle is invariably directed toward a point of the firmament about 10° west of the more brilliant of the two bright stars in the head of Gemini, therefore when the earth is opposite this point, and the center of the circle lies between them, the sun is seen at its greatest distance from the earth. In this circle, then, the earth revolves together with whatever else is included within the lunar sphere.

The second motion, which is peculiar to the earth, is the daily rotation on the poles in the order of the signs, that is, from west to east. On account of this rotation the entire universe appears to revolve with enormous speed. Thus does the earth rotate together with its circumjacent waters and encircling atmosphere.

The third is the motion in declination. For the axis of the daily rotation is not parallel to the axis of the great circle, but is inclined to it at an angle that intercepts a portion of a circumference, in our time about $23\frac{1}{2}°$. Therefore, while the center of the earth always remains in the plane of the ecliptic, that is, in the circumference of the great circle, the poles of the earth rotate, both of them describing small circles about centers equidistant from the axis of the great circle. The period of this motion is not quite a year and is nearly equal to the annual revolution on the great circle. But the axis of the great circle is invariably directed toward the points of the firmament which are called the poles of the ecliptic. In like manner the motion in declination, combined with the annual motion in their joint effect upon the poles of the daily rotation, would keep these poles constantly fixed at the same points of the heavens, if the periods of both motions were exactly equal. Now with the long passage of time it has become clear that this inclination of the earth to the firmament changes. Hence it is the common opinion that the firmament has several motions in conformity with a law not yet sufficiently understood. But the motion of the earth can explain all these changes in a less surprising way. I am not concerned to state what the path of the poles is. I am aware that, in lesser matters, a magnetized iron needle always points in the same direction. It has nevertheless seemed a better view to ascribe the changes to a sphere, whose motion governs the movements of the poles. This sphere must doubtless be sublunar.

Dedication of *On the Revolutions of the Heavenly Spheres* (1543)
Nicolaus Copernicus to Pope Paul III

I can easily conceive, most Holy Father, that as soon as some people learn that in this book which I have written concerning the revolutions of the heavenly bodies, I ascribe certain motions to the Earth, they will cry out at once that I and my theory should be rejected. For I am not so much in love with my conclusions as not to weigh what others will think about them, and although I know that the meditations of a philosopher are far removed from the judgment of the laity, because his endeavor is to seek out the truth in all things, so far as this is permitted by God to the human reason, I still believe that one must avoid theories altogether foreign to orthodoxy.

Accordingly, when I considered in my own mind how absurd a performance it must seem to those who know that the judgment of many centuries has approved the view that the Earth remains fixed as center in the midst of the heavens, if I should, on the contrary, assert that the Earth moves; I was for a long time at a loss to know whether I should publish the commentaries which I have written in proof of its motions, or whether it were not better to follow the example of the Pythagoreans and of some others, who were accustomed to transmit the secrets of Philosophy not in writing but orally, and only to their relatives and friends, as the letter from Lysis to Hipparchus bears witness. They did this, it seems to me, not as some think, because of a certain selfish reluctance to give their views to the world, but in order that the noblest truths, worked out by the careful study of great men, should not be despised by those who are vexed at the idea of taking great pains with any forms of literature except such as would be profitable, or by those who, if they are driven to the study of Philosophy for its own sake by the admonitions and the example of others, nevertheless, on account of their stupidity, hold a place among philosophers similar to that of drones among bees. Therefore, when I considered this carefully, the contempt which I had to fear because of the novelty and apparent absurdity of my view, nearly induced me to abandon utterly the work I had begun.

. . .

But perhaps Your Holiness will not so much wonder that I have ventured to publish these studies of mine, after having taken such pains in elaborating them that I have not hesitated to commit to writing my views of the motion of the Earth, as you will be curious to hear how it occurred to me to venture, contrary to the accepted view of mathematicians, and well-nigh contrary to common sense, to form a conception of any terrestrial motion whatsoever. Therefore, I would not have it unknown to your Holiness, that the only thing which induced me to look for another way of reckoning the movements of the heavenly bodies was that I knew that mathematicians by no means agree in their investigations thereof. For, in the first place, they are so much in doubt concerning the motion of the sun and the moon, that they cannot even demonstrate and prove by observation the constant length of a complete year; and in the second place, in determining the motions both of these and of the five other planets, they fail to employ consistently one set of first principles and hypotheses, but use methods of proof based only upon the apparent revolutions and motions. For some employ concentric circles only; others, eccentric circles and epicycles; and even by these means they do not completely attain the desired end. For, although those who have depended upon concentric circles have shown that certain diverse motions can be deduced from these, yet they have not succeeded thereby in laying down any sure principle, corresponding indisputably to the phenomena.

These, on the other hand, who have devised systems of eccentric circles, although they seem in great part to have solved the apparent movements by calculations which by these eccentrics are made to fit, have nevertheless introduced many things which seem to contradict the first principles of the uniformity of motion. Nor have they been able to discover or calculate from these the main point, which is the shape of the world and the fixed symmetry of its parts; but their procedure has been as if someone were to collect hands, feet, a head, and other members from various places, all very fine in themselves, but not proportionate to one body, and no single one corresponding in its turn to the others, so that a monster rather than a man would be formed from them.

Thus, in their process of demonstration which they term a "method," they are found to have omitted something essential, or to have included something foreign and not pertaining to the matter in hand. This certainly would never have happened to them if they had followed fixed principles; for if the hypotheses they assumed were not false, all that resulted therefrom would be verified indubitably. Those things which I am saying now may be obscure, yet they will be made clearer in their proper place.

Therefore, having turned over in my mind for a long time this uncertainty of the traditional mathematical methods of calculating the motions of the celestial bodies, I began to grow disgusted that no more consistent scheme of the movements of the mechanism of the universe, set up for our benefit by that best and most law abiding Architect of all things, was agreed upon by philosophers who otherwise investigate so carefully the most minute details of this world. Wherefore I undertook the task of rereading the books of all the philosophers I could get access to, to see whether any one ever was of the opinion that the motions of the celestial bodies were other than those postulated by the men who taught mathematics in the schools. And I found first, indeed, in Cicero, that Niceta perceived that the Earth moved; and afterward in Plutarch I found that some others were of this opinion, whose words I have seen fit to quote here, that they may be accessible to all:

> Some maintain that the Earth is stationary, but Philolaus the Pythagorean says that it revolves in a circle about the fire of the ecliptic, like the sun and moon. Heraklides of Pontus and Ekphantus the Pythagorean made the Earth move, not changing its position, however, confined in its falling and rising around its own center in the manner of a wheel.

Taking this as a starting point, I began to consider the mobility of the Earth; and although the idea seemed absurd, yet because I knew that the liberty had been granted to others before me to postulate all sorts of little circles for explaining the phenomena of the stars, I thought I also might easily be permitted to try whether by postulating some motion of the Earth, more reliable conclusions could be reached regarding the revolution of the heavenly bodies, than those of my predecessors.

And so, after postulating movements, which, farther on in the book, I ascribe to the Earth, I have found by many and long observations that if the movements of the other planets are assumed for the circular motion of the Earth and are substituted for the revolution of each star, not only do their phenomena follow logically therefrom, but the relative positions and magnitudes both of the stars and all their orbits, and of the heavens themselves, become so closely related that in none of its parts can anything be changed without causing confusion in the other parts and in the whole universe.

Therefore, in the course of the work I have followed this plan: I describe in the first book all the positions of the orbits together with the movements which I ascribe to the Earth, in order that this book might contain, as it were, the general scheme of the universe. Thereafter in the remaining books, I set forth the motions of the other stars and of all their orbits together with the movement of the Earth, in order that one may see from this to what extent the movements and appearances of the other stars and their orbits can be saved, if they are transferred to the movement of the Earth. Nor do I doubt that ingenious and learned mathematicians will sustain me, if they are willing to recognize and weigh, not superficially, but with that thoroughness which Philosophy demands above all things, those matters which have been adduced by me in this work to demonstrate these theories.

In order, however, that both the learned and the unlearned equally may see that I do not avoid anyone's judgment, I have preferred to dedicate these lucubrations of mine to Your Holiness rather than to any other, because, even in this remote corner of the world where I live, you are considered to be the most eminent man in dignity of rank and in love of all learning and even of mathematics, so that by your authority and judgment you can easily suppress the bites of slanderers, albeit the proverb hath it that there is no remedy for the bite of a sycophant. If perchance there shall be idle talkers, who, though they are ignorant of all mathematical sciences, nevertheless assume the right to pass judgment on these things, and if they should dare to criticize and attack this theory of mine because of some passage of Scripture which they have falsely distorted for their own purpose, I care not at all; I will even despise their judgment as foolish. For it is not unknown that Lactantius, otherwise a famous writer but a poor mathematician, speaks most childishly of the shape of the Earth when he makes fun of those who said that the Earth has the form of a sphere. It should not seem strange then to zealous students, if some such people shall ridicule us also.

Mathematics is written for mathematicians, to whom, if my opinion does not deceive me, our labors will seem to contribute something to the ecclesiastical state whose chief office Your Holiness now occupies; for when not so very long ago, under Leo X, in the Lateran Council the question of revising the ecclesiastical calendar was discussed, it then remained unsettled, simply because the length of the years and months, and the motions of the sun and moon were held to have been not yet sufficiently determined. Since that time, I have given my attention to observing these more accurately, urged on by a very distinguished man, Paul, Bishop of Fossombrone, who at that time had charge of the matter. But what I may have accomplished herein I leave to the judgment of Your Holiness in particular, and to that of all other learned mathematicians; and lest I seem to Your Holiness to promise more regarding the usefulness of the work than I can perform, I now pass to the work itself.

BACON

The New Organon **(1620)**   Aphorisms 31–46 (method of the new science, idols of the mind)

Aphorisms 95–96 (perception, reason, and experiment in science)

FRANCIS BACON (1561–1626) was the major English philosopher of the Renaissance period. He was born in 1561 and entered Cambridge University at twelve years of age. After studying Plato, Aristotle, and the Scholastics, he graduated at fifteen. One year later, he was an assistant ambassador to France. At twenty-five, he commenced a thirty-six-year active career in the English Parliament and was made Lord Chancellor in 1618. He was a career politician, but also wrote philosophical treatises, books on English history, and essays on numerous subjects, including the regulation of English Catholics, proper governorship of the Church of England, law reform, alliances against Spain, and unification of the kingdoms of Scotland and England.

Bacon's political and public life came to an abrupt end when, in 1621, a serious bribery case was laid against him after he accepted gifts from two people he had tried. He pleaded guilty, and his civic offices were stripped from him. After a brief illness caused by conducting an outdoor "experiment" in the cold of winter, he died on Easter Sunday, April 9, 1626.

The history of philosophy benefited from the court case: the final five years of Bacon's life were clear of all extraneous duties and pursuits, and he could devote his time to research, scholarship, manuscript corrections, and writing. His first major philosophical work, *The Advancement of Learning*, was published in 1605; his second, best-known, and most influential work, the *Novum Organum*, was published (in Latin) in 1620.

The title is an allusion to Aristotle's major work on logic and reasoning, the *Organum*. Bacon thought that the "Advancement of Learning" required not a correction, but an overthrowing, of the Aristotelian and Scholastic method. The book's subtitle was: *New organon, or true directions concerning the interpretation of nature.* The published work was originally planned as the second part of a major book, *The Great Instauration* (*Instauratio Magna*), but this was never completed. His *Novum Organum* laid out his proposed methodology for science and intimated his inductivist philosophy of science. Bacon thought that a new start was needed in the pursuit of knowledge of the world, and the pursuit was to be marked by observation, experiment, and cautious induction from samples to populations. Further, it was to be a communal and organized activity, no longer the quest of solitary isolated individuals, even when exceptionally gifted. Points of contention were not to be settled by rhetoric and argument but by experiment and modification of experiment.

How well Bacon understood the Scientific Revolution that he championed has been much debated. He clearly did not appreciate the powerful role that the newly introduced mathematical techniques had in science. He dismissed Copernicus as a "man who did not care what fictions he introduced into nature, provided his calculations answer." One can only conjecture what he would have made of Galileo's mature physics, with its many imaginary experiments, geometrically argued conclusions, and mathematical representations, which, as the Aristotelians recognized, did violence to the facts.

Bacon was the father of British empiricism. His "New Method" was the inductivist method. His epistemology was developed on the realist assumption that there is an external world that a perceiving subject confronts and gains knowledge of through sense impressions. The less the subject contributes, the more truthfully nature can speak. In the preface to *The Great Instauration*, a brief promissory note detailing his division of the sciences, he opines that success in science "all depends on keeping the eye steadily fixed upon the facts of nature and so receiving their images simply as they are." This idea of the "immaculate perception" became a leading motif of empiricism. Two centuries later, John Stuart Mill repeats it when he speaks of entry to the Kingdom of Knowledge being like entry to the Kingdom of Heaven—one has to become as unprejudiced as a child.

Bacon is highly regarded for detailing the causes of faulty cognition. His brief aphorisms on the "Idols of the Mind" are harbingers of modern studies in linguistics, social psychology, perception, ideology, and prejudice. We recognize clearly how language, class, race, gender, religion, and human interests all affect perception and judgment. Indeed, this recognition is now the cultural default position. In addition to social-psychological determiners, Bacon was also aware that theoretical frameworks determine what things are seen and how they are seen and conceptualized. His response became the hallmark of empiricism: try to find theory-free observational foundations upon which to inductively create a secure science, and where these cannot be found, try to compensate, or control for, the distorting effects. Auguste Comte and Ernst Mach developed this positivist program in the nineteenth century; it was further developed by the Vienna Circle and Logical Positivists in the twentieth.

Although Bacon contributed little to the new science, he was greatly esteemed by the succeeding generation of scientists and natural philosophers. The founding members of the Royal Society eulogized him and regarded their very formation and work as an instantiation of "Baconianism"; as the organized, collegial, experimental pursuit of natural philosophy (science). Voltaire, Diderot, and d'Alembert saw their *Encyclopédie* as a Baconian task. Immanuel Kant dedicated his most un-Bacon-like *Critique of Pure Reason* (1781) to him.

Bacon's star shone through the seventeenth and eighteenth centuries but began to dim in the mid to late nineteenth century. The relevance of empiricism, especially its associated inductivist method, to scientific practice, and as justification of laws and theories, was no longer as obvious as it once seemed. Further, the social cost of Baconian "industrial science" fueled many critics of science who saw Bacon's utopian novel, *New Atlantis* (1626), as the very harbinger of the Military-Industrial-Scientific complexes of the nineteenth and twentieth centuries.

REFERENCES

Gaukroger, Stephen. 2001. *Francis Bacon and the Transformation of Early-Modern Philosophy*. Cambridge: Cambridge University Press.

Giglioni, Guido. 2012. "Francis Bacon." Stanford Encyclopedia of Philosophy. Last modified December 7, 2012. https://plato.stanford.edu/entries/francis-bacon/.

Horton, Mary. 1973. "In Defence of Francis Bacon." *Studies in History and Philosophy of Science* 4: 241–278.

Peltonen, Markku, ed. 1996. *The Cambridge Companion to Bacon*. Cambridge: Cambridge University Press.

Sargent, Rose-Mary, ed. 1999. *Francis Bacon: Selected Philosophical Works*. Indianapolis: Hackett Publishing Company.

Urbach, Peter. 1987. *Francis Bacon's Philosophy of Science: An Account and a Reappraisal*. La Salle, IL: Open Court.

Zagorin, Perez. 1999. *Francis Bacon*. Princeton, NJ: Princeton University Press.

The New Organon (1620)
Aphorisms 31–46

XXXI

It is idle to expect any great advancement in science from the superinducing and engrafting of new things upon old. We must begin anew from the very foundations, unless we would revolve forever in a circle with mean and contemptible progress.

XXXII

The honor of the ancient authors, and indeed of all, remains untouched since the comparison I challenge is not of wits or faculties, but of ways and methods, and the part I take upon myself is not that of a judge, but of a guide.

XXXIII

This must be plainly avowed: no judgment can be rightly formed either of my method or of the discoveries to which it leads, by means of anticipations (that is to say, of the reasoning which is now in use) since I cannot be called on to abide by the sentence of a tribunal which is itself on trial.

XXXIV

Even to deliver and explain what I bring forward is no easy matter, for things in themselves new will yet be apprehended with reference to what is old.

XXXV

It was said by Borgia of the expedition of the French into Italy, that they came with chalk in their hands to mark out their lodgings, not with arms to force their way in. I, in like manner, would have my doctrine enter quietly into the minds that are fit and capable of receiving it—for confutations cannot be employed when the difference is upon first principles and very notions and even upon forms of demonstration.

XXXVI

One method of delivery alone remains to us, which is simply this: We must lead men to the particulars themselves, and their series and order. While men on their side must force themselves for awhile to lay their notions by and begin to familiarize themselves with facts.

XXXVII

The doctrine of those who have denied that certainty could be attained at all, has some agreement with my way of proceeding at the first setting out, but they end in being infinitely separated and opposed. For the holders of that doctrine assert simply that nothing can be known. I also assert that not much can be known in nature by the way which is now in use. But then they go on to destroy the authority of the senses and understanding, whereas I proceed to devise and supply helps for the same.

XXXVIII

The idols and false notions which are now in possession of the human understanding, and have taken deep root therein, not only so beset men's minds that truth can hardly find entrance, but even after entrance is obtained, they will again in the very instauration of the sciences meet and trouble us, unless men being forewarned of the danger fortify themselves as far as may be against their assaults.

XXXIX

There are four classes of Idols which beset men's minds. To these for distinction's sake I have assigned names—calling the first class Idols of the Tribe; the second, Idols of the Cave; the third, Idols of the Marketplace; the fourth, Idols of the Theater.

XL

The formation of ideas and axioms by true induction is no doubt the proper remedy to be applied for the keeping off and clearing away of idols. To point them out, however, is of great use—for the doctrine of idols is to the interpretation of nature what the doctrine of the refutation of sophisms is to common logic.

XLI

The Idols of the Tribe have their foundation in human nature itself, and in the tribe or race of men. For it is a false assertion that the sense of man is the measure of things. On the contrary, all perceptions as well of the sense as of the mind are according to the measure of the individual and not according to the measure of the universe. And the human understanding is like a false mirror, which receiving rays irregularly, distorts and discolors the nature of things by mingling its own nature with it.

XLII

The Idols of the Cave are the idols of the individual man. For everyone (besides the errors common to human nature in general) has a cave or den of his own, which refracts and discolors the light of nature, owing either to his own proper and peculiar nature; or to his education and conversation with others; or to the reading of books, and the authority of those whom he esteems and admires; or to the differences of impressions, accordingly as they take place in a mind preoccupied and predisposed or in a mind indifferent and settled; or the like. So that the spirit of man (according as it is meted out to different individuals) is in fact a thing variable and full of perturbation, and governed as it were by chance. Whence it was well observed by Heraclitus that men look for sciences in their own lesser worlds, and not in the greater or common world.

XLIII

There are also idols formed by the intercourse and association of men with each other, which I call Idols of the Marketplace on account of the commerce and consort of men there. For it is by discourse that men associate, and words are imposed according to the apprehension of the vulgar. And therefore the ill and unfit choice of words wonderfully obstructs the understanding. Nor do the definitions or explanations wherewith in some things learned men are wont to guard and defend themselves, by any means set the matter right. But words plainly force and overrule the understanding and throw all into confusion, and lead men away into numberless empty controversies and idle fancies.

XLIV

Lastly, there are idols which have immigrated into men's minds from the various dogmas of philosophies, and also from wrong laws of demonstration. These I call Idols of the Theater because in my judgment all the received systems are but so many stage plays, representing worlds of their own creation after an unreal and scenic fashion. Nor is it only of the systems now in vogue, or only of the ancient sects and philosophies, that I speak; for many more plays of the same kind may yet be composed and in like artificial manner set forth, seeing that errors the most widely different have nevertheless causes for the most part alike. Neither again do I mean this only of entire systems, but also of many principles and axioms in science, which by tradition, credulity, and negligence have come to be received. But of these several kinds of idols I must speak more largely and exactly, that the understanding may be duly cautioned.

XLV

[The Idols of the Tribe arise because] the human understanding is of its own nature prone to suppose the existence of more order and regularity in the world than it finds. And though there be many things in nature which are singular and unmatched, yet it devises for them parallels and conjugates and relatives which do not exist. Hence the fiction that all celestial bodies move in perfect circles; spirals and dragons being (except in name) utterly rejected. Hence too the element of fire with its orb is brought in, to make up the square with the other three which the sense perceives. Hence also the ratio of density of the so-called elements is arbitrarily fixed at ten to one. And so on of other dreams. And these fancies affect not dogmas only, but simple notions also.

XLVI

The human understanding when it has once adopted an opinion (either as being the received opinion or as being agreeable to itself) draws all things else to support and agree with it. And though there be a greater number and weight of instances to be found on the other side, yet these it either neglects and despises, or else by some distinction sets aside and rejects in order that by this great and pernicious predetermination, the authority of its former conclusions may remain inviolate. And therefore it was a good answer that was made by one who replied, when they showed him hanging in a temple a picture of those who had paid their vows as having escaped shipwreck, and would have him say whether he did not now acknowledge the power of the gods—"Aye," and asked in return, "but where are they painted that were drowned after their vows?" And such is the way of all superstition, whether in astrology, dreams, omens, divine judgments, or the like wherein men, having a delight in such vanities, mark the events where they are fulfilled, but where they fail, though this happen much oftener, neglect and pass them by. But with far more subtlety does this mischief insinuate itself into philosophy and the sciences, in which the first conclusion colors and brings into conformity with itself all that come after, though far sounder and better. Besides, independently of that delight and vanity which I have described, it is the peculiar and perpetual error of the human intellect to be more moved and excited by affirmatives than by negatives; whereas it ought properly to hold itself indifferently disposed towards both alike. Indeed in the establishment of any true axiom, the negative instance is the more forcible of the two.

Aphorisms 95–96

XCV

Those who have handled sciences have been either men of experiment or men of dogmas. The men of experiment are like the ant; they only collect and use. The reasoners resemble spiders who make cobwebs out of their own substance. But the bee takes a middle course. It gathers its material from the flowers of the garden and of the field, but transforms and digests it by a power of its own. Not unlike this is the true business of philosophy; for it neither relies solely or chiefly on the powers of the mind, nor does it take the matter which it gathers from natural history and mechanical experiments and lay it up in the memory whole as it finds it, but lays it up in the understanding altered and digested. Therefore from a closer and purer league between these two faculties, the experimental and the rational (such as has never yet been made), much may be hoped for.

XCVI

We have as yet no natural philosophy that is pure. All is tainted and corrupted; in Aristotle's school by logic; in Plato's by natural theology; in the second school of Platonists, such as Proclus and others, by mathematics, which ought only to give definiteness to natural philosophy, not to generate or give it birth. From a natural philosophy pure and unmixed, better things are to be expected.

III

GALILEO

GALILEO GALILEI (1564–1642) was born in Pisa in 1564 and died in Florence in the year of Newton's birth. Galileo was a contemporary of most of the great figures of the Scientific Revolution—Kepler, Brahe, Bacon, Gilbert, Hobbes, Descartes, Harvey— and also of John Donne and William Shakespeare. Galileo's preeminence in the history of science is assured. Immanuel Kant said in his *Critique of Pure Reason* that with Galileo, "a light broke upon all students of nature." Earlier, Newton had referred to Galileo as one of "the giants" upon whose shoulders he stood. Galileo's "science"— his physics and astronomy—contains developed methodological, epistemological, and ontological arguments. His contribution to philosophy deserves more than the brief mention, if any, he is given in standard histories of philosophy.

His intellectual life divides easily into three periods: from 1588 to 1592 at the University of Pisa, where he was a teacher of mathematics; from 1592 to 1610 at the University of Padua, where he taught mathematics and physics; and from 1610 to 1642 at Florence, where he was "Chief Mathematician and Philosopher" in the court of the Grand Duke of Tuscany. At Pisa, he was a well-versed teacher of Aristotelian philosophy and an enthusiast for the recently translated mathematical and physical work of the "superhuman" Archimedes, whose name Galileo never mentions "without a feeling of awe." He wrote a transitional medieval/modern treatise on motion (*De Motu* 1590), which utilized Euclidean and Archimedean mathematics in the description and analysis of such physical situations as flotation, balances, and the flight of projectiles (Drabkin and Drake 1960).

But the shadow of Aristotle was cast heavily over the pages of *De Motu*—for instance, Galileo kept the distinction of natural and violent motions. When dealing with free fall, he defined acceleration as the rate of change of speed with respect to *distance*. This is a very natural, intuitive, obvious, and immediate conceptualization. We see and experience speed changing with distance. But this understanding and definition inhibits scientific development. It was only years later, in his middle age, that Galileo defined acceleration in the modern terms of rate of change of speed with respect to *time*. This relatively simple conceptual point was a pivotal achievement in the history of mechanics; without it there would be no laws of fall, of collision, or much else, or at least mechanical laws as currently understood (Norton and Roberts 2012).

For eighteen years at the University of Padua, he laid the foundations of his new science of physics. He developed the notions of the relativity of perception, circular inertia, the correct law of free fall, and the parabolic analysis of projectile motion. Above all, he made his physics thoroughly mathematical, and consequently, he dealt with more and more abstract and ideal circumstances, such as perfect spheres rolling on frictionless surfaces with no air resistance. The Aristotelians said he was an increasingly better mathematician but a correspondingly poorer physicist—he was not describing and dealing with the world as it was given in experience. Inasmuch as philosophy is concerned with the type of world we know and with how we know that world, these developments in Galilean physics had philosophical consequences. They challenged Aristotelian naturalism (science tells us about a natural, undisturbed world), empiricism (knowledge of the world is gained through the senses), ontology (the planets and the earth are different substances), and methodology (physics and mathematics have different methods).

The Paduan period finished with Galileo's construction of the telescope in 1609 and his first observations of earth's moon and of the moons of Jupiter. The telescope occasioned his conversion to Copernican astronomy. Not just the instrumental value of Copernicanism, but its realist value; the solar system really was heliocentric; the sun really was immobile in the center. Immediately, in 1610, Galileo published his first astronomical work—*The Starry Messenger* (*Sideral Nuncius* Galileo [1610] 1989). This announced the first fruits of his telescopic work: mountains on the moon, Jupiter's moons and their periods, a range of new fixed stars, and the stellar composition of the Milky Way. He realized that the successful defense of the realist interpretation of the Copernican hypothesis required a new physics and an altered philosophy and theology. He already had the first; he began work on the latter two.

Having embraced the Copernican position and being aware of the likely ecclesiastical and Inquisitional reactions—in 1600 Giordano Bruno had been burned at the stake in Rome for suspect cosmological views—Galileo penned anticipatory defenses in two important letters. The first (1613) to Benedetto Castelli, a former student and professor of mathematics at Pisa; the second (1615) to the Grand Duchess Christina of Lorraine, wife of Grand Duke Ferdinando I de' Medici.[1] The second letter of thirty-six pages is a considered, abundantly referenced, richly informed, carefully argued, early approach to the reconciliation of scripture and science. When, in 1636, the letter was published as a book in Strasburg, its informative and comprehensive title was: *New and Old Doctrine of the Most Holy Fathers and Esteemed Theologians on Preventing the Reckless Use of the Testimony of the Sacred Scripture in Purely Natural Conclusions That Can Be Established by Sense Experience and Necessary Demonstrations.* The title says it all.

The letter ranges over issues of the appropriate spheres for the exercise of authority, the questionable evidence of senses, principles of hermeneutics, and much more. It is a compressed treatise on method in science and in theology. He compresses the anti-Copernican view as:

> So the reason they advance to condemn the opinion of the earth's mobility and sun's stability is this: since in many places in the Holy Scripture one reads that the sun moves and the earth stands still, and since Scripture can never lie or err, it follows as a necessary consequence that the opinion of those who want to assert the sun to be motionless and the earth moving is erroneous and damnable. (Finocchiaro 2008, 115).

Of this he says:

> The first thing to note about this argument is the following. It is most pious to say and most prudent to take for granted that Holy Scripture can never lie, as long as its true meaning has been grasped; but I do not think one can deny that this is frequently recondite and very different from what appears to be the literal meaning of the words. From this it follows that, if in interpreting it someone were to limit himself always to the pure literal meaning, and if the latter were wrong, then he could make Scripture appear to be full not only

---

1. Both letters are in Finocchiaro (2008).

of contradictions and false propositions, but also of serious heresies and blas-
phemies; for one would have to attribute to God feet, hands, eyes, and bodily
sensations, as well as human feelings like anger, contrition, and hatred. . . .
(Finocchiaro 2008, 115)

And, after elaboration of this position, he writes:

That is, I would say that the authority of Holy Scripture aims chiefly at
persuading men about those articles and propositions which, surpassing all
human reason, could not be discovered by scientific research or by any other
means than through the mouth of the Holy Spirit himself. (Finocchiaro
2008, 117)

Galileo concludes this portion of the letter with the much-quoted comment: "The
intention of the Holy Spirit is to teach us how one goes to heaven and not how heaven
goes" (Finocchiaro 2008, 119).

Needless to say, both letters came to the attention of Roman authorities. In 1615
Pope Paul V directed Cardinal Robert Bellarmine to order Galileo not to teach the
Copernican view. Shortly after, the Inquisition placed Copernicus's book on the Index
of Prohibited Books.

In 1618 three comets, in fairly quick succession, traversed the European night sky.
The flights prompted the usual widespread public reactions to such auguries. They
also drew both astronomical and philosophical responses. The comets appeared to
be in the *supra*-lunar, heavenly realm. But if true, then there was a problem for the
Aristotelian and long-established view that the heavens were perfect and unchange-
able. If they were *sub*-lunar phenomena, then containing their trajectories within the
orthodox earth-centered solar system was also problematic. Orazio Grassi, a professor
at the Roman College, wrote a pamphlet, *The Astronomical and Philosophical Balance*,
weighing up different sides of the debate. This prompted Galileo to, over four years,
write and publish in 1623 his *The Assayer (Il Saggiatore)*, extracts from which are
reproduced below.

The book considerably advanced debate in the philosophical domain of ontology,
with his distinction between primary and secondary qualities and its incipient atomism; in epistemology, with his questioning of sensory foundations for knowledge; and
in the methodology of science. Authorities did note the conflict between atomism
and Aristotelian hylomorphism, the doctrine that all existing things are a combina-
tion of matter and form. Atomism had the first but not the second, and it was the second alone that brought intelligibility to the Roman Catholic teaching about Christ's
real presence in the Eucharist. Galileo was on slippery astronomical, philosophical,
and theological slopes.[2]

---

2. See Redondi (1988).

In 1624 Galileo began work on the first of his great dialogues that would flesh out and defend the Copernican worldview and provide the new non-Aristotelian physics essential for the support of Copernicus. Since he had been admonished in 1615 not to teach or advocate Copernicanism, he had to look over his shoulder in presenting his case. The first work, *Dialogues Concerning the Two Chief World Systems* (Galileo [1632] 1967) was published in Florence. It presents the case for Copernicus in a very thinly disguised manner: so thinly disguised that Galileo was called before the Inquisition the following year and charged with breaching his instruction not to advocate the Copernican system. More specifically, teaching two false and heretical propositions:

> That the sun is the center of the world and motionless is a proposition which is philosophically absurd and false, and formally heretical, for being explicitly contrary to Holy Scripture.

> That the earth is neither the center of the world nor motionless but moves even with diurnal motion is philosophically equally absurd and false, and theologically at least erroneous in the Faith. (Finocchiaro 2008, 289)

He was duly found guilty and sentenced to comfortable house arrest in the sumptuous Villa Medici in Rome; and not very long after, in the Medici residence outside of Florence.[3] Posterity benefited from Galileo's confinement, as all his needs were met and, though struggling with progressive blindness, he was free to work on the second of his great dialogues, *Dialogues Concerning Two New Sciences* (Galileo [1638] 1954).

Galileo's work initiated much argument among astronomers, physicists, theologians, and philosophers (Palmerino and Thijssen 2004). He forged a new abstract, mathematical physics; he developed a near-modern understanding of the role of experiment in science; and he furthered knowledge of causality, perception, ontology, and epistemology. Within a few decades of his death, the Scientific (and philosophical) Revolution would triumph. Galileo's work was heterogeneous enough for empiricists (Stillman Drake), Platonic rationalists (Alexandre Koyré), modern Aristotelians (William Wallace), and methodological anarchists (Paul Feyerabend), to claim him as their champion.[4] Everyone wanted to be associated with a winner. Understandably Galileo was a transitional figure: two thousand years of Aristotelian philosophy and science—so compatible with common sense and everyday experience, social structures,

---

3. The trial of Galileo became a beacon for enlightened philosophical, theological, and political causes in the West right through to the present; it became "The Galileo Affair." The original issues of 1633 were multilayered, and the subsequent history of the trial has also been multilayered. Whole libraries have been filled with elaborations of the issues and the lessons to be drawn from them. The complexity of the affair is well documented in Finocchiaro (2005, 2019).
4. See Crombie (1981).

and entrenched religious belief—could not be surmounted by a single figure, no matter how illustrious they were.

REFERENCES

Crombie, Alastair C. 1981. "Philosophical Presuppositions and the Shifting Interpretations of Galileo." In *Theory Change, Ancient Axiomatics, and Galileo's Methodology*, edited by J. Hintikka et al., 271–286. Boston, MA: Reidel.

Drabkin, Israel E., and Stillman Drake, eds. 1960. *Galileo Galilei On Motion and On Mechanics*. Madison: University of Wisconsin Press.

Drake, Stillman. 1990. *Galileo: Pioneer Scientist*. Toronto: University of Toronto Press.

Finocchiaro, Maurice A. 1989. *The Galileo Affair: A Documentary History*. Berkeley: University of California Press.

———. 2005. *Retrying Galileo: 1633–1992*. Berkeley: University of California Press.

———, ed. 2008. *The Essential Galileo*. Indianapolis: Hackett Publishing Company.

———. 2019. *On Trial for Reason: Science, Religion and Culture in the Galileo Affair*. Oxford: Oxford University Press.

Galileo [Galileo Galilei]. (1610) 2016. *Sidereus Nuncius (The Starry Messenger)*. 2nd ed. Translated and edited by Albert van Helden. Chicago: The University of Chicago Press.

———. [Galileo Galilei]. (1632) 1967. *Dialogue Concerning the Two Chief World Systems*. Translated by S. Drake. Berkeley: University of California Press.

———. (1638) 1954. *Dialogues Concerning Two New Sciences*. Translated by H. Crew and A. de Salvio. New York: Dover Publications.

Machamer, Peter, ed. 1998. *The Cambridge Companion to Galileo*. Cambridge: Cambridge University Press.

Machamer, Peter, and David M. Miller. 2021. "Galileo Galilei." Stanford Encyclopedia of Philosophy. https://plato.stanford.edu/entries/galileo/.

McMullin, Ernan, ed. 2005. *The Church and Galileo*. Notre Dame, IN: University of Notre Dame Press.

Norton, John D., and Bryan W. Roberts. 2012. "Galileo's Refutation of the Speed-Distance Law of Fall Rehabilitated." *Centaurus* 54: 148–164.

Palmerino, Carla R., and J. M. M. Thijssen, eds. 2004. *The Reception of the Galilean Science of Motion in the Seventeenth-Century Europe*. Dordrecht: Springer.

Redondi, Pietro. 1988. *Galileo Heretic*. Translated by R. Rosenthal. London: Allen Lane.

Wallace, William A., ed. 1986. *Reinterpreting Galileo*. Washington, DC: Catholic University of America Press.

Weisheipl, James A. 1985. *Nature and Motion in the Middle Ages*. Edited by W. E. Carroll. Washington, DC: Catholic University of America Press.

Wootton, David. 2010. *Galileo: Watcher of the Skies*. New Haven, CT: Yale University Press.

The Assayer (1623)

In accordance with my earlier promise to Your Most Illustrious Lordship, there now remains for me to say what I think about the proposition "motion is the cause of heat," indicating in what sense I think it may be true. But first I must make a comment about what we call *heat*. I very much suspect that the conception which people generally form of it is very far from the truth inasmuch as it is believed to be a real attribute, property, and quality that truly inheres in the material by which we feel warmed.

Accordingly, I say that as soon as I conceive of a corporeal substance or material, I feel indeed drawn by the necessity of also conceiving that it is bounded and has this or that shape; that it is large or small in relation to other things; that it is in this or that location and exists at this or that time; that it moves or stands still; that it touches or does not touch another body; and that it is one, a few, or many. Nor can I, by any stretch of the imagination, separate it from these conditions. However, my mind does not feel forced to regard it as necessarily accompanied by such conditions as the following: that it is white or red, bitter or sweet, noisy or quiet, and pleasantly or unpleasantly smelling; on the contrary, if we did not have the assistance of our senses, perhaps the intellect and the imagination by themselves would never conceive of them. Thus, from the point of view of the subject in which they seem to inhere, these tastes, odors, colors, etc., are nothing but empty names; rather they inhere only in the sensitive body, such that if one removes the animal, then all these qualities are taken away and annihilated. However, since we have given them particular names different from those of the primary and real attributes, we have a tendency to believe that these qualities are truly and really different from the primary ones.

I think I can explain my meaning more clearly with some examples. Suppose I move my hand first over a marble statue and then over a living man. Regarding the action coming from my hand, from the point of view of the hand the action over one subject is the same as that over the other; it consists of primary attributes, namely, motion and touch, and we do not use any other names. But the animate body that receives such an action feels various sensations depending on where it is touched. For example, if it is touched on the soles of the feet, on the knees, or on the armpits, besides touch it feels another sensation to which we have given a particular name, calling it *tickling*. This sensation is entirely ours and not at all in the hand; I think it would be a great error to want to say that, besides motion and touching, the hand has within itself another property different from these, namely, the power to tickle, such that tickling is an attribute inherent in it. Similarly, a piece of paper or a feather lightly brushed over any part of our body performs exactly the same operation with regard to itself, namely, moving and touching. But with regard to us, by touching between the eyes, or on the nose, or under the nostrils, it produces an almost intolerable titillation, whereas in other parts it is hardly felt. That titillation is entirely in us and not in the feather, and if the animate and sensitive body is removed, it is nothing but an empty name. Now, I believe that many qualities that are attributed to natural bodies (such as tastes, odors, colors, and others) may have a similar and not greater reality.

A solid and, so to speak, highly material body, when moved and applied to any part of my person, produces in me a sensation which we call *touch*. Although this sensation covers the whole body, nevertheless it seems to reside chiefly in the palms of the hands, and especially in the fingertips, with which we feel extremely small differences of roughness, smoothness, softness, and hardness, whereas with other parts of the body we do not distinguish them as well. Some of these sensations are more pleasant, others less so, depending on the shapes of tangible bodies, whether they are smooth or rough, acute or obtuse, hard or soft. This sense, being more material than the others and deriving from the solidity of matter, seems to correspond to the element earth.

Now, some of these bodies are constantly being subdivided into tiny particles, of which some are heavier than air and fall downwards and others are lighter and rise upwards. And perhaps here is how two other senses are generated, when those particles go and strike two parts of our body that are much more sensitive than our skin, which does not feel the effect of materials that are so fine, delicate, and soft. The particles that go down are received by the upper part of the tongue, becoming mixed with its humidity and penetrating its substance; thus they produce taste, likable or disagreeable, depending on the kind of contact with the various shapes of the particles, on the greater or smaller number of particles, and on their velocity. The other particles, which go up, enter through the nostrils and strike some small nodules that are the instrument of our sense of smell; here likewise their touch and movements are recorded with pleasure or annoyance, depending on whether their shapes are these or those, their movements are slow or fast, and their number is small or large. And indeed we see that, with regard to their location, the tongue and the nasal passages are wisely arranged: the former is extended underneath in order to receive the descending signals; the latter are set up for the ascending ones. And perhaps there is an analogy between the production of tastes and the descent of fluids through air and between the production of odors and the ascent of fires.

There remains the question of the correspondence between the element air and sounds. These come to us equally from all parts (lower, higher, and lateral) since we are located in air, whose motion in its own region is propagated equally in all directions. And the placement of the ear is arranged as much as possible to respond to all positions. Sounds are produced in us and heard when, without any sonorous or sound-like qualities, a rapid vibration of the air in the form of extremely minute waves moves some cartilage in the tympanum that is in our ear. The external means capable of producing this rippling in the air are extremely numerous, but perhaps they reduce mostly to the vibration of bodies that strike the air and thereby ripple it; the waves propagate through it at great velocity, with higher frequencies generating sharper sounds and lower frequencies deeper tones.

However, I do not believe that in order to stimulate in us tastes, odors, and sounds, external bodies require anything other than sizes, shapes, quantity, and slow or fast motions. I think that if one takes away ears, tongues, and noses, there indeed remain the shapes, numbers, and motions, but not the odors, tastes, or sounds; outside the living animal these are nothing but names, just as tickling and titillation are nothing but names if we remove the armpits and the skin around the nose. And just as the four elements correspond to the four senses considered so far, I believe that light corresponds to vision, the sense that is the most eminent of all; indeed its excellence is such that the comparison is like that of finite to infinite, time consuming to instantaneous, divisible to indivisible, and dark to light. I understand very little about this sense and related matters, and to explain the little I do understand, or better to adumbrate it on paper, I would need a long time; so I pass it over in silence.

But let us return to my primary purpose here. We have already seen that many properties, which are considered to be qualities inherent in external objects, do not really have any other existence except in us, and that outside of us they are nothing but names. Now I say that I am inclined to believe that heat is of this kind. The materials which produce heat in us and make us feel it, and which we call by the general name *fire*, are large collections of tiny corpuscles shaped in such and such a manner and moving with such and such a speed; when they meet our body they penetrate it because of their extremely small size. Their contact, which they make as they pass through our bodily substance and which we feel, is the property we call *heat*, which is pleasing or hurtful depending on the lesser or greater number and speed of the particles that are pricking and penetrating us. Such penetration is pleasing when it facilitates our unfelt but necessary perspiration, and hurtful when it causes too much division and separation of our bodily substance. In short, the action of fire works exactly this way: because of its extreme flexibility, by moving it penetrates all bodies and so dissolves them sooner or later depending on the number and velocity of the igneous particles in it and on the density or rarity of the matter in those bodies; as they are being destroyed, the greater part of many bodies turns into tiny igneous particles, and the decomposition continues as long as there remains decomposable material.

However, I do not believe in the least that besides shape, quantity, motion, penetration, and touch, there is in fire another quality, and that this quality is heat. Rather, I think that heat is in us, so much so that if we remove the animate and sensitive body, heat remains nothing but a simple word. Furthermore, since this property is produced in us by the touch of the tiny igneous particles and their passing through our bodily substance, it is clear that if they were to stand still then their operation would remain null. Thus we see that the considerable amount of fire contained in the pores and cavities of a piece of quicklime does not warm us when we hold it in our hand, because the fire is standing still. But let us place the quicklime in water, where the fire has a greater propensity to move than it had in air because of the weight of the water, and where the cavities are opened more by the water as compared to the situation in air; then the tiny igneous particles escape and meet and penetrate our hand, and we feel the heat. Since, then, the presence of the igneous particles is not sufficient to stimulate heat, but their motion is also needed, therefore it seems to me very reasonable to say that motion is the cause of heat.

This is the motion that burns arrows and the wood of catapults and liquefies the lead of gunshots and other metals: moving at high speed, whether by their own power or by the strong blast of a bellows if that is insufficient, the tiny particles of fire penetrate all bodies; some of these are decomposed into flying igneous particles, others are decomposed into extremely minute dust, and still others are liquefied into fluids like water. But if this proposition is taken in its ordinary meaning (i.e., that moving a rock or a piece of iron or of wood heats them up), then I regard it as a solemn falsehood. Now, the friction and rubbing of two hard bodies does reduce them to motion, in the sense that either parts of them are decomposed into extremely fine flying particles, or the igneous particles contained in them are allowed to escape; as these moving particles meet our bodies, penetrate them, and pass through them, the sensitive soul feels their motion and touch and experiences the pleasing or hurtful sensation which we have named *heat*, *burning*, or *scorching*.

Perhaps while the rubbing and grinding are limited to producing particles that are tiny but still finite, their motion is temporal and their operation merely calorific. But then if one arrives at the ultimate and highest decomposition into really indivisible atoms, one creates light, whose motion (or rather, expansion or propagation) is instantaneous; and it is capable of filling immense spaces on account of its subtlety, rarefaction, and immateriality, although I do not know whether these words are correct or whether we should speak of some other property as yet unnamed and different from all these.

Your Most Illustrious Lordship, I do not want inadvertently to engulf myself in an infinite ocean such that I cannot get back to port. Nor do I want, while removing one doubt, to give rise to a hundred others, as I fear it may have happened as a result of my little departure from the shore. So I want to postpone further discussion to some other more appropriate occasion.

Dialogues Concerning the Two Chief World Systems (1632)

The Second Day

SALV. Yesterday's digressions from the direct path of our main discussions were many, and so I do not know whether I can get back and proceed further without your help.

. . .

SAGR. I am happy to do that. One day I was at the house of a highly respected physician in Venice; here various people met now and then, some to study, others for curiosity, in order to see anatomical dissections performed by an anatomist who was really no less learned than diligent and experienced. It happened that day that they were looking for the origin and source of the nerves, concerning which there is a famous controversy between Galenist and Peripatetic physicians. The anatomist showed how the great trunk of nerves started at the brain, passed through the nape of the neck, extended through the spine, and then branched out through the whole body, and how only a single strand as thin as a thread arrived at the heart. As he was doing this he turned to a gentleman, whom he knew was a Peripatetic philosopher and for whose sake he had made the demonstration; the physician asked the philosopher whether he was satisfied and sure that the origin of the nerves is in the brain and not in the heart, and the latter answered after some reflection: "You have made me see this thing so clearly and palpably that one would be forced to admit it as true, if Aristotle's texts were not opposed in saying plainly that the nerves originate in the heart."

SIMP. Gentlemen, I want you to know that this dispute about the origin of the nerves is not as settled and decided as some believe.

SAGR. Nor will it ever be decided as long as one has similar opponents. At any rate what you say does not diminish at all the absurdity of the answer of the Peripatetic, who against such a sensible experience did not produce other experiences or reasons of Aristotle, but mere authority and the simple *ipse dixit*.

SIMP. Aristotle has acquired such great authority only because of the strength of his arguments and the profundity of his discussions. However, you must understand him, and not only understand him, but also know his books so well that you have a complete picture of them and all his assertions always in mind. For he did not write for the common people, nor did he feel obliged to spin out his syllogisms by the well-known formal method; instead, using an informal procedure, he sometimes placed the proof of a proposition among passages that seem to deal with something else. Thus, you must have that whole picture and be able to combine this passage with that one and connect this text with another very far from it. There is no doubt that whoever has this skill will be able to draw from his books the demonstrations of all knowable things, since they contain everything.

SAGR. So, my dear Simplicio, you are not bothered by things being scattered here and there, and you think that by collecting and combining various parts you can squeeze their juice. But then, what you and other learned philosophers do with Aristotle's texts, I will do with the verses of Virgil or Ovid, by making patchworks of passages and explaining with them all the affairs of men and secrets of nature. But why even go to Virgil or other poets? I have a booklet much shorter than Aristotle or Ovid in which are contained all the sciences, and with very little study one can form a very complete picture of them: this is the alphabet. There is no doubt that whoever knows how to combine and order this and that vowel with this and that consonant will be able to get from them the truest answers to all questions and the teachings of all sciences and of all arts. In the same way a painter, given various simple colors placed separately on his palette, by combining a little of this with a little of that and that other, is able to draw men, plants, buildings, birds, fishes—in short, all visible objects—without having on his palette either eyes, or feathers, or scales, or leaves, or rocks; on the contrary, it is necessary that none of the things to be drawn nor any part of them be actually among the colors, which can serve to represent everything, for if there were, for example, feathers, they would not serve to depict anything but birds and bunches of feathers.

. . .

SIMP. But, if one abandons Aristotle, who will be the guide in philosophy? Name some author.

SALV. One needs a guide in an unknown and uncivilized country, but in a flat and open region only the blind need a guide; whoever is blind would do well to stay home, whereas anyone who has eyes in his head and in his mind should use them as a guide. Not that I am thereby saying that one should not listen to Aristotle; on the contrary, I applaud his being examined and diligently studied and only blame submitting to him in such a way that one blindly subscribes to all his assertions and accepts them as unquestionable dictates, without searching for other reasons for them. This abuse carries with it another extreme impropriety, namely, that no one makes an effort any longer to try to understand the strength of his demonstrations. Is there anything more shameful in a public discussion dealing with demonstrable conclusions than to see someone slyly appear with a textual passage (often written for some different purpose) and use it to shut the mouth of an opponent? If you want to persist in this manner of studying, lay down the name of philosophers and call yourselves either historians or memory experts, for it is not right that those who never philosophize should usurp the honorable title of philosopher.

However, we should get back to shore in order not to enter an infinite ocean from which we could not get out all day. So, Simplicio, come freely with reasons and demonstrations (yours or Aristotle's) and not with textual passages or mere authorities because our discussions are about the sensible world and not about a world on paper. In yesterday's discussions the earth was drawn out of darkness and brought to light in the open heavens, and we showed that to want to number it among those bodies called heavenly is not so doomed and prostrate a proposition as to be left devoid of any vital energy; and so today we should examine how much probability there is in holding it fixed and completely motionless (referring to the globe as a whole) and how much likelihood there is in making it move with any motion (and if so what type this is). I am undecided about this question, while Simplicio together with Aristotle is firmly on the side of immobility; because of this, he will present step-by-step the motives for their opinion, I will present the answers and arguments for the contrary side, and Sagredo will say what goes on in his mind and to which side he feels drawn.

SAGR. I am happy with this arrangement, but on the condition that I am free to introduce whatever simple common sense may suggest to me.

SALV. Indeed, I beg you to do exactly that; for I think the various authors have left out few of the easier and (so to speak) cruder considerations, so that only some of the more subtle and esoteric ones may be wanting and lacking; but to investigate these, what subtlety can be more appropriate than that of Sagredo's intellect, which is most acute and penetrating?

SAGR. I may be all that Salviati says, but please, let us not start on another sort of ceremonial digression because right now I am a philosopher and have come to school and not to city hall.

· · ·

SALV. As the strongest reason, everyone produces the one from heavy bodies, which when falling down from on high move in a straight line perpendicular to the earth's surface. This is regarded as an unanswerable argument that the earth is motionless. For, if it were in a state of diurnal rotation and a rock were dropped from the top of a tower, then during the time taken by the rock in its fall, the tower (being carried by the earth's turning) would advance many hundreds of cubits toward the east and the rock should hit the ground that distance away from the tower's base. They confirm this effect with another experiment. That is, they drop a lead ball from the top of the mast of a ship which is standing still, and they note that the spot where it hits is near the foot of the mast; but if one drops the same ball from the same place when the ship is moving forward, it will strike at a spot as far away from the first as the ship has moved forward during the time the lead was falling. This happens only because the natural motion of the ball in free fall is in a straight line toward the center of the earth.

This argument is strengthened with the experiment of a projectile thrown upward to a very great height, such as a ball shot by a cannon aimed perpendicular to the horizon. The time required for it to go up and down is such that at our latitude we, together with the cannon, would be carried by the earth many miles toward the east; thus the ball could never fall back near the gun, but rather would fall as far to the west as the earth would have moved forward.

Moreover, they add a third and very effective experiment, which is the following: if one shoots a cannon aimed at a great elevation toward the east, and then another with the same charge and the same elevation toward the west, the westward shot would range much farther than the eastward one. For, since the ball goes westward and the cannon (carried by the earth) goes eastward, the ball would strike the ground at a distance from the cannon equal to the sum of the two journeys (the westward one made by itself and the eastward one of the cannon carried by the earth); by contrast, from the journey made by the ball shot toward the east, one would have to subtract the one made by the cannon while following it; for example, given that the ball's journey in itself is five miles and that at that particular latitude the earth moves forward three during the ball's flight, in the westward shot the ball would strike the ground eight miles from the cannon (namely, its own westward five plus the cannon's eastward three), whereas the eastward shot would range two miles (which is the difference between the five of the shot and the three of the cannon's motion in the same direction). However, experience shows that the ranges are equal. Therefore, the cannon is motionless, and consequently so is the earth.

No less than this, shooting toward the south or toward the north also confirms the earth's stability. For one would never hit the mark aimed at, but instead the shots would always be off toward the west, due to the eastward motion of the target (carried by the earth) while the ball is in midair.

These shots along the meridians would not be the only ones that would hit off the mark. If one were shooting point-blank, the eastward shots would strike high and the westward ones low. For in such shooting, the ball's journey is made along the tangent, namely, along a line parallel to the horizon; moreover, if the diurnal motion should belong to the earth, the eastern horizon would always be falling and the western one rising (which is why the eastern stars appear to rise and the western ones to fall); therefore, the eastern target would drop below the shot and so the shot would strike high, while the rising of the western target would make the westward shot hit low. Thus, one could never shoot straight in any direction; but, because experience shows otherwise, one is forced to say that the earth stands still.

SIMP. Oh, these arguments are beautiful, and it will be impossible to find answers to them.

. . .

SALV. Before proceeding further, I must tell Sagredo that in these discussions I act as a Copernican and play his part with a mask, as it were. However, in regard to the internal effect on me of the reasons I seem to advance in his favor, I do not want to be judged by what I say while we are involved in the enactment of the play, but by what I say after I have put away the costume; for perhaps you will find me different from what you see when I am on stage. Now, let us go on.

Ptolemy and his followers advance another observation, similar to that of projectiles: it concerns things that are separate from the earth and remain at length in the air, such as clouds and birds in flight. Since clouds are not attached to the earth, they cannot be said to be carried by it, and so it does not seem possible that they could keep up with its speed; instead, they should all appear to us to be moving very fast toward the west. And, if we are carried by the earth and in twenty-four hours move along our parallel (which is at least sixteen thousand miles), how could birds keep up with so much drift? On the contrary, we see them fly toward the east as well as toward the west and toward any other direction, without any sensible difference.

. . .

SAGR. What do you say, Simplicio? Does it seem that Salviati knows and can explain the Ptolemaic and Aristotelian reasons? Do you think that any Peripatetic is equally knowledgeable of the Copernican demonstrations?

SIMP. If the discussions so far had not produced in me such a high opinion of Salviati's well-founded understanding and of Sagredo's sharp intelligence, I (with their permission) would be ready to leave without listening to anything else. For it seems to me impossible that one can contradict such palpable observations; moreover, I would like to keep my old opinion without having to hear anything else, because it seems to me that even if it were false, the fact that it is supported by such likely reasons would render it excusable. If these are fallacies, what true demonstrations were ever so beautiful?

SAGR. Still, it will be good to hear Salviati's answers. If these should be true, they must be even more beautiful and infinitely more beautiful, and those others must be ugly, indeed very ugly; this would follow if there is truth in the metaphysical proposition that truth and beauty are the same thing, as falsehood and ugliness also are. However, Salviati, let us not lose any more time.

. . .

SIMP. By means of the senses: they assure us that the tower is straight and perpendicular; they show us that the falling rock grazes it without inclining so much as a hairbreadth to one side or the other; and they show that the rock lands at the foot of the tower exactly under the place from which it was dropped.

SALV. But if by chance the terrestrial globe were rotating and consequently were also carrying the tower along with it, and if the falling rock were still seen to graze the edge of the tower, what would its motion have to be?

SIMP. In that case one would rather have to speak of "its motions"; for there would be one that would take it from above downwards, and it would have to have another in order to follow the course of the tower.

SALV. Therefore, its motion would be a compound of two, namely, one with which it grazes the edge of the tower, and another one with which it follows the tower; the result of this compound would be that the rock would no longer describe a simple straight and perpendicular line, but rather an inclined, and perhaps not straight, one.

SIMP. I am not sure about its not being straight; but I understand well that it would have to be inclined and different from the straight perpendicular one it would describe on a motionless earth.

SALV. Therefore, from just seeing the falling rock graze the tower, you cannot affirm with certainty that it describes a straight and perpendicular line unless you first assume the earth to be standing still.

SIMP. That is correct; for if the earth were moving, the rock's motion would be inclined and not perpendicular.

SALV. Here, then, is the paralogism of Aristotle and Ptolemy made clear and evident, and discovered by yourself; the argument is assuming as known what it is trying to prove.

SIMP. In what way? To me it seems to be a syllogism in proper form and not a fallacy of question begging.

SALV. Here is how. Tell me: does not the demonstration regard the conclusion as unknown?

SIMP. Yes, unknown, for otherwise it would be superfluous to demonstrate it.

SALV. But, should not the middle term be known?

SIMP. That is necessary, for otherwise it would be an attempt to prove the unknown by means of what is equally unknown.

SALV. Is not the conclusion to be proved, and which is unknown, the proposition that the earth stands still?

SIMP. It is.

SALV. Is not the middle term, which must be already known, the straight and perpendicular fall of the rock?

SIMP. That is the middle term.

SALV. But, did we not just conclude that we can have no knowledge that this fall is straight and perpendicular unless we first know that the earth is standing still? Therefore, in your syllogism the certainty of the middle term is inferred from the uncertain conclusion. So you see the type and the seriousness of the paralogism.

Dialogues Concerning the Two New Sciences (1638)

The Third Day

SALV. The present does not seem to be the proper time to investigate the cause of the acceleration of natural motion, concerning which various opinions have been expressed by various philosophers. That is, some explain it by attraction to the center; others reduce it to the gradual decrease of the amount of medium to be overcome; still others attribute it to a certain pressure of the surrounding medium, which closes in behind the falling body and drives it from one position to another. Now, all these fantasies, and others too, ought to be examined; but it is not really worthwhile. At present it is the purpose of our Author merely to investigate and to demonstrate some of the properties of an accelerated motion such that (whatever the cause of this acceleration may be) the moments of its velocity go on increasing after departure from rest in simple proportionality to the time, which is the same as saying that in equal time intervals the body receives equal increments of velocity; and if we find that the properties to be demonstrated later are realized in freely falling and accelerated bodies, we may conclude that the assumed definition includes such a motion of falling bodies, and that it is true that their speed goes on increasing as the time and the duration of the motion.

SAGR. So far as I see at present, the definition might have been put a little more clearly perhaps without changing the fundamental idea. That is, uniformly accelerated motion is motion such that its speed increases in proportion to the space traversed; so that, for example, the speed acquired by a body in falling four cubits would be double that acquired in falling two cubits, and this latter speed would be double that acquired in the first cubit. For there is no doubt but that a heavy body falling from the height of six cubits has, and strikes with, an impetus double that which it had at the end of three cubits, triple that which it had at the end of two, and six times that which it had at the end of one.

SALV. It is very comforting to me to have had such a companion in error. Moreover, let me tell you that your reasoning seems so highly likely and probable that our Author himself admitted, when I put it forward to him, that he had for some time shared the same fallacy. But what most surprised me was to see two propositions proven in a few simple words to be not only false but also impossible, even though they are so inherently likely that they have commanded the assent of everyone to whom I have presented them.

SIMP. I am one of those who accept them. I believe that a falling body acquires force in its descent, its velocity increasing in proportion to the space, and that the moment of the same striking body is double when it falls from a double height. These propositions, it appears to me, ought to be conceded without hesitation or controversy.

SALV. And yet they are as false and impossible as that motion should be completed instantaneously. Here is a very clear demonstration of it. When the velocities are in proportion to the spaces traversed or to be traversed, these spaces are traversed in equal intervals of time; if, therefore, the velocities with which the falling body traverses a space of four cubits were double the velocities with which it covered the first two cubits (since the one distance is double the other), then the time intervals required for these passages would be equal; but for one and the same body to move four cubits and two cubits in the same time is possible only in the case of instantaneous motion; but observation shows us that the motion of a falling body takes time, and less of it in covering a distance of two cubits than of four cubits; therefore, it is false that its velocity increases in proportion to the space.

The falsity of the other proposition may be shown with equal clearness. For if we consider a single striking body, the difference in the moment of its percussions can depend only upon a difference of velocity; thus, if the striking body falling from a double height were to deliver a percussion of double moment, it would be necessary for this body to strike with a double velocity; with this double speed it would traverse a double space in the same time interval; but observation shows that the time required for fall from the greater height is longer.

SAGR. You present these recondite matters with too much evidence and ease. This great facility makes them less appreciated than they would be had they been presented in a more abstruse manner. For, in my opinion, people esteem more lightly that knowledge which they acquire with so little labor than that acquired through long and obscure discussion.

SALV. If those who demonstrate with brevity and clearness the fallacy of many popular beliefs were treated with contempt instead of gratitude, the injury would be quite bearable. But on the other hand, it is very unpleasant and annoying to see men who claim to be peers of anyone in a certain field of study take for granted conclusions that later are quickly and easily shown by another to be false. I do not call such a feeling envy, which usually degenerates into hatred and anger against those who discover such fallacies; I would call it a strong desire to maintain old errors, rather than accept newly discovered truths. This desire at times induces them to unite against these truths, although at heart believing in them, merely for the purpose of lowering the esteem in which certain others are held by the unthinking crowd. Indeed, I have heard our Academician talk about many such false propositions, held as true but easily refutable; and I have even made a list of some of them.

SAGR. You must not withhold them from us, but must tell us about them at the proper time, even though an extra session be necessary. For now, continuing the thread of our discussion, it would seem that so far we have formulated the definition of the uniformly accelerated motion to be treated in what follows. It is this: *A motion is said to be equally or uniformly accelerated when, starting from rest, its velocity receives equal increments in equal times.*

SALV. This definition established, the Author assumes the truth of a single principle, namely: *The speeds acquired by one and the same body moving down planes of different inclinations are equal when the heights of these planes are equal.*

Galileo's Inquisition's Sentence (1633)

[We] by the grace of God, Cardinals of the Holy Roman Church, and especially commissioned by the Holy Apostolic See as Inquisitors-General against heretical depravity in all of Christendom.

Whereas you, Galileo, son of the late Vincenzio Galilei, Florentine, aged seventy years, were denounced to this Holy Office in 1615 for holding as true the false doctrine taught by some that the sun is the center of the world and motionless and the earth moves even with diurnal motion; for having disciples to whom you taught the same doctrine; for being in correspondence with some German mathematicians about it; for having published some letters entitled *On Sunspots*, in which you explained the same doctrine as true; for interpreting Holy Scripture according to your own meaning in response to objections based on Scripture which were sometimes made to you; and whereas later we received a copy of an essay in the form of a letter, which was said to have been written by you to a former disciple of yours and which in accordance with Copernicus's position contains various propositions against the authority and true meaning of the Holy Scripture;

And whereas this Holy Tribunal wanted to remedy the disorder and the harm which derived from it and which was growing to the detriment of the Holy Faith, by order of His Holiness and the Most Eminent and Most Reverend Lord Cardinals of this Supreme and Universal Inquisition, the Assessor Theologians assessed the two propositions of the sun's stability and the earth's motion as follows:

That the sun is the center of the world and motionless is a proposition which is philosophically absurd and false, and formally heretical, for being explicitly contrary to Holy Scripture.

That the earth is neither the center of the world nor motionless but moves even with diurnal motion is philosophically equally absurd and false, and theologically at least erroneous in the Faith.

. . .

And whereas a book has appeared here lately, printed in Florence last year, whose inscription showed that you were the author, the title being *Dialogue by Galileo Galilei on the two Chief World Systems, Ptolemaic and Copernican*; and whereas the Holy Congregation was informed that with the printing of this book the false opinion of the earth's motion and sun's stability was being disseminated and taking hold more and more every day, the said book was diligently examined and was found to violate explicitly the above-mentioned injunction given to you; for in the same book you have defended the said opinion already condemned and so declared to your face, although in the said book you try by means of various subterfuges to give the impression of leaving it undecided and labeled as probable; this is still a very serious error since there is no way an opinion declared and defined contrary to divine Scripture may be probable.

. . .

Therefore, having seen and seriously considered the merits of your case, together with the above-mentioned confessions and excuses and with any other reasonable matter worth seeing and considering, we have come to the final sentence against you given below.

Therefore, invoking the Most Holy name of Our Lord Jesus Christ and of his most glorious Mother, ever Virgin Mary; and sitting as a tribunal, with the advice and counsel of the Reverend Masters of Sacred Theology and the Doctors of both laws, our consultants; in this written opinion we pronounce final judgment on the case pending before us between the Magnificent Carlo Sinceri, Doctor of both laws, and Prosecuting Attorney of this Holy Office, on one side, and you the above-mentioned Galileo Galilei, the culprit here present, examined, tried, and confessed as above, on the other side:

We say, pronounce, sentence, and declare that you, the above-mentioned Galileo, because of the things deduced in the trial and confessed by you as above, have rendered yourself according to this Holy Office vehemently suspected of heresy, namely of having held and believed a doctrine which is false and contrary to the divine and Holy Scripture: that the sun is the center of the world and does not move from east to west, and the earth moves and is not the center of the world, and that one may hold and defend as probable an opinion after it has been declared and defined contrary to Holy Scripture. Consequently, you have incurred all the censures and penalties imposed and promulgated by the sacred canons and all particular and general laws against such delinquents. We are willing to absolve you from them provided that first, with a sincere heart and unfeigned faith, in front of us you abjure, curse, and detest the above-mentioned errors and heresies, and every other error and heresy contrary to the Catholic and Apostolic Church, in the manner and form we will prescribe to you.

Furthermore, so that this serious and pernicious error and transgression of yours does not remain completely unpunished, and so that you will be more cautious in the future and an example for others to abstain from similar crimes, we order that the book *Dialogue* by Galileo Galilei be prohibited by public edict.

Galileo's Abjuration (1633)

I, Galileo, son of the late Vincenzio Galilei of Florence, seventy years of age, arraigned personally for judgment, kneeling before you Most Eminent and Most Reverend Cardinals Inquisitors-General against heretical depravity in all of Christendom, having before my eyes and touching with my hands the Holy Gospels, swear that I have always believed, I believe now, and with God's help I will believe in the future all that the Holy Catholic and Apostolic Church holds, preaches, and teaches. However, whereas, after having been judicially instructed with injunction by the Holy Office to abandon completely the false opinion that the sun is the center of the world and does not move and the earth is not the center of the world and moves, and not to hold, defend, or teach this false doctrine in any way whatever, orally or in writing; and after having been notified that this doctrine is contrary to Holy Scripture; I wrote and published a book in which I treat of this already condemned doctrine and adduce very effective reasons in its favor, without refuting them in any way; therefore, I have been judged vehemently suspected of heresy, namely of having held and believed that the sun is the center of the world and motionless and the earth is not the center and moves.

Therefore, desiring to remove from the minds of Your Eminences and every faithful Christian this vehement suspicion, rightly conceived against me, with a sincere heart and unfeigned faith I abjure, curse, and detest the above-mentioned errors and heresies, and in general each and every other error, heresy, and sect contrary to the Holy Church; and I swear that in the future I will never again say or assert, orally or in writing, anything which might cause a similar suspicion about me; on the contrary, if I should come to know any heretic or anyone suspected of heresy, I will denounce him to this Holy Office, or to the Inquisitor or Ordinary of the place where I happen to be.

Furthermore, I swear and promise to comply with and observe completely all the penances which have been or will be imposed upon me by this Holy Office; and should I fail to keep any of these promises and oaths, which God forbid, I submit myself to all the penalties and punishments imposed and promulgated by the sacred canons and other particular and general laws against similar delinquents. So help me God and these Holy Gospels of His, which I touch with my hands.

I, the above-mentioned Galileo Galilei, have abjured, sworn, promised, and obliged myself as above; and in witness of the truth I have signed with my own hand the present document of abjuration and have recited it word for word in Rome, at the convent of the Minerva, this twenty-second day of June 1633.

I, Galileo Galilei, have abjured as above, by my own hand.

DESCARTES

RENÉ DESCARTES (1596–1650) was born in 1596 in the Brittany area of France. From 1604 to 1612 he was educated at the illustrious Jesuit college of La Flèche, where he met a fellow student, Father Marin Mersenne, who was to be his lifelong friend and philosophical correspondent. After nine years of travel (1620–1628) in Holland, Germany, and Italy, he settled to a quiet life in Holland. There he proceeded to write major works in mathematics, philosophy, and science and carried on a voluminous correspondence with the major scholars of his day. Though remembered as a philosopher, Descartes was first, and perhaps foremost, a scientist.[1] In 1649, he went to Sweden to tutor Queen Christina, whose habit of 5:00 a.m. classes in the northern winter agreed more with her mind than with Descartes's body—he caught a fever and died in February 1650.

Following upon some disturbing dreams in late 1619, Descartes's life work became the creation of a systematic philosophy that would encompass all branches of knowledge. The system would be based on a few undeniable principles, and all knowledge would be deduced from them, so that metaphysics, physics, mathematics, morals, and

---

1. On Descartes's science see Gaukroger (1978). On his philosophy of science, see Clarke (1982).

politics would all cohere. Knowledge is an organic whole, in which all fields have the same method. Descartes repeatedly used the metaphor of a tree:

> Thus philosophy as a whole is like a tree whose roots are metaphysics, whose trunk is physics, and whose branches, which issue from this trunk, are all the other sciences.[2]

This doctrine of a single, all-embracing method is contrary to that of Aristotle, for whom the different fields of human knowledge all have their own subject matter and appropriate method.

Just like Francis Bacon, his contemporary in England, Descartes thought that a new beginning was needed for the acquisition of knowledge, for the project of social knowledge creation. The Aristotelian philosophy of the schools, Scholastic philosophy, could not be reformed: it had to be rejected in toto. Of the greatest consequence was his rejection of the core Aristotelian ontological notion of hylomorphism, the contention that all existing things were an admixture of matter and substantial form.

For Aristotle, matter did not and could not exist by itself; it was always "informed," so to speak, with a substantial form. The form characterized the individual; it dictated the motion, including transformations, of the body. Tigers were animated by a tiger form; diamonds by a diamond form; species of fish by specific fish forms, and so on. In a collection of identical-looking seeds, it was their different inherent forms that, with nutrition, directed their development into orange, lemon, grapefruit, apple, and whatever other varieties of trees. And humans were animated by a human form, something that the Christian tradition could seamlessly identify as a soul.

The Catholic tradition explicitly called on hylomorphism to make understandable the substantial transformation that occurred when the Eucharistic host was consecrated in the Mass. Descartes's rejection of the doctrine, and his turn to atomism, resulted in his books being placed on the Index of Prohibited Books in 1663.

What survived from his Catholic schooling was an abiding enthusiasm and respect for mathematics, or, more specifically, Euclidean geometry. This was systematic, deductive, and methodical. From a few self-evident principles, knowledge of distant and complicated theorems could be generated, provided only that the correct method was followed.

Descartes was not the only person in the history of philosophy to be mesmerized by mathematics: to see in the structure, method, and certainty of mathematics the model for all human knowledge. Galileo and Newton were also convinced that physics (natural philosophy) should follow the geometrical method of analysis and synthesis.

Descartes's project was assisted by and perhaps indeed gave rise to his division of the world into mental and physical substances, thinking and corporeal substances.

---

2. "Author's Letter" for French translation of *Principles of Philosophy.*

Physics dealt with corporeal substances. The nature and essence of corporeal sub-stance, or matter, was "extension in length, breadth, and depth." Thus geometry was able to represent faithfully and without omission the very essence of the subject mat-ter of physics. Physics could be geometrical; there were no forms for which physics needed to account.

Just as Galileo before and Robert Boyle and John Locke after, Descartes made a distinction between the primary and secondary qualities of matter. Colors, odors, and heat were all the product of interaction between corporeal bodies and feeling subjects. Physics could ignore them; the secondary qualities did not exist in nature; they were an artifact of humans being about. A tree falling in a deserted forest does not make a sound; it creates airwaves but not sounds. Physics was the science of determined, extended bodies in motion. Much later, psychophysics would become the science of subjective responses and experiences of physical events and processes.

Along with Pierre Gassendi, Descartes revived corpuscularian philosophy.[3] The objects of experience—tables, chairs, stones—might be in essence extended and capa-ble of geometrical representation, but what of the unseen and unseeable tiny corpus-cules, the supposed building blocks of the universe? To these he assigns "determinate figures, magnitudes, and motions . . . as if I had seen them." (Descartes 1644, Pt. 4 §203) There is clearly something of a leap of faith here, a leap made more perilous because Descartes so clearly wants certainty in his architectonic system of knowledge. What happens to the tree if the roots contain such a major unsupported hypothesis? Robert Boyle, another atomist, would later face the same question. Depending upon answers to this question, different positions in epistemology, or the theory of knowl-edge, are derived. Instrumentalism, whereby theories such as the atomic hypothesis are believed not to tell us about unseen deep structures, but about how to manipu-late surface events, is one answer; fallibilism—whereby theories are believed to be about deep structures, but we only provisionally believe them until a better theory is developed—is another; absolutism, whereby we believe that our theories are true and will remain so, is yet another.

Hypotheses and experiments in science were matters of which Descartes had even-tually to give an account. Some of the better-known early works of his project—*Rules for the Direction of Mind* (1628), *Discourse on Method* (1637), and *Meditations on First Philosophy* (1641)—were all to a large extent programmatic. While other early works, such as *Geometry, Opticks,* and *Meteorology,* were more specific and substantive. These better-known works were statements of an idea, expressions of a hope. There the vision of a deductive, coherent, certain body of all-encompassing knowledge could be safely entertained.

---

3. Descartes was an ambiguous corpuscularian: he did not believe in discrete atoms and, along with Aristotle, he did not believe in a void. Atoms could always be further divided; space was everywhere filled with the plenum in which his vortices revolved.

In his last major work, *Principles of Philosophy* (1644), the promises were kept, the program fulfilled, the vision given flesh. In *Principles*, he deals with subjects such as God's attributes, freedom of will, prejudice, laws of motion, laws of impact, planetary orbits, comets, rainbows, the moon, the formation of mountains, tides, minerals, combustion, glass making, gravitation, magnets and attraction in glass, among other things. Indeed, so extensive is the list that Descartes claimed, "That there is no phenomenon in nature which has not been dealt with in this treatise." (Descartes 1644, Pt. 4 §199). Could he maintain his earlier confidence in a completely deductive, systematic, and certain science?

On the basis of the early methodological books, many see Descartes's science as entirely *a prioristic*. But clearly this cannot be so when the later *Principles* are considered. No one, not even Descartes, could pretend to spin out the explanation of mineral formation or the laws of free fall totally *a priori*. Guesses, hypotheses, experiments had to enter into the system at some place. How were these accommodated, given his concern for certainty and his goal of a systematic science?

Descartes's problem was recognized much earlier by Aristotle and by Thomas Aquinas; although one hypothesis might well account for the phenomena, so might many others (Gilby 1951, 18). To argue from an effect to a cause was always problematic unless one could, first, fully enumerate all the possible causes and, second, eliminate all but the chosen one. The second task is, in practice, difficult; the first is conceptually impossible. Aristotle called the problem the "fallacy of affirming the consequent."

Although the point is much debated, some see that logic and the complexity of experimentation forced Descartes in the end to moderate his epistemological position: certainty in science is given up in favor of fallibilism.[4] At the end of the *Principles*, he says he has done all that is required of him (and of science) if the causes I have assigned are such that they correspond to all the phenomena manifested by nature [without inquiring whether it is by their means or by others that they are produced]. (Descartes 1644, Pt. 4 §204)

Descartes's relationship with Galileo is informative.[5] He knew of Galileo but does not mention him in his major works; comment is confined to some letters. One in particular gives a good picture of Descartes's priorities, his views about the mathematizing of physics and his commitment to a systematic philosophy. Writing to Mersenne (June 29, 1638), Descartes says of Galileo:

> I find that in general he philosophizes much better than the usual lot for he leaves as much as possible the errors of the School and strives to examine physical matters with mathematical reasons. In this I am completely in agreement with him and I hold that there is no other way of finding the truth. But

---

4. See Garber (1978).
5. See Shea (1978) and Ariew (1986).

I see a serious deficiency in his constant digressions and his failure to stop and explain a question fully. This shows that he has not examined them in order and that, without considering the first causes of nature, he has merely looked for the causes of some particular effects, and so has built without any foundation. (Shea 1978, 148)

It is most interesting that when Descartes dealt with the problem of free fall—a problem at the heart of physics since Aristotle's time—he repeated exactly the mistake that had so dogged the early attempts of Galileo to solve the problem. Everyone knew that bodies went faster as they fell, that they accelerated. Descartes assumed that acceleration uniformly increased with the distance traversed rather than with the time elapsed. This mistake was so easy, so seemingly in accord with experience, yet it prevented Descartes's discovery of the law of free fall—distance traversed is as the square of time elapsed.[6] This well illustrates the difficulty for the whole Cartesian program, which depended upon not introducing any assumptions that were not absolutely certain and proven. Descartes's radical doubt did, in fact, leave many everyday assumptions untouched—assumptions so seemingly well founded that they were not seriously examined.

One lasting and monumental scientific achievement of Descartes was his creation of analytic geometry. Up to his time, the mathematization of science, so vital to the New Science, meant the Archimedean-like rendering of scientific problems into Euclidean-geometric form. This was the method of Galileo. Distance (say) was represented by a line, time by another, and solutions to unknowns were derived by geometric construction. Newton used this method in his *Principia*. In contrast, Descartes, in his *Geometry* represented different line lengths by different variables and converted geometry to algebra. Laborious proofs that took pages of Euclidean constructions were now reduced to a few clear, easy-to-follow algebraic steps. The long hoped for program of mathematizing science was now well and truly launched.

References

Ariew, Roger. 1986. "Descartes as Critic of Galileo's Scientific Methodology." *Synthese* 67, no. 1: 77–90.

Clarke, Desmond M. 1982. *Descartes' Philosophy of Science*. Manchester: Manchester University Press.

———. 2006. *Descartes: A Biography*. Cambridge: Cambridge University Press.

Cottingham, John, ed. 1992. *The Cambridge Companion to Descartes*. Cambridge: Cambridge University Press.

---

6. See Norton and Roberts (2012).

Descartes, René. (1644) 1983. *Principles of Philosophy*. Translated by V. R. Miller and R. P. Miller. Dordrecht: Reidel.

———. 1998. *Discourse on Method; Meditations on First Philosophy*. 4th ed. Translated by Donald A. Cress. Indianapolis: Hackett Publishing Company.

———. 1998. *Philosophical Essays and Correspondence*. Translated and edited by Roger Ariew. Indianapolis: Hackett Publishing Company.

Garber, Daniel. 1978. "Science and Certainty in Descartes." In *Descartes: Critical and Interpretative Essays*, edited by Michael Hooker, 114–151. Baltimore: Johns Hopkins University Press.

Gaukroger, Stephen. 1995. *Descartes: An Intellectual Biography*. Oxford: Oxford University Press.

———. 1998. *René Descartes: The World and Other Writings*. Translated and edited by Stephen Gaukroger. Cambridge: Cambridge University Press.

Gilby, Thomas, ed. 1951. *St. Thomas Aquinas Philosophical Texts*. Oxford: Oxford University Press.

Norton, John D., and Bryan W. Roberts. 2012. "Galileo's Refutation of the Speed-Distance Law of Fall Rehabilitated." *Centaurus* 54: 148–164.

Shea, William R. 1978. "Descartes as Critic of Galileo." In *New Perspectives on Galileo*, edited by R. E. Butts and J. C. Pitt, 139–159. Dordrecht: Reidel.

Discourse on the Method of Rightly Conducting the Reason (1637)

But, like a man who walks alone and in the dark, I resolved to go so slowly and to use so much circumspection in all things that, if I advanced only very slightly, at least I would effectively keep myself from falling. Nor did I want to begin to reject totally any of the opinions that had once been able to slip into my head without having been introduced there by reason, until I had first spent sufficient time planning the work I was undertaking and seeking the true method for arriving at the knowledge of everything of which my mind would be capable.

When I was younger, I had studied, among the parts of philosophy, a little logic, and among those of mathematics, a bit of geometrical analysis and algebra—three arts or sciences that, it seemed, ought to contribute something to my plan. But in examining them, I noticed that, in the case of logic, its syllogisms and the greater part of its other lessons served more to explain to someone else the things one knows, or even, like the art of Lully, to speak without judgment concerning matters about which one is ignorant, than to learn them. And although, in effect, it might well contain many very true and very good precepts, nevertheless there are so many others mixed up with them that are either harmful or superfluous, that it is almost as difficult to separate the latter precepts from the former as it is to draw a Diana or a Minerva from a block of marble that has not yet been hewn. Then, as to the analysis of the ancients and the algebra of the moderns, apart from the fact that they apply only to very abstract matters and seem to be of no use, the former is always so closely tied to the consideration of figures that it cannot exercise the understanding without greatly fatiguing the imagination; and in the case of the latter, one is so subjected to certain rules and to certain symbols, that out of it there results a confused and obscure art that encumbers the mind, rather than a science that cultivates it. That is why I thought it necessary to search for some other method embracing the advantages of these three yet free from their defects. And since the multiplicity of laws often provides excuses for vices, so that a state is much better ruled when it has but very few laws and when these are very strictly observed; likewise, in place of the large number of precepts of which logic is composed, I believed that the following four rules would be sufficient for me, provided I made a firm and constant resolution not even once to fail to observe them:

The first was never to accept anything as true that I did not plainly know to be such; that is to say, carefully to avoid hasty judgment and prejudice; and to include nothing more in my judgments than what presented itself to my mind so clearly and so distinctly that I had no occasion to call it in doubt.

The second, to divide each of the difficulties I would examine into as many parts as possible and as was required in order better to resolve them.

The third, to conduct my thoughts in an orderly fashion, by commencing with those objects that are simplest and easiest to know, in order to ascend little by little, as by degrees, to the knowledge of the most composite things, and by supposing an order even among those things that do not naturally precede one another.

And the last, everywhere to make enumerations so complete and reviews so general that I was assured of having omitted nothing.

Those long chains of utterly simple and easy reasonings that geometers commonly use to arrive at their most difficult demonstrations had given me occasion to imagine that all the things that can fall within human knowledge follow from one another in the same way, and that, provided only that one abstain from accepting any of them as true that is not true, and that one always adheres to the order one must follow in deducing the ones from the others, there cannot be any that are so remote that they are not eventually reached nor so hidden that they are not discovered. And I was not very worried about trying to find out which of them it would be necessary to begin with; for I already knew that it was with the simplest and easiest to know. And considering that, of all those who have hitherto searched for the truth in the sciences, only mathematicians have been able to find any demonstrations, that is to say, certain and evident reasonings, I did not at all doubt that it was with these same things that they had examined [that I should begin].

Principles of Philosophy (1644)

Following on this, and in order to make very clear the end I have had in view in publishing them, I would like to explain here what seems to me to be the order that should be followed in our self-instruction. To begin with, a man who as yet has merely the common and imperfect knowledge that may be acquired by the four methods before mentioned, should above all try to form for himself a code of morals sufficient to regulate the actions of his life, because this does not permit any delay, and we ought above all other things to endeavor to live well. After that he should likewise study logic—not the logic of the Schools, because properly speaking it is only a dialectic that teaches how to make the things we know understood by others, or even to repeat, without forming any judgment on them, many words respecting those we do not know, thus corrupting rather than increasing good sense—but the logic that teaches us how best to direct our reason in order to discover those truths of which we are ignorant. And since this is very dependent on custom, it is good for him to practice the rules for a long time on easy and simple questions such as those of mathematics.

Then, when he has acquired a certain skill in discovering the truth in these questions, he should begin seriously to apply himself to the true philosophy, the first part of which is metaphysics, containing the principles of knowledge, among which is the explanation of the principal attributes of God, the immateriality of our souls, and all the clear and simple notions that are in us. The second is physics, in which, after having found the true principles of material things, we examine generally how the whole universe is composed, and then in particular what is the nature of this earth and of all the bodies most commonly found around it, like air, water, and fire, magnetic ore, and other minerals. It is then necessary to inquire individually into the nature of plants, animals, and above all of man, so that we may afterwards be able to discover the other sciences useful to man.

Thus, philosophy as a whole is like a tree whose roots are metaphysics, whose trunk is physics, and whose branches, which issue from this trunk, are all the other sciences. These reduce themselves to three principal ones, namely, medicine, mechanics, and morals—by morals I mean the highest and most perfect moral science which, presupposing a complete knowledge of the other sciences, is the ultimate degree of wisdom.

But just as it is not from the roots or the trunk of trees that one gathers the fruit, but only from the extremities of their branches, so the main use of philosophy is dependent on those of its parts that we cannot learn until the end. Although, however, I am ignorant of almost all of these, the zeal I have always shown in trying to render service to the public caused me to print ten or twelve years ago certain essays on things I appeared to have learned. The first part of these essays was a *Discourse on the Method of Rightly Conducting One's Reason and Seeking Truth in the Sciences*, in which I summarized the principal rules of logic and of an imperfect system of morals which may be followed provisionally while we still know none better. The other parts were three treatises: the first *Dioptrics*, the second *Meteors*, and the last *Geometry*. In the *Dioptrics* I intended to show that we could make sufficient progress in philosophy to attain by its means a knowledge of those arts useful to life, because the invention of the telescope, which I there explained, is one of the most difficult ever attempted. In the treatise on *Meteors* I endeavored to make clear the difference between the philosophy I cultivate and that taught in the Schools, where the same subject is usually treated. Finally in the *Geometry* I professed to show that I had found certain matters of which men were previously ignorant, and thus to afford occasion for believing that many more may yet be discovered, in order by this means to incite all men to the search after truth.

From this time onwards, foreseeing the difficulty which would be felt by many in understanding the foundations of metaphysics, I tried to explain the principal points in a book of *Meditations* which is not very large, but whose volume has been increased, and whose matter has been much illuminated, by the objections many very learned persons have sent me in regard to them, and by the replies I have made to them.

Then, finally, when it appeared to me that these preceding treatises had sufficiently prepared the mind of readers to accept the *Principles of Philosophy*, I likewise published them, and I divided the book containing them into four parts, the first of which contains the principles of knowledge, which is what may be called First Philosophy or Metaphysics. That is why it is better to read beforehand the *Meditations* which I have written on the same subject, in order that it may be properly understood. The other three parts contain what is most general in physics, that is, an explanation of the first laws or principles of nature, the manner in which the heavens, fixed stars, planets, comets, and generally all the universe are composed. Then the nature of this earth, and of air, water, fire, and magnetic ore is dealt with more particularly, for these are the bodies that may most commonly be found everywhere around it, as also all the qualities observed in these bodies, such as light, heat, weight, and the like. By this means I believe myself to have begun to explain the whole of philosophy in order, without having omitted anything that ought to precede the last things of which I have written. But in order to carry this plan to a conclusion, I should afterwards in the same way explain in further detail the nature of each of the other bodies on the earth, that is, minerals, plants, animals, and above all man, then finally treat exactly of medicine, morals, and mechanics. All this I should have to do in order to give to mankind a complete body of philosophy; I do not feel myself to be so old, I do not so much despair of my strength, and I do not find myself so far removed from a knowledge of what remains that I should not venture to endeavor to achieve this design, if I had the means of making all the experiments I would need in order to support and justify my reasoning. But seeing that great expense is requisite for this end, to which the resources of an individual like myself could not attain if he were not given assistance by the public, and not seeing that I can expect that aid, I conceive it to be henceforth my duty to content myself with studying for my own private instruction, trusting that posterity will excuse me if I fail henceforth to work on its behalf.

51. What substance is: a name we cannot attribute in the same sense to God and to his creatures.

With respect to those matters we consider as being things or modes of things, it is necessary that we should examine them here one by one. By substance, we can understand nothing else than a thing which so exists that it needs no other thing in order to exist. And in fact only one substance can be understood which clearly needs nothing else, namely, God. We perceive that all other things can exist only by the help of God's concurrence. That is why the word substance does not pertain *univocally* to God and to other things, as they say in the Schools, that is, there is no meaning that can be distinctly understood as common to God and to his creatures.

52. It may be attributed univocally to soul and to body; how we know substance.

Created substances, however, whether corporeal or thinking, may be understood under this common concept; for they are things that need only the concurrence of God in order to exist. But yet substance cannot be first discovered merely from the fact that it is an existing thing, for that fact alone is not observed by us. We may, however, easily discover it by means of any one of its attributes, because it is a common notion that nothing is possessed of no attributes, properties, or qualities. For this reason, when we perceive any attribute, we can conclude that some existing thing or substance to which it may be attributed is necessarily present.

53. Each substance has a principal attribute: the attribute of the mind is thought, while that of body is extension.

But although any one attribute is sufficient to give us a knowledge of substance, there is always one principal property of substance which constitutes its nature and essence, and to which all other properties are referred. Thus extension in length, breadth, and depth constitutes the nature of corporeal substance; and thought constitutes the nature of thinking substance. For all else that may be attributed to body presupposes extension, and is but a mode of an extended thing; as everything that we find in mind is but so many diverse forms of thinking. Thus, for example, shape is unintelligible except in an extended thing, and motion likewise in an extended space; so imagination, feeling, and will are unintelligible except in a thinking thing. But, on the other hand, we can understand extension without shape or action, and thinking without imagination or sensation, and so on with the rest; as is quite clear to anyone who attends to the matter.

198. There is nothing known of external objects by the senses but their shape, size, or motion.

In addition, we observe no difference in the nerves that may cause us to judge that some convey one thing rather than another to the brain from the organs of the external sense, nor again that anything is conveyed there except the local motion of the nerves themselves. And we see that this local motion excites in us not only the sensations of pleasure or pain, but also those of sound and light. For if we receive a blow in the eye hard enough for the vibration to reach the retina, we see myriads of sparks which are still not outside our eye; and when we place our finger on our ear, we hear a murmuring sound whose cause cannot be attributed to anything but the agitation of the air trapped within it. Finally we can likewise frequently observe that heat and other sensible qualities, inasmuch as they are in objects, and also the forms of purely material things, such as those of fire, are produced in them by the motions of certain other bodies, and that these again also produce other motions in other bodies. And we can very well conceive how the motion of one body can be caused by that of another, and diversified by the size, shape, and motion of its parts, but we can in no way understand how these same things (namely, size, shape, and motion) can produce something entirely different in nature from themselves, like those substantial forms and real qualities many suppose to exist in bodies; nor likewise can we understand how these forms or qualities have the power to produce motion in other bodies.

But since we know that our soul is of such a nature that the various motions of body suffice to produce in it all the various sensations it has, and as we see by experience that some of the sensations are really caused by such motions, though we do not find anything but these motions to pass through the organs of the external senses to the brain, we may conclude that we in no way likewise apprehend that in external objects like light, color, smell, taste, sound, heat, cold, and the other tactile qualities, or what are called their substantial forms, there is anything but the various dispositions of these objects which have the power of moving our nerves in various ways.

199. There is no phenomenon in nature that has not been dealt with in this treatise.

And thus, by a simple enumeration, it may be deduced that there is no phenomenon in nature whose treatment has been omitted in this treatise. For there is nothing that can be counted as a phenomenon of nature, except what is apprehended by the senses. And with the exception of motion, size, and shape, which are to be found in every body, we perceive nothing outside us by means of our senses, but light, color, smell, taste, sound, and tactile qualities; and I have just proved that these are nothing more, as far as is known to us, than certain dispositions of objects consisting of size, shape, and motion so that there is nothing in all the visible world, insofar as it is merely visible or sensible, but the things I have explained there.

203. How we may arrive at a knowledge of the shapes, sizes, and motions of the imperceptible particles of bodies.

But since I assign determinate shapes, sizes, and motions to the imperceptible particles of bodies, as if I had seen them, but admit that they do not fall under the senses, someone will perhaps ask how I have come to my knowledge of them. To this I reply that I first considered generally the simplest and best understood principles implanted in our mind by nature, and examined the principal differences that could be found between the sizes, shapes, and positions of bodies imperceptible on account of their smallness alone, and what observable effects could be produced by the various ways in which they impinge on one another. And finally, when I found like effects in the bodies perceived by our senses, I considered that they might have been produced from a similar interaction of such bodies, especially as no other way of explaining them could be suggested. And for this end the example of certain artifacts was of use to me, for I can see no difference between these and natural bodies, except that the effects of machines depend for the most part on the operation of certain tubes, springs, or other instruments, which, since men necessarily make them, must always be large enough to be capable of being easily perceived by the senses.

The effects of natural causes, on the other hand, almost always depend on certain organs minute enough to escape our senses. And it is certain that there are no rules in mechanics that do not hold good in physics, of which mechanics forms a part or species so that all that is artificial is also natural; for it is not less natural for a clock, made of the proper number of wheels, to indicate the hours, than for a tree which has sprung from this or that seed, to produce a particular fruit. Accordingly, just as those who apply themselves to the consideration of automata, when they know the use of a certain machine and see some of its parts, easily infer from these the manner in which others they have not seen are made, so from considering the sensible effects and parts of natural bodies, I have tried to discover the nature of the imperceptible causes and particles contained in them.

204. With regard to the things our senses do not perceive, it is sufficient to explain their possible natures, though perhaps they are not what we describe them to be and this is all that Aristotle has tried to do.

But here it may be said that although I have shown how all natural things can be formed, we have no right to conclude on this account that they were produced by these causes. For just as there may be two clocks made by the same craftsman, which although they indicate the time equally well and are externally in all respects alike, yet in no way resemble one another in the composition of their wheels, so doubtless there are many different ways in which all things we see could be formed by the great artificer without its being possible for the mind of man to be aware which of these means he has chosen to use. This I most freely admit; and I believe that I have done all that is required of me if the causes I have assigned are such that they correspond to all the phenomena manifested by nature without inquiring whether it is by their means or by others that they are produced. And it will be sufficient for the needs of life to know such causes, for medicine and mechanics, and in general all these arts that can be developed with the use of physics, have for their end only perceptible effects that are accordingly to be counted among the phenomena of nature. And in case it is supposed that Aristotle did, or desired to do, more than this, it must be remembered that he expressly says in the first book of the *Meteorology*, in the beginning of the seventh chapter, that with regard to things not manifest to the senses, he considers that he supplies sufficient explanations and demonstrations of them, if he merely shows that they may be such as he explains them to be.

V

BOYLE

Of the Excellency and Grounds of the Corpuscular or Mechanical Philosophy (1674)

(corpuscularian philosophy, criticism of Aristotelian science)

ROBERT BOYLE (1627–1691) was among the foremost English philosophers, scientists, and theologians of the seventeenth century. He was born in 1627 as the second to last of his independently wealthy mother's fifteen children. His father, Lord Cork, owed his own wealth and numerous estates to the sixteenth-century Tudor colonization, exploitation, and expropriation of Ireland. As was common for aristocratic families, he was tutored at home in French, Latin, and Greek, but tellingly not in Gaelic. At age eight, he was sent to Eton. At age twelve, he began the Continental Grand Tour, as was customary for young aristocrats. He was accompanied by an older brother and a tutor, Isaac Marcombes, a Calvinist Huguenot who had fled France. At age fourteen, he was in Florence reading Galileo (probably illegal editions since Galileo's work had been banned), at the time of Galileo's death.

Boyle was immediately convinced of the "righteousness" of Galileo's mathematical and experimental approach to physics and his rejection of Scholastic philosophy. He returned to Ireland in 1647 with these teenage convictions about natural philosophy and with dismay about the Roman Catholic Church, but with renewed Christian faith following a period in Geneva, staying with the family of his Calvinist tutor. The seamless unity of faith, theology, philosophy, and science characterized the remainder of Boyle's life and work.

In 1654 he left Ireland for Oxford, and as a gentleman of leisure, his first works were on ethics and theology, though increasingly he turned to natural philosophy and came into close contact with notable philosophers and scientists. In 1657, with Robert Hooke, he commenced experiments with a refined version of Otto von

Guericke's newly made air pump. He was a participant in the "Invisible College" of natural philosophers who were to establish, in 1663, the Royal Society. For the three decades after his return from Ireland, he produced a new science of chemistry and advanced the philosophy of corpuscularianism, or atomism, as the most fitting philosophical base for the new science of his age. He died, aged sixty-four years, in 1691.

His life was almost coterminous with those of Christiaan Huygens, Robert Hooke, Isaac Newton, and John Locke. He died six years after the birth of another prominent Irish theologian and philosopher: George Berkeley (1685–1753). Boyle was one of the jewels of the English late Renaissance.

It is standard to date modern chemistry from 1661, the year of Boyle's *The Skeptical Chymist* (Boyle [1661] 2003). In this book Boyle rejected the Aristotelian assumption of forms being responsible for chemical changes and the doctrine of the four basic elements: earth, fire, water, and air. He also rejected the alchemy of Paracelsus for its lack of systematic theory and the work of some contemporary chemists that was based on an assumption of three prime elements: salt, sulfur, and mercury.

Because chemistry dealt directly with the properties of matter, Boyle thought it ought to have a privileged place in the curriculum of natural philosophy. *The Origin of Forms and Qualities* (Stewart 1991) well illustrates how he used science as a tool in philosophical argument. At the end of a litany of experimental results, he concluded that neither Aristotelian substantial forms nor the principles of his contemporary chemists were adequate for the explanatory job at hand. Instead, he advocated basing chemistry on the "catholic and fertile principle" that change results from the "motion, bulk, shape, and texture of the minute parts of matter" (Stewart 1991). This was corpuscularianism. It was the corporeal side of the metaphysics developed earlier on the Continent by René Descartes and, in a different fashion, by Pierre Gassendi. Boyle's position, prestige, and ceaseless experimentation gave an enormous impetus to the development and extension of the corpuscularian, mechanical, anti-Aristotelian worldview.

Along with advocacy of the mechanical worldview went advocacy of the Christian religion. Boyle was a champion of natural theology, in which properties of the world supported inferences about the creator of the world. From beginning to end, he was convinced of the strength of the Design Argument for God's existence. Boyle, at one point, said there was incomparably more art expressed in the structure of a dog's foot than in the famous clock at Strasbourg (Boyle [1688] 2000).[1] He saw each scientific advance as further glorifying the handiwork of God. He endowed the Boyle lectures "for proving the Christian religion against notorious infidels" and left monies to Harvard University and to William and Mary College for the education of missionaries.

---

1. The clock metaphor was widely adduced: just as the regular and elaborate Strasbourg clock required a maker, so also did the universe; just as the workings of the clock were deterministic, so too were the workings of the universe. See Larry Laudan (1981).

Of the Excellency and Grounds of the Corpuscular or Mechanical Philosophy (1674), which follows, was originally published as an appendix to a major theological work, *The Excellency of Theology* (1664). The former rehearses the advantages of corpuscularianism for chemistry and for science more generally. It deals, as well, with issues in the methodology of science—the role and status of hypotheses in science, the degree of certainty they command, and the evaluation of competing scientific claims. These methodological questions have remained central to the philosophy of science; they are part of the border zone between philosophy and science.

REFERENCES

Alexander, Peter. 1985. *Ideas, Qualities and Corpuscles: Locke and Boyle on the External World.* Cambridge: Cambridge University Press.

Boyle, Robert. (1661) 2003. *The Sceptical Chymist.* New York: Dover Publications.

———. (1688) 2000. "A Disquisition about the Final Causes of Natural Things." In *The Works of Robert Boyle*, edited by Michael C.W. Hunter and Edward B. Davis, vol. 11. London: Pickering & Chatto.

Hunter, Michael, ed. 1994. *Robert Boyle Reconsidered.* Cambridge: Cambridge University Press.

———. 2000. *Robert Boyle, 1627–91: Scrupulosity and Science.* Woodbridge, Suffolk: Boydell Press.

———. 2009. *Boyle: Between God and Science.* New Haven, CT: Yale University Press.

Laudan, L. 1981. "The Clock Metaphor and Hypotheses: The Impact of Descartes on English Methodological Thought." In *Science and Hypothesis*, 27–58. Dordrecht: Reidel.

Shapin, Steven, and Simon Schaffer. 1985. *Leviathan and the Air-Pump: Hobbes, Boyle, and the Experimental Life.* Princeton, NJ: Princeton University Press.

Stewart, M. A., ed. 1991. *Selected Philosophical Papers of Robert Boyle.* Indianapolis: Hackett Publishing Company.

Wojcik, Jan W. 1997. *Robert Boyle and the Limits of Reason.* New York: Cambridge University Press.

Of the Excellency and Grounds of the Corpuscular or Mechanical Philosophy (1674)

By embracing the corpuscular or mechanical philosophy, I am far from supposing with the Epicureans that atoms accidentally meeting in an infinite vacuum were able, of themselves, to produce a world and all its phenomena; nor do I suppose, when God had put into the whole mass of matter an invariable quantity of motion, he needed do no more to make the universe, the material parts being able by their own unguided motions to throw themselves into a regular system. The philosophy I plead for reaches only to purely corporeal things; and distinguishing between the first origin of things and the subsequent course of nature teaches that God indeed gave motion to matter, but that in the beginning he so guided the various motion of the parts of it as to contrive them into the world he designed they should compose, and established those rules of motion and that order among corporeal things which we call the laws of nature. Thus, the universe being once framed by God, and the laws of motion settled and all upheld by his perpetual concourse and general providence, the same philosophy teaches that the phenomena of the world are physically produced by the mechanical properties of the parts of matter, and that they operate upon one another according to mechanical laws. It is of this kind of corpuscular philosophy that I speak.

And the first thing that recommends it is the intelligibleness or clearness of its principles and explanations. Among the Peripatetics[2] there are many intricate disputes about matter, privation, substantial forms, their eductions, etc. And the chemists are puzzled to give such definitions and accounts of their hypostatical principles, as are consistent with one another, and to some obvious phenomena; and much more dark and intricate are their doctrines about the Archeus, Astral Beings, and other odd notions, which perhaps have in part occasioned the darkness and ambiguity of their expressions, that could not be very clear when the conceptions were obscure.[3] And if the principles of the Aristotelians and chemists are thus obscure, it is not to be expected that the explications made by the help of such principles only should be intelligible. And, indeed, many of them are so general and slight, or otherwise so unsatisfactory, that, granting their principles, it is very hard to understand or admit their applications of them to particular phenomena.

And, I think, even in some of the more ingenious and subtle of the Peripatetic discourses, the authors, upon their superficial and narrow theories, have acted more like painters than philosophers and only shown their skill in making men fancy they see castles, cities, and other structures, that appear solid, magnificent, and extensive, when the whole piece is superficial, artificially made up of colors, and comprised within a frame. But, as to the corpuscular philosophy, men do so easily understand one another's meaning when they talk of local motion, rest, magnitude, shape, order, situation, and contexture of material substances; and these principles afford such clear accounts of those things that are rightly deduced from them alone that even such Peripatetics or chemists as maintain other principles acquiesce in the explications made

2. Aristotelians, especially the reactionary formalists of the sixteenth and seventeenth centuries.
3. The reference is to the followers of Paracelsus and Jan Baptist van Helmont. The "Archeus" is a vital spirit responsible for both chemical and physiological changes.

by these, when they can be had, and seek no further; though, perhaps, the effect is so admirable as to make it pass for that of a hidden form or an occult quality.

Those very Aristotelians who believe the celestial bodies to be moved by intelligences have no recourse to any peculiar agency of theirs to account for eclipses; and we laugh at those East Indians who, to this day, go out in multitudes with some instruments to relieve the distressed luminary whose loss of light, they fancy, proceeds from some fainting fit, out of which it must be roused. For no intelligent man, whether chemist or Peripatetic, flies to his peculiar principles after he is informed that the moon is eclipsed by the interposition of the earth between her and it, and the sun by that of the moon between him and the earth. And when we see the image of a man cast into the air by a concave spherical mirror, though most men are amazed at it, and some suspect it to be no less than an effect of witchcraft, yet he who is skilled enough in catoptrics will, without consulting Aristotle or Paracelsus or flying to hypostatical principles or substantial forms, be satisfied that the phenomenon is produced by rays of light reflected and made to converge according to optical and mathematical laws.

I next observe that there cannot be fewer principles than the two grand ones of our philosophy, matter and motion; for matter alone, unless it is moved, is wholly inactive, and, while all the parts of a body continue in one state without motion, that body will not exercise any action or suffer any alteration, though it may, perhaps, modify the action of other bodies that move against it.

Nor can we conceive any principles more primary than matter and motion; for either both of them were immediately created by God, or, if matter is eternal, motion must either be produced by some immaterial supernatural agent or it must immediately flow, by way of emanation, from the nature of the matter it appertains to.

There cannot be any physical principles more simple than matter and motion, neither of them being resoluble into any other thing.

The next thing which recommends the corpuscular principles is their extensiveness. The genuine and necessary effect of the strong motion of one part of matter against another is either to drive it on in its entire bulk or to break and divide it into particles of a determinate motion, figure, size, posture, rest, order, or texture. The two first of these, for instance, are each of them capable of numerous varieties; for the figure of a portion of matter may either be one of the five regular geometrical figures, some determinate species of solid figures, or irregular, as the grains of sand, feathers, branches, files, etc. And, as the figure, so the motion of one of these particles may be exceedingly diversified, not only by the determination to a particular part of the world but by several other things, as by the almost infinitely different degrees of celerity, by the manner of its progression, with or without rotation, etc., and more yet by the line in which it moves, as circular, elliptical, parabolic, hyperbolic, spiral, etc. For, as later geometers have shown that these curves may be compounded of several motions, that is, described by a body whose motion is mixed and results from two or more simple motions; so, how many more curves may be made by new compositions and recompositions of motion is not easy to determine.

Now, since a single particle of matter, by virtue of only two mechanical properties that belong to it, may be diversified so many ways, what a vast number of variations may we suppose capable of being produced by the compositions and recompositions of myriads of single invisible corpuscles that may be contained and concreted in one small body, and each of them be endowed with more than two or three of the fertile universal principles above mentioned? And the aggregate of those corpuscles may be further diversified by the texture resulting from their convention into a body, which, as so made up, has its own magnitude, shape, pores, and many capacities of acting and suffering, upon account of the place it holds among other bodies in a world constituted like ours; so that, considering the numerous diversifications that compositions and recompositions may make of a small number, those who think the mechanical principles may serve, indeed, to account for the phenomena of some particular part of natural philosophy, as statics, the theory of planetary motions, etc., but prove inapplicable to all the phenomena of things corporeal, seem to imagine that by putting together the letters of the alphabet one may, indeed, make up all the words to be found in Euclid or Virgil, or in the Latin or English language, but that they can by no means supply words to all the books of a great library, much less to all the languages in the world.

There are other philosophers who, observing the great efficacy of magnitude, situation, motion, and connection in engines, are willing to allow those mechanical principles a great share in the operations of bodies of a sensible bulk and manifest mechanism and, therefore, to be usefully employed in accounting for the effects and phenomena of such bodies, though they will not admit that these principles can be applied to the hidden transactions among the minute particles of bodies and, therefore, think it necessary to refer these to what they call nature, substantial forms, real qualities, and the like unmechanical agents.

But this is not necessary, for the mechanical properties of matter are to be found, and the laws of motion take place, not only in the great masses and the middle-sized lumps, but in the smallest fragments of matter—a less portion of it being as much a body as a greater must as necessarily as the other have its determinate bulk and figure. And whoever views sand through a good microscope will easily perceive that each minute grain has its own size and shape as well as a rock or a mountain. Thus too, when we let fall a large stone and a pebble from the top of a high building, they both move conformably to the laws of acceleration in heavy descending bodies, and the rules of motion are observed not only in cannon-bullets but in small shot; and the one strikes down a bird according to the same laws as the other batters a wall. And though nature works with much finer materials and employs more curious contrivances than art, yet an artist, according to the quantity of the matter he employs, the exigency of the design he undertakes, and the magnitude and shape of the instruments he uses, is able to make pieces of work of the same nature or kind, of extremely different bulks, where yet the like art, contrivance, and motion may be observed.

. . .

And therefore, to say that though in natural bodies, whose bulk is manifest and their structure visible, the mechanical principles may be usefully admitted but are not to be extended to such portions of matter whose parts and texture are invisible, is like allowing that the laws of mechanism may take place in a town clock and not in a pocket watch, or, because the terraqueous globe is a vast magnetic body, one should affirm that magnetic laws are not to be expected manifest in a small spherical piece of lodestone; yet experience shows us that, notwithstanding the immense disproportion between these two spheres, the terella[4] as well as the earth has its poles, equator, and meridians, and in several other magnetic properties resembles the terrestrial globe.

When, to solve the phenomena of nature, agents are made use of which, though they involve no contradiction in their notions, as many think substantial forms and real qualities do, yet are such that we conceive not how they operate to produce effects—such agents I mean, as the soul of the world, the universal spirit, the plastic power, etc.—the curiosity of an inquisitive person who seeks not so much to know what is the general agent that produces a phenomenon, as by what means, and after what manner it is produced, is not satisfied hereby.

Sennert and other physicians tell us of diseases which proceed from incantation; but surely, it is very trivial to a sober physician who comes to visit a patient reported to be bewitched, to hear only that the strange symptoms he meets with, and would have an account of, are produced by a witch or the devil; and he will never be satisfied with so short an answer if he can by any means reduce those extravagant symptoms to any more known and stated diseases; as epilepsies, convulsions, hysteric fits, etc., and if he cannot, he will confess his knowledge of this distemper to come far short of what might be expected and attained in other diseases, in which he thinks himself bound to search into the morbific matter, and will not be satisfied, until he can, probably, deduce from that, and the structure of the human body, and other concurring physical causes, the phenomena of the malady.

And it would be of little satisfaction to one who desires to understand the causes of the phenomena in a watch and how it comes to point at and strike the hours to be told that a certain watchmaker so contrived it or, to him who would know the true causes of an echo, to be answered that it is a man, a vault, or a wood, that makes it.

I come now to consider that which I observe most alienates other sects from the mechanical philosophy, namely, a supposition that it pretends to have principles so universal and mathematical that no other physical hypothesis can be tolerated by it.

---

4. William Gilbert's spherical lodestone.

This I look upon as an easy, indeed, but an important mistake, for the mechanical principles are so universal and applicable to so many purposes that they are rather fitted to take in than to exclude any other hypothesis founded on nature. And such hypotheses, if prudently considered, will be found, as far as they have truth on their side, to be either legitimately deducible from the mechanical principles or fairly reconcilable to them. For such hypotheses will, probably, attempt to account for the phenomena of nature, either by the help of a determinate number of material ingredients, such as the *tria prima* of the chemists[5] or else by introducing some general agents, as the Platonic soul of the world and the universal spirit, asserted by some chemists, or by both these ways together.

Now, the chief thing that a philosopher should look after in explaining difficult phenomena is not so much what the agent is or does, as what changes are made in the patient to bring it to exhibit the phenomena proposed, and by what means, and after what manner those changes are effected. So that the mechanical philosopher being satisfied, one part of matter can act upon another only by virtue of local motion or its effects and consequences; he considers if the proposed agent is not intelligible and physical, it can never physically explain the phenomena, and if it is intelligible and physical, it will be reducible to matter and some or other of its universal properties. And the indefinite divisibility of matter, the wonderful efficacy of motion, and the almost infinite variety of coalitions and structures that may be made of minute and insensible corpuscles being duly weighed, why may not a philosopher think it possible to make out, by their help, the mechanical possibility of any corporeal agent, however subtle, diffused, or active, that can be solidly proved to have a real existence in nature?

Though the Cartesians are mechanical philosophers, yet their subtle matter which the very name declares to be a corporeal substance is, for all I know, little less diffused through the universe, or less active in it than the universal spirit of some chemists, not to say the world soul of the Platonists. But whatever is the physical agent, whether it is inanimate or living, purely corporeal or united to an intellectual substance, the above mentioned changes wrought in the body made to exhibit the phenomena may be brought about by the same or the like means, or after the same, or the like manner, as for instance, if corn is reduced to meal, the materials and shape of the millstones and their peculiar motion and adaptation will be much of the same kind; and, to be sure, the grains of corn will suffer various attritions and pulverizations in their passage to the form of meal, whether the corn is ground by a watermill, or a windmill, a horsemill, or a handmill, that is, a mill whose stones are turned by inanimate, by brute, or by rational agents.

And if an angel himself should work a real change in the nature of a body, it is scarcely conceivable to men how he could do it without the assistance of local motion,

---

5. The Paracelsan elements of salt, sulfur, and mercury.

since, if nothing were displaced or otherwise moved than before, it is hardly conceivable how it should be, in itself, different from what it was before.

But if the chemists or others who would deduce a complete natural philosophy from salt, sulfur, and mercury, or any determined number of ingredients of things, would well consider what they undertake, they might easily discover that the material parts of bodies can reach but to a few phenomena of nature, while these things are considered but as quiescent things; whence they would find themselves to suppose them active, and that things purely corporeal cannot but by means of local motion, and the effects that may result from it, be very variously shaped, sized, and combined parts of matter, so that the chemists must leave the greatest part of the phenomena of the universe unexplained by means of the ingredients of bodies, without taking in the mechanical and more comprehensive properties of matter, especially local motion.

I willingly grant that salt, sulfur, and mercury, or some substances analogous to them, are obtainable by the action of the fire from a very great many bodies able to be dissipated here below. Nor do I deny that in explaining several phenomena of such bodies, it may be of use to a naturalist to know and consider that as sulfur, for instance, abounds in the body proposed, it may be, thence, probably argued that the qualities usually attending that principle, when predominant, may be also upon its account found in the body that so largely partakes of it. But, though chemical explications are sometimes the most obvious, yet they are not the most fundamental and satisfactory: for the chemical ingredient itself, whether sulfur or any other, must owe its nature and other qualities to the union of insensible particles in a convenient size, shape, motion, or rest, and texture, all which are but mechanical properties of convening corpuscles.

. . .

And here let me add that it would not at all overthrow the corpuscularian hypothesis, though, either by more exquisite purifications or by some other operations than the usual analysis by fire, it should appear that the material principles of mixed bodies are not the *tria prima* of the vulgar chemists, but either substances of another nature or fewer in number, or if it were true that the Helmontians had such a resolving menstruum as their master's alkahest,[6] by which he affirms that he could reduce stones into salt of the same weight with the mineral, and bring both that salt and all other mixed and tangible bodies into insipid water. For whatever is the number or qualities of the chemical principles, if they really exist in nature, it may very possibly be shown that they are made up of insensible corpuscles of determinate bulks and shapes, and by the various coalitions and textures of such corpuscles, many material ingredients may be composed or made to result.

6. A universal solvent.

But though the alkahestical reductions newly mentioned should be admitted, yet the mechanical principles might well be accommodated even to them. For the solidity, taste, etc., of salt may be fairly accounted for by the stiffness, sharpness, and other mechanical properties of the minute particles of which salt consists; and if, by a further action of the alkahest, the salt or any other solid body is reduced into insipid water, this also may be explained by the same principles, supposing a further comminution of its parts and such an attrition as wears off the edges and points that enabled them to strike briskly upon the organ of taste; for as to fluidity and firmness, they principally depend upon two of our grand principles, motion and rest. And it is certain that the agitation or rest and the looser contact or closer cohesion of the particles, is able to make the same portion of matter at one time a firm and at another a fluid body. So that, though future sagacity and industry of chemists should obtain from mixed bodies, homogeneous substances, different in number, nature, or both, from their vulgar salt, sulfur, and mercury, yet the corpuscular philosophy is so general and fertile as to be fairly reconcilable to such a discovery and also so useful that these new material principles will, as well as the old *tria prima*, stand in need of the more universal principles of the corpuscularians, especially of local motion.

And, indeed, whatever elements or ingredients men have pitched upon, yet if they do not take in the mechanical properties of matter, their principles are so deficient that I have observed both the materialists and chemists not only leave many things unexplained, to which their narrow principles will not extend, but even in the particulars they presume to give an account of, they either content themselves to assign such common and indefinite causes as are too general to be satisfactory, or, if they venture to give particular causes, they assign precarious or false ones, liable to be easily disproved by circumstance or instances to which their doctrines will not agree.

The chemists, however, need not be frightened from acknowledging the prerogative of the mechanical philosophy, since that may be reconcilable with the truth of their own principles, so far as they agree with the phenomena they are applied to; for these more confined hypotheses may be subordinate to those more general and fertile principles, and there can be no ingredient assigned that has a real existence in nature but may be derived either immediately or by a row of compositions from the universal matter, modified by its mechanical properties. For if with the same bricks, differently put together and ranged, several bridges, vaults, houses, and other structures may be raised merely by a various contrivance of parts of the same kind, what a great variety of ingredients may be produced by nature from the various coalitions and contextures of corpuscles that need not be supposed, like bricks, all of the same size and shape, but to have, both in the one and the other, as great a variety as could be wished for? And the primary and minute concretions that belong to these ingredients may, without opposition from the mechanical philosophy, be supposed to have their particles so minute and strongly coherent that nature of herself scarce ever tears them asunder.

Thus, mercury and gold may be successively made to put on a multitude of disguises, and yet so retain their nature as to be reducible to their pristine forms.

From hence it is probable if, besides rational souls, there are any immaterial substances, such as the heavenly intelligences and the substantial forms of the Aristotelians that are regularly to be numbered among natural agents, their way of working being unknown to us, they can only help to constitute and effect things, but will very little help us to conceive how things are effected, so that, by whatever principles natural things are constituted, it is by the mechanical principles that their phenomena must be clearly explained.

For instance, though we grant with the Aristotelians that the planets are made of a quintessential matter and moved by angels or immaterial intelligences, yet to explain the stations, progressions and retrogradations, and other phenomena of the planets, we must have recourse either to eccentrics, epicycles, etc., or to motions made in elliptical or other peculiar lines, and, in a word, to theories in which the motion, figure, situation, and other mathematical or mechanical properties are chiefly employed. But if the principles proposed are corporeal, they will then be fairly reducible or reconcilable to the mechanical principles, these being so general and fertile that, among real material things, there is none but may be derived from or reduced to them.

And when the chemists shall show that mixed bodies owe their qualities to the predominance of any one of their three grand ingredients, the corpuscularians will show that the very qualities of this or that ingredient flow from its peculiar texture and the mechanical properties of the corpuscles that compose it. And to affirm that because the chemical furnaces afford a great number of uncommon productions and phenomena, that there are bodies or operations among purely corporeal things not derivable from or reconcilable to the principles of mechanical philosophy is to say, because there are many and various hymns, pavanes, threnodies, courantes, gavottes, sarabands, etc. in a music book, many of the tunes or notes have no dependence on the scale of music, or as if because excepting rhomboids, squares, pentagons, chiliagons, and numerous other polygons, one should affirm there are some rectilinear figures not reducible to triangles or that have properties which overthrow Euclid's doctrine of triangles and polygons.

I shall only add that as mechanical principles and explanations, where they can be had, are preferred by materialists themselves for their clearness, so the sagacity and industry of modern naturalists and mathematicians, having happily applied them to several of those difficult phenomena which before were referred to occult qualities, it is probable that when this philosophy is more scrutinized and further improved, it will be found applicable to the solution of still more phenomena of nature. And it is not always necessary that he who advances an hypothesis in astronomy, chemistry, anatomy, etc., be able, *a priori*, to prove it true or demonstratively to show that the other hypothesis proposed about the same subject must be false, for as Plato said that the world is God's epistle to mankind and might have added in his own way that it was written in mathematical characters, so, in the physical explanations of the parts of the system of the world, I think there is somewhat like what happens when men conjecturally frame several keys to read a letter written in ciphers. For though one man by his sagacity finds the right key, it will be very difficult for him either to prove, otherwise than by trial, that any particular word is not such as it is guessed to be by others according to their keys or to show *a priori* that theirs are to be rejected and his to be preferred, yet, if due trial being made, the key he proposes be found so agreeable to the characters of the letter as to enable one to understand them and make coherent sense of them, its suitableness to what it should decipher is, without either confutations or foreign positive proofs, alone sufficient to make it accepted as the right key of that cipher.

Thus, in physical hypotheses, there are some that, without falling foul upon others, peaceably obtain the approbation of discerning men only by their fitness to solve the phenomena for which they were devised, without thwarting any known observation or law of nature; and therefore, if the mechanical philosophy shall continue to explain corporeal things, as it has of late, it is scarce to be doubted but that in time unprejudiced persons will think it sufficiently recommended by its being consistent with itself and applicable to so many phenomena of nature.

VI

HUYGENS

Treatise on Light **(1690)**   Preface (the hypothetico-deductive method)
                                    Chapter 1 (an argument with Descartes)

CHRISTIAAN HUYGENS (1629–1695) was born in 1629 into an esteemed Dutch family of scholars and diplomats during the Dutch "Golden Age," which was blessed with luminaries such as: Grotius, Rembrandt, Vermeer, Steen, Beeckman, Descartes, Spinoza, Bayle, Stevin, and numerous explorers and prominent merchants.[1] He developed skills and interests in mathematics and manual arts early in his life. At seventeen, he entered into philosophical and scientific correspondence with Mersenne and Descartes. By his mid-twenties, he was the foremost lens grinder in Europe, perfecting telescopes and microscopes. With the latter, he discovered Titan, a moon of Saturn, and made numerous other novel stellar and planetary observations, including determining the length of a Martian day (twenty-four hours and thirty minutes), which is only a few minutes removed from the contemporary figure (twenty-four hours and thirty-seven minutes). Needless to say, he was a champion of Copernicus's heliocentric theory, designing an orrery to display sun-centered planetary positions and rotational periods—something not easily done in a seventeenth-century Catholic country.

Among Huygens's many achievements, one that stands out for its immediate social consequence was his invention of the first reliable and accurate pendulum clock (*Horologium Oscillatorium*, 1673). The first step was mathematical: he corrected Galileo's slightly inaccurate claim that pendulums swinging on a circular curve were isochronic. Huygens established mathematically that movement on a cycloid, rather than circular, curve was isochronic. Following this theoretical advance, which was part of his overall mastery of the geometry of curves, he

---

1. See Schama (1987).

oversaw the making of the first accurate pendulum clock by his friend and fellow technician, Salomon Coster.[2]

In the period between Descartes and Leibniz, Huygens was justly acclaimed as Europe's greatest mathematician. He was a founding member of both the English Royal Society (established 1660) and the French Académie des Sciences (established 1666). He made original and lasting contributions to optics, mechanics, geometry, hydrostatics, horology, and astronomy. He died, aged sixty-six years, in 1695.

Although remembered as a scientist (his wave theory of light is familiar to most neophyte physics students), Huygens's work was infused with philosophical concerns; it was a work of natural philosophy. He dealt with issues in ontology, epistemology, methodology, and theology. Although differing from Descartes in some respects, he developed the Cartesian program of explaining all phenomena—gravitational, magnetic, optical, electric, and chemical—from the "two catholic principles" of matter and motion. In this he had no equal in the seventeenth century.

In Huygens's time, the telescope and microscope played major roles in the arbitration of scientific disputes and of borderline philosophical disputes, such as the possibility of living things being generated from the nonliving. Because both instruments depended on the transmission and amplification of light, it was natural that the nature and properties of light should be the subject of earnest inquiry. As a mathematician and optical-instrument maker, Huygens was ideally suited to advance these inquiries.

Huygens's *Treatise on Light* was written in 1678 and published in 1690. Its full title continues: *in which is explained the causes of that which occurs in reflection and in refraction and particularly in the strange refraction of Iceland Crystal.* The "strange refraction" was the just-discovered property of polarization. He explains this and other optical phenomena by the principles of the "true philosophy, in which one conceives the causes of all natural effects in terms of mechanical motions" (Huygens [1690] 1945, 3). For Huygens, philosophical theories about the nature and constitution of the world were subject to scientific and experimental testing. Again, what at one time is philosophical, speculative, and programmatic becomes at a later time scientific if the research based on the "philosophy" is fruitful.

The Preface of his *Treatise* contains one of the earliest and clearest statements of the hypothetical-deductive method in science. It occurs in the context of contrasting the probabilism and fallibilism of science with the certainty of geometry. Although often not recognized, this was the view of Descartes, for whom the hypotheses of science were at best only highly probable.

---

2. On pendulum clocks and their immense social ramifications in exploration, science, philosophy, and culture, see contributions to Matthews, Gauld, and Stinner (2005).

REFERENCES

Andriesse, Cornelis D. 2013. *Huygens: The Man Behind the Principle*. Cambridge: Cambridge University Press.

Bos, Henk J. M. 1980. "Huygens and Mathematics." In *Studies on Christiaan Huygens*, edited by Henk J. M. Bos et al., 126–146. Lisse: Swets & Zeitlinger.

———. 1986. Introduction to *Christiaan Huygens' The Pendulum Clock*. Translated by R. J. Blackwell. Ames, IA: Iowa State University Press.

Bos, Henk J. M., M. J. S. Rudwick, and H. A. M. Snelders, eds. 1980/2004. *Studies on Christiaan Huygens*. London: Routledge.

Huygens, Christiaan. (1673) 1986. *Horologium Oscillatorium: The Pendulum Clock or Geometrical Demonstrations Concerning the Motion of Pendula as Applied to Clocks*. Translated by R. J. Blackwell. Ames, IA: Iowa State University Press.

———. (1690) 1945. *Treatise on Light*. Translated and edited by Silvanus P. Thompson. Chicago: University of Chicago Press.

Matthews, Michael R., Colin F. Gauld, and Arthur Stinner, eds. 2005. *The Pendulum: Scientific, Historical, Philosophical and Educational Perspectives*. Dordrecht: Springer.

Schama, Simon. 1987. *The Embarrassment of Riches: An Interpretation of Dutch Culture in the Golden Age*. New York: Alfred Knopf.

Thompson, Silvanus P., ed. 1945. *Huygens: Treatise on Light*. Chicago: University of Chicago Press.

Treatise on Light (1690)
Preface

This treatise was written during my stay in Paris twelve years ago, and in the year 1678 was presented to the Royal Academy of Sciences, to which the king had been pleased to call me. Several of this body who are still living, especially those who have devoted themselves to the study of mathematics, will remember having been at the meeting at which I presented the paper; of these I recall only those distinguished gentlemen Messrs. Cassini, Römer, and De la Hire. Although since then I have corrected and changed several passages, the copies which I had made at that time will show that I have added nothing except some conjectures concerning the structure of Iceland spar and an additional remark concerning refraction in rock-crystal. I mention these details to show how long I have been thinking about these matters which I am only just now publishing, and not at all to detract from the merit of those who, without having seen what I have written, may have investigated similar subjects: as, indeed, happened in the case of two distinguished mathematicians, Newton and Leibniz, regarding the question of the proper figure for a converging lens, one surface being given.

It may be asked why I have so long delayed the publication of this work. The reason is that I wrote it rather carelessly in French, expecting to translate it into Latin, and, in the meantime, to give the subject still further attention. Later I thought of publishing this volume together with another on dioptrics in which I discuss the theory of the telescope and the phenomena associated with it. But soon the subject was no longer new and was therefore less interesting. Accordingly I kept putting off the work from time to time, and now I do not know when I shall be able to finish it, for my time is largely occupied either by business or by some new investigation.

In view of these facts I have thought wise to publish this manuscript in its present state rather than to wait longer and run the risk of its being lost.

One finds in this subject a kind of demonstration which does not carry with it so high a degree of certainty as that employed in geometry; and which differs distinctly from the method employed by geometers in that they prove their propositions by well-established and incontrovertible principles, while here principles are tested by the inferences which are derivable from them. The nature of the subject permits of no other treatment. It is possible, however, in this way to establish a probability which is little short of certainty. This is the case when the consequences of the assumed principles are in perfect accord with the observed phenomena, and especially when these verifications are numerous; but above all when one employs the hypothesis to predict new phenomena and finds his expectations realized.

If in the following treatise all these evidences of probability are present, as, it seems to me, they are, the correctness of my conclusions will be confirmed; and, indeed, it is scarcely possible that these matters differ very widely from the picture which I have drawn of them. I venture to hope that those who enjoy finding out causes and who appreciate the wonders of light will be interested in these various speculations and in the new explanation of that remarkable property upon which the structure of the human eye depends and upon which are based those instruments which so powerfully aid the eye. I trust also there will be some who, from such beginnings, will push these investigations far in advance of what I have been able to do; for the subject is not one which is easily exhausted. This will be evident especially from those parts of the subject which I have indicated as too difficult for solution; and still more evident from those matters upon which I have not touched at all, such as the various kinds of luminous bodies and the whole question of color, which no one can yet boast of having explained.

Finally, there is much more to be learned by investigation concerning the nature of light than I have yet discovered; and I shall be greatly indebted to those who, in the future, shall furnish what is needed to complete my imperfect knowledge.

The Hague, 8th of January, 1690.

Chapter I: On the Rectilinear Propagation of Rays

Demonstrations in optics, as in every science where geometry is applied to matter, are based upon experimental facts; as, for instance, that light travels in straight lines, that the angles of incidence and reflection are equal, and that rays of light are refracted according to the law of sines. For this last fact is now as widely known and as certainly known as either of the preceding.

Most writers upon optical subjects have been satisfied to assume these facts. But others, of a more investigating turn of mind, have tried to find the origin and the cause of these facts, considering them in themselves interesting natural phenomena. And although they have advanced some ingenious ideas, these are not such that the more intelligent readers do not still want further explanation in order to be thoroughly satisfied.

Accordingly, I here submit some considerations on this subject with the hope of elucidating, as best I may, this department of natural science, which not undeservedly has gained the reputation of being exceedingly difficult. I feel myself especially indebted to those who first began to make clear these deeply obscure matters, and to lead us to hope that they were capable of simple explanations.

But, on the other hand, I have been astonished to find these same writers accepting arguments which are far from evident as if they were conclusive and demonstrative. No one has yet given even a probable explanation of the fundamental and remarkable phenomena of light, *viz.* why it travels in straight lines and how rays coming from an infinitude of different directions cross one another without disturbing one another.

I shall attempt, in this volume, to present in accordance with the principles of modern philosophy, some clearer and more probable reasons, first, for the rectilinear propagation of light, and secondly, for its reflection when it meets other bodies. Later I shall explain the phenomenon of rays which are said to undergo refraction in passing through transparent bodies of different kinds. Here I shall treat also of refraction effects due to the varying density of the earth's atmosphere. Afterwards I shall examine the causes of that peculiar refraction occurring in a certain crystal which comes from Iceland. And lastly, I shall consider the different shapes required in transparent and in reflecting bodies to converge rays upon a single point or to deflect them in various ways. Here we shall see with what ease are determined, by our new theory, not only the ellipses, hyperbolas, and other curves which M. Descartes has so ingeniously devised for this purpose, but also the curve which one surface of a lens must have when the other surface is given, as spherical, plane, or of any figure whatever.

We cannot help believing that light consists in the motion of a certain material. For when we consider its production, we find that here on the earth it is generally produced by fire and flame which, beyond doubt, contain bodies in a state of rapid motion, since they are able to dissolve and melt numerous other more solid bodies.

And if we consider its effects, we see that when light is converged, as, for instance, by concave mirrors, it is able to produce combustion just as fire does. That is, it is able to tear bodies apart; a property that surely indicates motion, at least in the true philosophy where one believes all natural phenomena to be mechanical effects. And, in my opinion, we must admit this, or else give up all hope of ever understanding anything in physics.

Since, according to this philosophy, it is considered certain that the sensation of sight is caused only by the impulse of some form of matter upon the nerves at the base of the eye, we have here still another reason for thinking that light consists in a motion of the matter situated between us and the luminous body.

When we consider, further, the very great speed with which light is propagated in all directions, and the fact that when rays come from different directions, even those directly opposite, they cross without disturbing each other, it must be evident that we do not see luminous objects by means of matter translated from the object to us, as a shot or an arrow travels through the air. For certainly this would be in contradiction to the two properties of light which we have just mentioned, and especially to the latter. Light is then propagated in some other manner, an understanding of which we may obtain from our knowledge of the manner in which sound travels through the air.

We know that through the medium of the air, an invisible and impalpable body, sound is propagated in all directions, from the point where it is produced, by means of a motion which is communicated successively from one part of the air to another; and since this motion travels with the same speed in all directions, it must form spherical surfaces which continually enlarge until finally they strike our ear. Now there can be no doubt that light also comes from the luminous body to us by means of some motion impressed upon the matter which lies in the intervening space; for we have already seen that this cannot occur through the translation of matter from one point to the other.

If, in addition, light requires time for its passage—a point we shall presently consider—it will then follow that this motion is impressed upon the matter gradually, and hence is propagated, as that of sound, by surfaces and spherical waves. I call these *waves* because of their resemblance to those which are formed when one throws a pebble into water and which represent gradual propagation in circles, although produced by a different cause and confined to a plane surface.

As to the question of light requiring time for its propagation, let us consider first whether there is any experimental evidence to the contrary.

What we can do here on the earth with sources of light placed at great distances (although showing that light does not occupy a sensible time in passing over these distances) may be objected to on the ground that these distances are still too small, and that, therefore, we can conclude only that the propagation of light is exceedingly rapid. M. Descartes thought it instantaneous, and based his opinion upon much better evidence, furnished by the eclipse of the moon. Nevertheless, as I shall show, even this evidence is not conclusive. I shall state the matter in a manner slightly different from his in order that we may more easily arrive at all the consequences.

Let A be the position of the sun; BD a part of the orbit or annual path of the earth; ABC a straight-line intersecting in C the orbit of the moon, which is represented by the circle CD.

If, now, light requires time—say one hour—to traverse the space between the earth and the moon, it follows that when the earth has reached the point B, its shadow, or the interruption of light, will not yet have reached the point C, and will not reach it until one hour later. Counting from the time when the earth occupies the position B, it will be one hour later that the moon arrives at the point C and is there obscured; but this eclipse or interruption of light will not be visible at the earth until the end of still another hour. Let us suppose that during these two hours the earth has moved to the position E. From this point the moon will appear to be eclipsed at C, a position which it occupied one hour before, while the sun will be seen at A. For I assume with Copernicus that the sun is fixed and, since light travels in straight lines, must always be seen it its true position. But it is a matter of universal observation, we are told, that the eclipsed moon appears in that part of the ecliptic directly opposite the sun; while according to our view its position ought to be behind this by the angle GEC, the supplement of the angle AEC. But this is contrary to the fact, for the angle GEC will be quite easily observed, amounting to about 33°. Now according to our computation, which will be found in the memoir on the causes of the phenomena of Saturn, the distance, BA, between the earth and the sun is about 12,000 times the diameter of the earth, and consequently 400 times the distance of the moon, which is 30 diameters. The angle ECB will, therefore, be almost 400 times as great as BAE, which is 5′ *viz.*, the angular distance traversed by the earth in its orbit during an interval of two hours. Thus the angle BCE amounts to almost 33°, and likewise the angle CEG, which is 5′ greater.

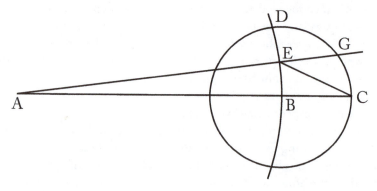

But it must be noted that in this argument the speed of light is assumed to be such that the time required for it to pass from here to the moon is one hour. If, however, we suppose that it requires only a minute of time, then evidently the angle CEG will amount to only 33′; and if it requires only ten seconds of time, this angle will amount to less than 6′. But so small a quantity is not easily observed in a lunar eclipse, and consequently it is not allowable to infer the instantaneous propagation of light.

It is somewhat unusual, we must confess, to assume a speed one hundred thousand times as great as that of sound, which, according to my observations, travels about 180 toises [1151 *feet*] in a second, or during a pulse-beat; but this supposition appears by no means impossible, for it is not a question of carrying a body with such speed, but of a motion passing successively from one point to another.

I do not therefore, in thinking of these matters, hesitate to suppose that the propagation of light occupies time, for on this view all the phenomena can be explained, while on the contrary view none of them can be explained. Indeed, it seems to me, and to many others also, that M. Descartes, whose object has been to discuss all physical subjects in a clear way, and who has certainly succeeded better than anyone before him, has written nothing on light and its properties which is not either full of difficulty or even inconceivable.

But this idea which I have advanced only as a hypothesis has recently been almost established as a fact by the ingenious method of Römer, whose work I propose here to describe, expecting that he himself will later give a complete confirmation of this view.

VII

NEWTON

***Principia* (1687)**	Scholium (on absolute space and time)
	General Scholium (Design Argument, hypotheses in science)
***Opticks* (1704)**	Query 31 (nature, corpuscularianism, gravity, the Design Argument, hypotheses in science)

ISAAC NEWTON (1643–1727) was born, according to the then-used Julian calendar, on Christmas Day 1642 (January 4, 1643 in the Gregorian calendar). He was the towering figure of the Scientific Revolution. In a period blessed with so many outstanding thinkers, Newton was simply the most outstanding. With good reason, Goethe labeled 1642 the "Christmas of the modern age." English enthusiasm for Newton was captured in Alexander Pope's epitaph, composed for Newton's Westminster Abbey tomb:

> Nature and Nature's laws lay hid in night:
> God said, Let Newton be! and all was light.

This enthusiasm spread rapidly through the Western world, eventually becoming the modern scientific norm—at least until twentieth-century relativity and quantum theories necessitated some adjustments.

John Locke memorably, and with understatement, wrote in the introduction of his 1690 *An Essay Concerning Human Understanding*:

> The Commonwealth of Learning is not at this time without Master-Builders, whose mighty designs, in advancing the sciences, will leave lasting monuments to the admiration of posterity; but every one must not hope to be

a Boyle, or a Sydenham; and in an age that produces such masters, as the great Huygenius, and the incomparable Mr. Newton, with some other of that strain; 'tis ambition enough to be employed as an under-labourer in clearing ground a little, and removing some of the rubbish, that lies in the way to knowledge. (Locke [1690] 1975, 10)

Newtonian thought met initial resistance from followers of Descartes, Huygens, and Leibniz, who objected that Newton's gravitational attraction violated a basic tenet of the nascent mechanical worldview, namely that things affect other things only by contact, not by contactless "pulls" or attractions. It also met some resistance from "rearguard" Aristotelians who saw in Newton's world no recognition of hylomorphism. They could not accept a literally formless world of moving, bumping, aimless, brute matter. However, by the end of the eighteenth century, Newtonianism had triumphed in natural philosophy (Ducheyne 2012; Schliesser 2021), and the thought-to-be Newtonian method was widely employed in social and historical studies. The reception of Newtonianism is a case study of the perennial interaction, nay conflict, of physics (science) and metaphysics (including religion): Which of the two has priority when there is a clash?[1]

Newton is universally known and esteemed for his foundational three laws of motion and theory of universal gravitation. Yet he also made fundamental contributions in many fields—much more in mechanics, optics, astronomy, mathematics, geodesy, and chemistry—any of which would have assured him an honored place in the histories of science and mathematics.

In addition, Newton wrote substantial works in theology and scriptural studies; indeed, 1.3 million words on these subjects. During three decades of his life, he wrote many thousands of folio pages explicating an accurate chronology of biblical and Middle Eastern history: he wrote nearly 90,000 words for a manuscript, *The Chronology of Ancient Kingdoms Amended*, which was published shortly after his death in 1728.

Newton was a serious biblical scholar who paid exacting attention to the translation history, and thus authenticity, of scriptural texts (Popkin 2000). In 1704 he composed a long letter to John Locke arguing that the translation of central scriptural passages in the epistles of John (1 John 5:7) and Timothy (1 Timothy 3:16) had been corrupted by the Trinitarian prejudices, or ideology, of the early Roman Church.

Despite his preeminence and social standing, Newton never publicly avowed his non-Trinitarian, basically Arian-Unitarian, beliefs.[2] In England, such revelation

---

1. This conflict played out in Scholastic/Aristotelian reaction to Galileo's physics, Christian/Islamic reaction to Darwinian evolution, Marxist/Leninist reaction to Mendel's theory, Maoist reaction to quantum theory, and numerous indigenous cultures' responses to modern science.

2. On Newton's religious belief, see Brooke (1988), and contributions to Force and Popkin (1998).

would have led to immediate dismissal from public employment, and assuredly from his fellowship at, of all colleges, Trinity College. Newton's manuscript/letter to Locke was not published until 1785, nearly sixty years after his death. In Scotland, the Act against Blasphemy (1661) made denial of the Trinity a hanging offense and this remained in force until the passing of the Doctrine of the Trinity Act (1813), which gave relief primarily to Unitarian Christians. Though not an orthodox Christian, Newton was a staunch theist, writing in a 1692 letter to his friend Richard Bentley:

> When I wrote my treatise about our system, I had an eye upon such principles
> as might work with considering men, for the belief of a Deity, and nothing
> can rejoice me more than to find it useful for that purpose.[3]

Newton wrote over a half million words on alchemy. Indeed, he wrote much more on theology, scriptural studies, and alchemy than he did on what we recognize as science.[4] And he was not just a scholar: Newton was a member of Parliament, a long-time president of the Royal Society (1703–1727), Master of the Royal Mint for thirty years, and a home counties magistrate. He died in 1727, aged eighty-four years, and was buried in Westminster Abbey.[5]

Newton corresponded and argued with all of the prominent philosophers of his age: Robert Boyle, Robert Hooke, Christiaan Huygens, Henry More, George Berkeley, John Wallis, John Locke, Gottfried Leibniz, and the followers of René Descartes who were advancing Cartesian natural philosophy. Both the debates with Leibniz (over the possibility of absolute space and time and the consequence thereof for science, religion, and cognition) and those with Cartesians (concerning how gravitational attraction could be reconciled with a mechanical, effects-only-by-contact worldview) illustrate the unavoidable interaction between science and philosophy mentioned earlier.

Newton's influence on the history of science is unequaled, but his influence extended well beyond science. His achievements set a standard whereby knowledge-seeking in all fields was judged, and his methodology was consequently adopted. Newton, in his *Opticks*, had himself indicated the path:

> If natural Philosophy in all its Parts, by pursuing this Method, shall at length
> be perfected, the Bounds of Moral Philosophy will be also enlarged.[6]

In the preface to his 1739 *Treatise*, David Hume claimed he was following Newton's path and chose as the work's subtitle: *An Attempt to Introduce the Experimental Method*

---

3. Letter to Bentley, December 10, 1692 in Thayer (1953, 46).
4. See Newman (2018).
5. For biographies of Newton, see Gleick (2003) and Westfall (1980).
6. Newton (1730/1979), 405. Here "moral philosophy" means social/historical studies.

of Reasoning into Moral Subjects. Immanuel Kant based the philosophy of his *Critique of Pure Reason* partly upon the assumption that Newton had discovered the correct system of the world and, consequently, philosophy had to be reconciled to that system. A great many theologians, moralists, economists, and chemists did their best to emulate what they saw as Newton's method.[7]

At the urging of, and with the support of, Edmund Halley, Britain's Astronomer Royal, Newton published his monumental *The Mathematical Principles of Natural Philosophy* in 1687.[8] A clue to its method is contained in a piece originally meant as its preface but not published until its appearance as Query 31 in the second edition of the *Opticks* (1717). He says:

> As in mathematics, so in natural philosophy, the investigation of difficult things by the method of analysis ought ever to precede the method of composition. This analysis consists in making experiments and observations and in drawing general conclusions from them by induction and in admitting of no objections against the conclusions but such as are taken from experiments or other certain truths.[9]

As stated here, mathematics and physics have similar methods. This is a most un-Aristotelian position: the Aristotelian separation of mathematics and physics greatly limited medieval science.

A further clue to the method of the *Principia* occurs in the published preface to the first edition. In talking of the difference between geometrical objects (the perfect figures of Euclid and Pythagoras) and material objects made by artisans, he follows Galileo in saying, "errors are not in the art but in the artificers." (Newton [1726] 1999, 381). If technology and craft could produce a perfect sphere, its properties would be exactly as the mathematicians tell us. More generally, Newton sees the scientific experiment as an attempt at, or approximation to, the objectification of scientific theory. The scientist does not merely look at undisturbed nature as Aristotle urged: the experiment is an attempt to create a part of nature in the image of the theory—to objectify the theory by removing impediments, impurities, confounding causes, and the like.[10]

Newton's procedure is a development of the revolutionary "scientific" program of idealization introduced by Galileo. He deals with the mathematics of ideal and abstracted situations *before* he considers the properties of real objects. This is the reverse of Aristotelian empiricism. The structure of the *Principia* displays the procedure.

---

7. See contributions to Butts and Davis (1970) and Cohen and Smith (2002).

8. Second edition 1713, third edition 1726. The best English translation is Newton (1999).

9. Newton ([1730] 2019) Query 31, reproduced in *Opticks* selection included here.

10. One of the earliest statements of experiment as objectification of theory is Bachelard (1984). There is copious philosophical literature on experiment. See at least Franklin (1999).

The first four hundred pages are entirely mathematical and deal with clearly idealized situations: a body considered as a point mass moving in a circle, pendulums moving in voids, two-body universes, and so on. It is not until the third and final book that he considers how actual bodies move in the world around us.[11] Many of Newton's early empiricist supporters—Bacon, Locke, Hume, Mill—and subsequent empiricists and positivists did not appreciate this essential component of the Newtonian method.[12]

Newton's second major work was his *Opticks*. Published in 1704, it was the result of many years of investigative work and Royal Society presentations. The book displays in marvelous sweep and detail his experimental genius. Consistent with the mechanical worldview, he developed a corpuscular, or particle, theory of light. In a second edition (1717), he added a lengthy series of philosophical and methodological reflections (see the selection of text below). These dealt with gravity, the theory of matter, the Design Argument, the role of hypotheses in natural philosophy, and other topics.

The Design Argument was important to Newton, who understood his scientific work as advancing the tradition of natural theology and said in the General Scholium to his *Principia* that discourse about God "from the appearances of things does certainly belong to natural philosophy." He rejected the claim (later made famous by Pierre-Simon Laplace's reply "I have no need for that hypothesis" in response to a question from Napoleon) that the theory of gravitation obviates the need for a creator to design the solar system. Newton's view was that gravitation explains how the planets go, but not how they came to be in a planar orbit, with separations that gave just the right atmospheric conditions for sustaining life on earth. Out of chaos, gravitational attraction could not, alone, produce such a circumstance; only a designer could.

The arguments that raged with his opponents on the Continent demonstrate the intertwining of physics, philosophy, and theology so characteristic of not only Newton but of all natural philosophy of the period. In rejecting Newton's claim that the amount of motion in the world is steadily decreasing, Leibniz said that it requires that:

> God Almighty wants to wind up his watch (the universe) from time to time: otherwise it would cease to move. (Alexander 1956, 11)

Understanding this debate, so crucial to the emergence of the "scientific" idea of the conservation of energy, requires an appreciation of science, theology, and philosophy. Something that liberal education informed by the history and philosophy of science provides.[13]

---

11. On idealization in science, see Rice (2021) and Potochnik (2017).
12. See Mittelstrass (1972) and contributions to Butts and Davis (1970).
13. See Matthews (2015).

A further example of these interconnections was Newton's grand unifying theory of gravitation. This monumental achievement combined Kepler's laws for planetary motion and Galileo's law of falling bodies into the single inverse-square law of universal gravitational attraction. Yet it was immediately attacked by Leibniz and Cartesian physicists as being occult, as turning the clock back to Aristotelian physics. The idea of attraction at a distance, without any intermediary mechanism, was seen as incompatible with the hard-won, new, mechanical-by-contact worldview.

John Locke, Newton's self-styled "under-laborer," had said in the first edition of his *Essay Concerning Human Understanding* that "Bodies operate one upon another by impulse and nothing else . . . it is impossible to conceive that Body should operate upon what it does not touch" (Locke 1975, Book II, Ch. 8, #11). This was a metaphysical "certain truth," yet his adoption of Newton's physics caused the metaphysics to be soon amended, if not rejected.[14] In his 1698 third letter to Bishop Stillingfleet of Worcester, defending himself against anti-Trinitarian innuendo, Locke writes:

> You ask, "how can my way of liberty agree with the idea that bodies can operate only by motion and impulse?" *Answ.* By the omnipotency of God, who can make all things agree, that involve not a contradiction. It is true, I say, "that bodies operate by impulse, and nothing else." And so I thought when I writ it, and can yet conceive no other way of their operation. But I am since convinced by the judicious Mr. Newton's incomparable book, that it is too bold a presumption to limit God's power, in this point, by my narrow conceptions. The gravitation of matter towards matter, by ways inconceivable to me, is not only a demonstration that God can, if he pleases, put into bodies powers and ways of operation, above what can be derived from our idea of body, or can be explained by what we know of matter, but also an unquestionable and every where visible instance, that he has done so. And therefore in the next edition of my book, I shall take care to have that passage rectified. (Locke 1997)

Gravitational attraction was a core metaphysical question in the late seventeenth century. It was at the heart of Kant's eighteenth-century philosophy, it was "wished away" by Mach in the nineteenth century, and was reasserted by Einstein's 1915 general theory of relativity that "required" the existence of then-unknown gravitational waves.[15] The very concept of gravitation—as with other foundational scientific concepts such as force, matter, time, and evolution—is at once scientific and philosophical.

---

14. On Newton's impact on Locke, see Rogers (1978) and Stein (1990).
15. The existence of gravitational waves was only confirmed in 2016 by the LIGO research team (Kennefick, 2007).

Just what the law of gravitation entails are scientific questions: What is the relation between gravitational strength and the distance between bodies? Does it vary inversely with the square of distance, with the cube, or fractional cube of distance? Does it hold between all bodies or just solid bodies, not gaseous bodies? If the latter, how does the sun fit into the gravitational picture? A more philosophical question is: Does the attraction operate over empty space, in a celestial vacuum? A connected question is: Can the law just be asserted without attention to mediums or mechanisms? If so, how does the assertion differ from claims that devils, angels, or spirits are responsible for individual events or patterns of events?

A more outright metaphysical question is the one Locke acknowledged in his foregoing exchange with Stillingfleet: Is the power of attracting other bodies something essential to matter? Is the power part of the divine, or otherwise ordained, ontology of the world? Is "attracting power" a primary quality of matter along with extension, impenetrability, inertia, and mass? In Newton's Rule III of "Rules of Reasoning in Philosophy," he rhetorically asks and then affirms: "All bodies whatsoever are endowed with a principle of mutual gravitation." (Newton [1726] 1999, 796)

Careful reading of the following selections from Newton's *Principia* and *Opticks* will illustrate most of the philosophical matters touched upon in this Introduction.

REFERENCES

Alexander, H. G., ed. 1956. *The Leibniz-Clarke Correspondence*. Manchester: Manchester University Press.

Bachelard, Gaston. (1934) 1984. *The New Scientific Spirit*. Boston: Beacon Books.

Brooke, John H. 1988. "The God of Isaac Newton." In *Let Newton Be! A New Perspective on His Life and Works*, edited by John Fauvel et al., 169–183. Oxford: Oxford University Press.

Butts, Robert E., and John Davis, eds. 1970. *The Methodological Heritage of Newton*. Toronto: University of Toronto Press.

Cohen, I. Bernard. 1980. *The Newtonian Revolution*. Cambridge: Cambridge University Press.

Cohen, I. Bernard, and George E. Smith, eds. 2002. *The Cambridge Companion to Newton*. Cambridge: Cambridge University Press.

Ducheyne, Steffen. 2012. *The Main Business of Natural Philosophy: Isaac Newton's Natural-Philosophical Methodology*. Dordrecht: Springer.

Fauvel, John, Raymond Flood, Michael Shortland, and Robin Wilson, eds. 1988. *Let Newton Be!: A New Perspective on His Life and Works*. Oxford: Oxford University Press.

Force, James E., and Richard H. Popkin, eds. 1998. *Newton and Religion: Context, Nature, and Influence*. Dordrecht: Kluwer Academic Publishers.

Franklin, Allan. 1999. *Can That Be Right?: Essays on Experiment, Evidence, and Science*. Dordrecht: Kluwer Academic Publishers.

Gleick, James. 2003. *Isaac Newton*. New York: Random House.

Janiak, Andrew. 2008. *Newton as Philosopher*. Cambridge: Cambridge University Press.

Janiak, Andrew, and Eric Schliesser, eds. 2012. *Interpreting Newton: Critical Essays*. Cambridge: Cambridge University Press.

Kennefick, Daniel. 2007. *Travelling at the Speed of Thought: Einstein and the Quest for Gravitational Waves*. Princeton, NJ: Princeton University Press.

Locke, John. (1690) 1975. *An Essay Concerning Human Understanding*. Edited by Peter H. Nidditch. Oxford: Oxford University Press.

———. (1698) 1997. "Letter to Stillingfleet, Bishop of Worcester." In *Collected Works of John Locke*. London: Routledge.

Matthews, Michael R. 2015. *Science Teaching: The Contribution of History and Philosophy of Science*. 2nd ed. New York: Routledge.

Mittelstrass, Jürgen. 1972. "The Galilean Revolution: The Historical Fate of a Methodological Insight." *Studies in the History and Philosophy of Science* 2, no. 4: 297–328.

Newman, William R. 2018. *Newton the Alchemist: Science, Enigma, and the Quest for Nature's "Secret Fire."* Princeton, NJ: Princeton University Press.

Newton, Isaac. (1726) 1999. *The Principia: Mathematical Principles of Natural Philosophy*. Translated by I. Bernard Cohen and Anne Whitman, preceded by "A Guide to Newton's *Principia*" by I. Bernard Cohen. Berkeley: University of California Press.

———. (1730) 1979. *Opticks or A Treatise of the Reflections, Refractions, Inflections & Colours of Light*. New York: Dover Publications.

Popkin, Richard H. 2000. "Newton, Spinoza and Biblical Scholarship." In *Rethinking the Scientific Revolution*, edited by Margaret J. Osler, 297–311. Cambridge: Cambridge University Press.

Potochnik, Angela. 2017. *Idealization and the Aims of Science*. Chicago: The University of Chicago Press.

Rice, Collin. 2021. *Leveraging Distortions: Explanation, Idealization, and Universality in Science*. Cambridge, MA: MIT Press.

Rogers, G. A. J. 1978. "Locke's *Essay* and Newton's *Principia*." *Journal for the History of Ideas* 39, no. 2: 217–232.

Schilt, Cornelis J. 2021. *Isaac Newton and the Study of Chronology: Prophecy, History, and Method*. Amsterdam: Amsterdam University Press.

Schliesser, Eric. 2021. *Newton's Metaphysics: Essays*. Oxford: Oxford University Press.

Stein, Howard. 1990. "On Locke, 'The Great Huygenius, and the Incomparable Mr. Newton.'" In *Philosophical Perspectives on Newtonian Science*, edited by Phillip Bricker and R. I. G. Hughes, 17–47. Cambridge, MA: MIT Press.

Thayer, H. S., ed. 1953. *Newton's Philosophy of Nature: Selections from His Writings*. New York: Hafner Press.

Westfall, Richard S. 1980. *Never at Rest: A Biography of Isaac Newton*. Cambridge: Cambridge University Press.

Principia (1687)
Scholium on Absolute Space and Time

Up to now I have defined terms that are less known and explained the sense I would have them understood in the following discourse. I do not define time, space, place, and motion, since they are well known to all. Only I must observe that the common people conceive those quantities under no other notions than from their relation to sensible objects. And from this certain prejudices arise, for the removing of which it will be convenient to distinguish the terms into absolute and relative, true and apparent, mathematical and common.

I. Absolute, true, and mathematical time, of itself, and from its own nature, flows uniformly without relation to anything external, and by another name is called *duration*. Relative, apparent, and common time is some sensible and external (whether accurate or varying in rate) measure of duration by the means of motion, which is commonly used instead of true time, such as an hour, a day, a month, a year.

II. Absolute space, in its own nature, without relation to anything external, always remains similar and immovable. Relative space is some movable dimension or measure of the absolute spaces, which our senses determine by its position to bodies and is commonly taken for immovable space, such as the dimension of subterraneous, aerial, or celestial space, determined by its position with respect to earth. Absolute and relative space are the same in form and magnitude, but they do not always remain numerically the same. For if the earth, for instance, moves, a space of our air, which relatively and with respect to the earth always remains the same, will at one time be one part of the absolute space into which the air passes, at another time it will be another part of the same, and so, absolutely understood, it will be continually changed.

III. Place is a part of space which a body takes up, and is absolute or relative according to the space. I say, a part of space, not the situation nor the external surface of the body. For the places of equal solids are always equal, but their surfaces, by reason of their dissimilar figures, are often unequal. Positions properly have no quantity, nor are they so much the places themselves as the properties of places. The motion of the whole is the same as the sum of the motions of the parts; that is, the translation of the whole out of its place is the same thing as the sum of the translations of the parts out of their places; and therefore the place of the whole is the same as the sum of the places of the parts, and for that reason it is internal and in the whole body.

IV. Absolute motion is the translation of a body from one absolute place into another, and relative motion the translation from one relative place into another. Thus in a ship under sail, the relative place of a body is that part of the ship the body possesses, or that part of the cavity the body fills, and which therefore moves together with the ship; and relative rest is the continuance of the body in the same part of the ship or of its cavity. But real, absolute rest is the continuance of the body in the same part of that immovable space, in which the ship itself, its cavity, and all that it contains, is moved. For that reason, if the earth is really at rest, the body which relatively rests in the ship will really and absolutely move with the same velocity which the ship has on the earth. But if the earth also moves, the true and absolute motion of the body will arise, partly from the true motion of the earth in immovable space, partly from the relative motion of the ship on the earth; and if the body moves also relatively in the ship, its true motion will arise, partly from the true motion of the earth in immovable space, and partly from the relative motions as well of the ship on the earth as of the body in the ship; and from these relative motions will arise the relative motion of the body on the earth. As if that part of the earth, where the ship is, was truly moved towards the east with a velocity of 10,010 units, while the ship itself, with a fresh gale and full sails, is carried towards the west with a velocity expressed by ten of those units, while a sailor walks in the ship towards the east, with one unit of the said velocity, then the sailor will be moved truly in immovable space towards the east with a velocity of 10,001 units, and relatively on the earth towards the west with a velocity of nine of those units.

Absolute time is distinguished from relative in astronomy by the equation or correction of the apparent time. For the natural days are truly unequal, though they are commonly considered as equal and used for a measure of time; astronomers correct this inequality that they may measure the celestial motions by a more accurate time. It may be that there is no such thing as a uniform motion by which time may be accurately measured. All motions may be accelerated and retarded, but the flowing of absolute time is not liable to any change. The duration or perseverance of the existence of things remains the same, whether the motions are swift or slow or none at all; and therefore this duration ought to be distinguished from what are only sensible measures of it, and from which we deduce it by means of the astronomical equation. The necessity of this equation for determining the times of a phenomenon is established as well from the experiments of the pendulum clock as by eclipses of the satellites of Jupiter.

As the order of the parts of time is immutable, so also is the order of the parts of space. Suppose those parts to be moved out of their places, and they will be moved (if the expression may be allowed) out of themselves. For times and spaces are, as it were, the places as well of themselves as of all other things. All things are placed in time as to order of succession, and in space as to order of situation. It is from their essence or nature that they are places, and it is absurd that the primary places of things should be movable. These are therefore the absolute places, and translations out of those places are the only absolute motions.

But because the parts of space cannot be seen or distinguished from one another by our senses, we use sensible measures of them in their stead. For from the positions and distances of things from any body considered as immovable, we define all places, and then with respect to such places, we estimate all motions, considering bodies as transferred from some of those places into others. And so, instead of absolute places and motions, we use relative ones, and that without any inconvenience in common affairs; but in philosophical disquisitions, we ought to abstract from our senses and consider things themselves, distinct from what are only sensible measures of them. For it may be that there is no body really at rest to which the places and motions of others may be referred.

But we may distinguish rest and motion, absolute and relative, one from the other by their properties, causes, and effects. It is a property of rest that bodies really at rest do rest in respect to one another. And therefore as it is possible that in the remote regions of the fixed stars, or perhaps far beyond them, there may be some body absolutely at rest, but impossible to know, from the position of bodies to one another in our regions, whether any of these do keep the same position to that remote body, it follows that absolute rest cannot be determined from the position of bodies in our regions.

It is a property of motion that the parts, which retain given positions to their wholes, do partake of the motions of those wholes. For all the parts of revolving bodies endeavor to recede from the axis of motion, and the impetus of bodies moving forwards arises from the joint impetus of all the parts. Therefore, if surrounding bodies are moved, those that are relatively at rest within them will partake of their motion. Because of this, the true and absolute motion of a body cannot be determined by the translation of it from those which only seem to rest; for the external bodies should not only appear at rest, but be really at rest. For otherwise, all included bodies, besides their translation from near the surrounding ones, partake likewise of their true motions; and though that translation were not made, they would not be really at rest, but only seem to be so. For the surrounding bodies stand in the like relation to the surrounded as the exterior part of a whole does to the interior, or as the shell does to the kernel; but if the shell moves, the kernel will also move, as being part of the whole, without any removal from near the shell.

A property related to the preceding is that if a place is moved, whatever is placed in it moves along with it; and therefore a body which is moved from a place in motion partakes also of the motion of its place. Upon which account, all motions, from places in motion, are no other than parts of entire and absolute motions, and every entire motion is composed of the motion of the body out of its first place, and the motion of this place out of its place, and so on, until we come to some immovable place, as in the aforementioned example of the sailor. Because of this, entire and absolute motions can be no otherwise determined than by immovable places; and for that reason I did before refer those absolute motions to immovable places, but relative ones to movable places. Now no other places are immovable but those that, from infinity to infinity, do all retain the same given position one to another, and upon this account must ever remain unmoved, and do as a result constitute immovable space.

The causes by which true and relative motions are distinguished from one another are the forces impressed upon bodies to generate motion. True motion is neither generated nor altered, but by some force impressed upon the body moved; but relative motion may be generated or altered without any force impressed upon the body. For it is sufficient only to impress some force on other bodies with which the former is compared, that by their giving way, that relation in which the relative rest or motion of this other body did consist may be changed. Again, true motion always suffers some change from any force impressed upon the moving body; but relative motion does not necessarily undergo any change by such forces. For if the same forces are likewise impressed on those other bodies, with which the comparison is made, that the relative position may be preserved, then that condition will be preserved in which the relative motion consists. And therefore any relative motion may be changed when the true motion remains unaltered, and the relative may be preserved when the true suffers some change. Thus, true motion by no means consists in such relations.

The effects which distinguish absolute from relative motion are the forces of receding from the axis of circular motion. For there are no such forces in a circular motion purely relative, but in a true and absolute circular motion, they are greater or less, according to the quantity of the motion. If a vessel hung by a long cord is so often turned about that the cord is strongly twisted, then filled with water and held at rest together with the water, at once, by the sudden action of another force, it is whirled about the contrary way, and while the cord is untwisting itself, the vessel continues for some time in this motion, the surface of the water will at first be even, as before the vessel began to move; but after that the vessel, by gradually communicating its motion to the water, will make it begin to revolve sensibly and recede gradually from the middle, and ascend to the sides of the vessel, forming itself into a concave figure (as I have experienced); and the swifter the motion becomes, the higher will the water rise, until at last, performing its revolutions in the same times with the vessel, it becomes relatively at rest in it. This ascent of the water shows its endeavor to recede from the axis of its motion, and the true and absolute circular motion of the water, which is here directly contrary to the relative, becomes known and may be measured by this endeavor.

At first, when the relative motion of the water in the vessel was greatest, it produced no endeavor to recede from the axis; the water showed no tendency to the circumference, nor any ascent towards the sides of the vessel, but remained of an even surface, and therefore its true circular motion had not yet begun. But afterwards, when the relative motion of the water had decreased, its ascent towards the sides of the vessel proved its endeavor to recede from the axis; and this endeavor showed the real circular motion of the water continually increasing, until it had acquired its greatest quantity when the water rested relatively in the vessel. And therefore this endeavor does not depend upon any translation of the water in respect of the ambient bodies, nor can true circular motion be defined by such translation. There is only one real circular motion of any one revolving body corresponding to only one power of endeavoring to recede from its axis of motion as its proper and adequate effect; but relative motions in one and the same body are innumerable, according to the various relations it bears to external bodies, and like other relations are altogether destitute of any real effect, except insofar as they may perhaps partake of that unique true motion.

And therefore, in the system of those who suppose that our heavens revolving below the sphere of the fixed stars carry the planets along with them, the several parts of those heavens and the planets, which are indeed relatively at rest in their heavens, do yet really move. For they change their position one to another (which never happens to bodies truly at rest), and being carried together with their heavens, partake of their motions, and as parts of revolving wholes, endeavor to recede from the axis of their motions.

For that reason, relative quantities are not the quantities themselves, whose names they bear, but those sensible measures of them (either accurate or inaccurate), which are commonly used instead of the measured quantities themselves. And if the meaning of words is to be determined by their use, then by the names time, space, place, and motion, their sensible measures are properly to be understood; and the expression will be unusual, and purely mathematical, if the measured quantities themselves are meant. On this account, those who interpret these words for the measured quantities violate the accuracy of language, which ought to be kept precise. Nor do those who confound real quantities with their relations and sensible measure defile the purity of mathematical and philosophical truths any less.

It is indeed a matter of great difficulty to discover and effectually to distinguish the true motions of particular bodies from the apparent, because the parts of that immovable space in which those motions are performed do by no means come under the observation of our senses. Yet the thing is not altogether desperate; for we have some arguments to guide us, partly from the apparent motions, which are the differences of the true motions, partly from the forces, which are the causes and effects of the true motions. For instance, if two globes, kept at a given distance one from the other by means of a cord that connects them, were revolved about their common center of gravity, we might, from the tension of the cord, discover the endeavor of the globes to recede from the axis of their motion, and from thence we might compute the quantity of their circular motions. And then if any equal forces should be impressed at once on the alternate faces of the globes to augment or diminish their circular motions, from the increase or decrease of the tension of the cord, we might infer the increment or decrement of their motions; and hence would be found on what faces those forces ought to be impressed, that the motions of the globes might be most augmented; that is, we might discover their hindmost faces, or those which do follow in the circular motion. But the faces which follow being known, and consequently the opposite ones that precede, we should likewise know the determination of their motions. And thus we might find both the quantity and the determination of this circular motion, even in an immense vacuum, where there was nothing external or sensible with which the globes could be compared.

But now, if some remote bodies that kept always a given position one to another were placed in that space, as the fixed stars do in our regions, we could not indeed determine from the relative translation of the globes among those bodies, whether the motion did belong to the globes or to the bodies. But if we observed the cord and found that its tension was that very tension which the motions of the globes required, we might conclude the motion to be in the globes and the bodies to be at rest; and then, lastly, from the translation of the globes among the bodies, we should find the determination of their motions. But how we are to obtain the true motions from their causes, effects, and apparent differences, and the converse, shall be explained more at large in the following treatise. For to this end it was that I composed it.

General Scholium

The hypothesis of vortices [Descartes] is pressed by many difficulties. In order that any planet may describe areas proportional to the time by a radius drawn to the sun, the periodic times of the parts of the vortices should observe the square of their distances from the sun; but in order that the periodic times of the planets may obtain the 3/2th power of their distances from the sun, the periodic times of the parts of the vortex ought to be as the 3/2th power of their distances. In order that the smaller vortices may maintain their lesser revolutions about Saturn, Jupiter, and other planets and float quietly and undisturbed in the greater vortex of the sun, the periodic times of the parts of the solar vortex should be equal. But the rotation of the sun and planets about their axes, which ought to correspond with the motions of their vortices, are in disagreement with all these ratios. The motions of the comets are exceedingly regular, are governed by the same laws as the motions of the planets, and cannot be accounted for by the hypothesis of vortices. For comets are carried in highly eccentric motions through all parts of the heavens, which is incompatible with the notion of a vortex.

Projectiles in our air feel only the resistance of the air. If the air is removed, as is done in Mr. Boyle's vacuum, the resistance ceases, for a bit of fine down and a piece of solid gold fall with equal velocity in this void. And the same argument must apply to the celestial spaces above the earth's atmosphere; in these spaces, where there is no air to resist their motions, all bodies will move with complete freedom, and the planets and comets will constantly revolve in orbits given in shape and position, according to the laws above explained. But although these bodies may, indeed, carry on in their orbits by the mere laws of gravity, they could by no means have attained the regular position of the orbits through these laws.

The six primary planets revolve about the sun in circles concentric with the sun, in the same direction of motion and almost in the same plane. Ten moons revolve about the earth, Jupiter, and Saturn in concentric circles in the same direction of motion and nearly in the planes of the orbits of those planets. But it is not to be conceived that mere mechanical causes could give birth to so many regular motions, since the comets range over all parts of the heavens in very eccentric orbits. In this kind of motion, the comets pass easily through the orbits of the planets and with great rapidity; and at their aphelions, where they move the slowest and delay the longest, they recede to the greatest distances from each other and hence suffer the least disturbance from their mutual attractions. This most beautiful system of the sun, planets, and comets could only proceed from the counsel and dominion of an intelligent and powerful Being. And if the fixed stars are the centers of similar other systems, since these are formed by the same counsel, they must all be subject to the dominion of One, especially since the light of the fixed stars is of the same nature as the light of the sun and light passes into all the other systems from every system; and so that the systems of the fixed stars should not fall on each other by their gravity, he has placed those systems at immense distances from one another.

This Being governs all things, not as the soul of the world, but as Lord over all; and because of his dominion he is usually called Lord God *Pantokrator*, or Universal Ruler. For *God* is a relative word and is relative to servants, and Deity is the dominion of God, not over his own body, as those imagine who imagine God to be the world soul, but over servants. The supreme God is a Being eternal, infinite, absolutely perfect; but a being, however perfect, without dominion cannot be said to be Lord God. For we say, "my God, your God, the God of Israel, the God of Gods, and Lord of Lords," but we do not say, "my Eternal, your Eternal, the Eternal of Israel, the Eternal of Gods"; we do not say, "my Infinite or my Perfect." These are titles which have no relation to servants. The word *God* usually signifies Lord, but not every Lord is God. It is the dominion of a spiritual being that constitutes God—a true, supreme, or imaginary dominion makes a true, supreme, or imaginary God.

From his true dominion it follows that the true God is a living, intelligent, and powerful Being, and from his other perfections, that he is supreme or most perfect. He is eternal and infinite, omnipotent and omniscient; that is, he endures from eternity to eternity and is present from infinity to infinity; he governs all things and knows all things that are or can be done. He is not eternity and infinity, but eternal and infinite; he is not duration and space, but he endures and is present. He endures forever and is present everywhere, and, by existing always and everywhere, he constitutes duration and space. Since every particle of space is always, and every indivisible moment of duration is everywhere, certainly the Maker and Lord of all things cannot be never and nowhere. Every sentient soul is still the same indivisible person at different times and in different organs of sense and motion. Successive parts are given in duration, coexistent parts in space, but neither is given in the person of a man or his thinking principle, and much less can they be found in the thinking substance of God. Every person, insofar as he is a sentient being, is one and the same person during his whole life, in each and all of his organs of sense. God is the same God always and everywhere. . . .

But, by way of allegory, God is said to see, to speak, to laugh, to love, to hate, to desire, to give, to receive, to rejoice, to be angry, to fight, to frame, to work, to build. For all our notions of God are taken from the ways of mankind by a certain similitude, which, though not perfect, has some likeness, however. And this much concerning God, about whom a discourse from the appearances of things does certainly belong to natural philosophy.

Up to now we have explained the phenomena of the heavens and of our sea through the force of gravity but have not yet assigned the cause for this. It is certain that it must proceed from a cause that penetrates to the very centers of the sun and planets with no diminution of force, and that operates not according to the quantity of the surfaces of the particles upon which it acts (as mechanical causes usually do) but according to the quantity of the solid matter they contain, and which acts at immense distances, extended everywhere, always decreasing as the inverse square of the distances. Gravitation toward the sun is made up out of the gravitations toward the individual particles of the body, and in receding from the sun decreases precisely as the inverse square of the distances as far as the orbit of Saturn, as is evident from the aphelions of the planets being at rest, and even to the remotest aphelions of the comets, if those aphelions are also at rest.

But up to now I have not been able to deduce the reason for these properties of gravity from phenomena, and I frame no hypotheses. For whatever is not deduced from the phenomena is to be called a hypothesis, and hypotheses, whether metaphysical or physical, whether of occult qualities or mechanical, have no place in experimental philosophy. In this philosophy, particular propositions are deduced from the phenomena and are rendered general by induction. The impenetrability, mobility, and impetus of bodies and the laws of motion and of gravitation were discovered in this way. And it is enough that gravity does really exist and acts according to the laws we have explained, and abundantly serves to account for all the motions of the celestial bodies and of our sea.

Opticks (1704)
Query 31

And thus nature will be very conformable to herself and very simple, performing all the great motions of the heavenly bodies by the attraction of gravity that intercedes between those bodies, and almost all the small ones of their particles by some other attractive and repelling powers which intercede between the particles. The *vis inertiae* is a passive principle by which bodies persist in their motion or rest, receive motion in proportion to the force impressing it, and resist as much as they are resisted. By this principle alone there never could have been any motion in the world. Some other principle was necessary for putting bodies into motion; and now that they are in motion, some other principle is necessary for conserving the motion. For from the various composition of two motions, it is very certain that there is not always the same quantity of motion in the world. For if two globes joined by a slender rod revolve about their common center of gravity with a uniform motion, while that center moves on uniformly in a right line drawn in the plane of their circular motion, the sum of the motions of the two globes, as often as the globes are in the right line described by their common center of gravity, will be bigger than the sum of their motions, when they are in a line perpendicular to that right line. By this instance it appears that motion may be gotten or lost.

But by reason of the tenacity of fluids and attrition of their parts, and the weakness of elasticity in solids, motion is much more apt to be lost than gotten, and is always upon the decay. For bodies which are either absolutely hard or so soft as to be void of elasticity will not rebound from one another. Impenetrability makes them only stop. If two equal bodies meet directly *in vacuo*, they will, by the laws of motion, stop where they meet and lose all their motion and remain in rest unless they are elastic and receive new motion from their spring. If they have so much elasticity as suffices to make them rebound with a quarter or half or three quarters of the force with which they come together, they will lose three quarters or half or a quarter of their motion.

And this may be tried by letting two equal pendulums fall against one another from equal heights. If the pendulums are of lead or soft clay, they will lose all or almost all their motions; if they are of elastic bodies they will lose all but what they recover from their elasticity. If it is said that they can lose no motion but what they communicate to other bodies, the consequence is that *in vacuo* they can lose no motion, but when they meet they must go on and penetrate one another's dimensions.

If three equal round vessels are filled, the one with water, the other with oil, the third with molten pitch, and the liquors are stirred about alike to give them a vortical motion, the pitch by its tenacity will lose its motion quickly, the oil being less tenacious will keep it longer, and the water being less tenacious will keep it longest but yet will lose it in a short time. From this it is easy to understand that if many contiguous vortices of molten pitch were each of them as large as those which some suppose to revolve about the sun and fixed stars, as large as the Cartesian vortices, yet these and all their parts would, by their tenacity and stiffness, communicate their motion to one another until they all rested among themselves. Vortices of oil or water or some more fluid matter might continue longer in motion, but unless the matter were void of all tenacity and attrition of parts, and communication of motion (which is not to be supposed), the motion would constantly decay.

Seeing therefore the variety of motion that we find in the world is always decreasing, there is a necessity of conserving and recruiting it by active principles, such as are the cause of gravity, by which planets and comets keep their motions in their orbs and bodies acquire great motion in falling, and the cause of fermentation, by which the heart and blood of animals are kept in perpetual motion and heat, the inward parts of the earth are constantly warmed and in some places grow very hot, bodies burn and shine, mountains take fire, the caverns of the earth are blown up, and the sun continues violently hot and lucid and warms all things by his light. For we meet with very little motion in the world besides what is owing either to these active principles or to the dictates of a will. And if it were not for these principles, the bodies of the earth, planets, comets, sun, and all things in them would grow cold and freeze and become inactive masses, and all putrefaction, generation, vegetation, and life would cease, and the planets and comets would not remain in their orbs.

All these things being considered, it seems probable to me that God in the beginning formed matter in solid, massy, hard, impenetrable, moveable particles of such sizes and figures and with such other properties and in such proportion to space as was most conducive to the end for which he formed them; and that these primitive particles being solids are incomparably harder than any porous bodies compounded of them, even so very hard as never to wear or break in pieces, no ordinary power being able to divide what God himself made one in the first creation. While the particles continue entire, they may compose bodies of one and the same nature and texture in all ages; but should they wear away or break in pieces, the nature of things depending on them would be changed. Water and earth, composed of old worn particles and fragments of particles, would not be of the same nature and texture now with water and earth composed of entire particles in the beginning. And therefore, that nature may be lasting, the changes of corporeal things are to be placed only in the various separations and new associations and motions of these permanent particles, since compound bodies are apt to break, not in the midst of solid particles, but where those particles are laid together and only touch in a few points.

It seems to me further that these particles have not only a *vis inertia* accompanied with such passive laws of motion as naturally result from that force but also that they are moved by certain active principles, such as is that of gravity and that which causes fermentation and the cohesion of bodies. These principles I consider not as occult qualities supposed to result from the specific forms of things, but as general laws of nature, by which the things themselves are formed, their truth appearing to us by phenomena though their causes are not yet discovered. For these are manifest qualities, and their causes are only occult. And the Aristotelians gave the name of occult qualities not to manifest qualities but to such qualities only as they supposed to lie hidden in bodies and to be the unknown causes of manifest effects such as would be the causes of gravity and of magnetic and electric attractions and of fermentations if we should suppose that these forces or actions arose from qualities unknown to us and incapable of being discovered and made manifest. Such occult qualities put a stop to the improvement of natural philosophy and therefore of late years have been rejected.

To tell us that every species of things is endowed with an occult specific quality by which it acts and produces manifest effects is to tell us nothing, but to derive two or three general principles of motion from phenomena and afterwards to tell us how the properties and actions of all corporeal things follow from those manifest principles would be a very great step in philosophy, though the causes of those principles were not yet discovered; and therefore I do not hesitate to propose the principles of motion above mentioned, since they are of very general extent, and leave their causes to be found out.

Now by the help of these principles all material things seem to have been composed of the hard and solid particles mentioned above, variously associated in the first creation by the counsel of an intelligent agent. For it became him who created them to set them in order. And if he did so, it is unphilosophical to seek for any other origin of the world or to pretend that it might arise out of a chaos by the mere laws of nature, though being once formed it may continue by those laws for many ages. For while comets move in very eccentric orbs in all manner of positions, blind fate could never make all the planets move one and the same way in concentric orbs, some inconsiderable irregularities excepted which may have arisen from the mutual actions of comets and planets upon one another and which will be apt to increase until this system needs a reformation. . . .

As in mathematics, so in natural philosophy, the investigation of difficult things by the method of analysis ought ever to precede the method of composition. This analysis consists in making experiments and observations and in drawing general conclusions from them by induction and in admitting of no objections against the conclusions but such as are taken from experiments or other certain truths. For hypotheses are not to be regarded in experimental philosophy. And although the arguing from experiments and observations by induction is no demonstration of general conclusions, yet it is the best way of arguing which the nature of things admits of, and may be looked upon as so much the stronger by how much the induction is more general. And if no exception occurs from phenomena, the conclusion may be pronounced generally. But if at any time afterwards any exception shall occur from experiments, it may then begin to be pronounced with such exceptions as occur. By this way of analysis we may proceed from compounds to ingredients and from motions to the forces producing them and in general from effects to their causes and from particular causes to more general ones, until the argument ends in the most general. This is the method of analysis; and the synthesis consists in assuming the causes discovered and established as principles, and by them explaining the phenomena proceeding from them and proving the explanations. . . .

And if natural philosophy in all its parts, by pursuing this method, shall at length be perfected, the bounds of moral philosophy will be also enlarged. For so far as we can know by natural philosophy what is the First Cause, what power he has over us, and what benefits we receive from him, so far our duty toward him as well as that toward one another will appear to us by the light of nature. And no doubt, if the worship of false gods had not blinded the heathen, their moral philosophy would have gone further than to the four cardinal virtues; and instead of teaching the transmigration of souls, and to worship the sun and moon and dead heroes, they would have taught us to worship our true Author and Benefactor, as their ancestors did under the government of Noah and his sons before they corrupted themselves.

VIII

D'ALEMBERT

| *Preliminary Discourse to the* | Part I (the achievements of natural philosophy) |
| *Encyclopédie* (1751) | Part II (the need for public education) |

JEAN-BAPTISTE LE ROND D'ALEMBERT (1717–1783) was a mathematical genius and one of the foremost physicists of his era. He was named after the Parisian church of Saint-Jean-le-Rond, where he had been abandoned due to his illegitimate birth. His thought-to-be father, a lieutenant general of artillery, arranged for a kindly lady to raise him and provide for his education. By his mid-twenties, d'Alembert had submitted six mathematical papers to the Paris Académie des Sciences and solved mathematical problems related to the precession of the equinoxes that had defeated Newton; by utilization of partial differential equations, he had also beaten the famed Leonhard Euler (1707–1783) to a solution of the Vibrating String problem.

D'Alembert was much more than a mathematician. In 1743, at the age of twenty-four, he published *Traité de dynamique*, which laid out his laws of motion and systematized the science of mechanics; he wrote a book on the principles of music (1752); papers on probability; produced a French translation of Tacitus's Latin text; and much else. He was also an energetic member of several significant Parisian salons, where he mixed with the leaders of progressive thought, including Voltaire, whom he admired. Progressive rulers, such as Frederick of Prussia and Catherine of Russia, sought his advice, extended invitations, and provided him with generous pensions.

D'Alembert was a leading figure in the European Enlightenment, a momentous period of intellectual ferment and advance that shaped intellectual, political, and religious life in the West and eventually beyond. It formulated and championed liberalism, democracy, anti-autocracy, and freedom of thought, religion, and conscience.[1]

---

1. For elaboration see Berlin (1956), Dupré (2004), Fleischacker (2013), Gay (1970), Hankins (1970), Israel (2006), Pagden (2013), and Porter (2000).

Historically, the Enlightenment occurred between the bloodless 1688 Glorious Revolution in England and the 1815 defeat of Napoleon at Waterloo. Philosophically, it began with three remarkable publications by John Locke written over a two-year period—*A Letter Concerning Toleration* (1689), *An Essay Concerning Human Understanding* (1690), and *Two Treatises of Government* (1690)—and, notionally, closed with Mary Wollstonecraft's *An Historical and Moral View of the Origin and Progress of the French Revolution* (1794).

This chronological period is referred to as the "long eighteenth century." The Enlightenment philosophers of the period, or *philosophes* in France,[2] were inspired by the New Science of the seventeenth century—the work of Galileo, Huygens, Harvey, Newton, Boyle, Hooke, and others—whose dramatic achievements in mechanics, astronomy, horology, chemistry, medicine, mathematics, and other fields, were widely known, admired, and appreciated. These "natural philosophers" (scientists) were seen as exemplars of correct reasoning and inquiry, whose fruitful methods of discovery should be followed not only in inquiries about the natural world but also in investigating the historical and social worlds. David Hume reflected this commitment in the subtitle of his 1739 *Treatise of Human Nature: Being an Attempt to Introduce the Experimental Method of Reasoning into Moral Subjects* (Hume [1739] 1888). Of the Enlightenment writers, Isaiah Berlin well-noted:

> The intellectual power, honesty, lucidity, courage, and disinterested love of the truth of the most gifted thinkers of the eighteenth century remain to this day without parallel. Their age is one of the best and most hopeful episodes in the life of mankind. (Berlin 1956, 29)

D'Alembert captured the thought and enthusiasm of Enlightenment thinkers when he wrote in his 1759 essay "Elements of Philosophy":

> Our century is called . . . the century of philosophy par excellence. . . . The discovery and application of a new method of philosophizing, the kind of enthusiasm which accompanies discoveries, a certain exaltation of ideas which the spectacle of the universe produces in us—all these causes have brought about a lively fermentation of minds, spreading through nature in all directions like a river which has burst its dams. (Cassirer [1932] 1951, 3–4)

---

2. The principal figures listed in birth order are: John Locke (1632–1704), Baruch Spinoza (1632–1677); Pierre Bayle (1647–1706); John Toland (1670–1722); Voltaire (1694–1778); Benjamin Franklin (1706–1790); Julien Offray de La Mettrie (1709–1751); David Hume (1711–1776); Denis Diderot (1713–1784); Étienne Bonnot de Condillac (1714–1780); Jean le Rond d'Alembert (1717–1783); Paul-Henri Thiry, Baron d'Holbach (1723–1789); Adam Smith (1723–1790); Immanuel Kant (1724–1804); Joseph Priestley (1733–1804); Marquis of Condorcet (1743–1794); and Thomas Jefferson (1743–1826).

The philosophers were committed to education: outreach, or "public engagement," was built into their program (Matthews 2015, ch. 2). In current vocabulary, they were all public intellectuals.

D'Alembert's historical reputation is indelibly linked to his collaboration with Denis Diderot in founding in 1751, then co-editing until 1771, the famed *Encyclopédie*, which became the Enlightenment's widely subscribed to and extensively read standard reference work to which he contributed over one thousand entries. Of overwhelming importance is his two-hundred-plus-page book, *Preliminary Discourse to the* Encyclopédie *of Diderot* (1751), which functioned as a *Prospectus* for the project that he and Diderot labeled a *Reasoned Dictionary of the Sciences, Arts and Trades*. His esteem for the empiricism of Bacon, Locke, and Hume is clear from the outset.

Elsewhere, d'Alembert identifies liberty and freedom of speech as a condition for the growth of knowledge, writing: "For liberty of action and thought alone is capable of producing great things, and liberty requires only enlightenment to preserve itself from excess." This was later famously argued by John Stuart Mill and became an epistemological argument for an open, liberal society.

Selections of the *Discourse* follow.

References

Berlin, Isaiah, ed. 1956. *The Age of Enlightenment: The Eighteenth Century Philosophers.* New York: Mentor Books.

Cassirer, Ernst. (1932) 1951. *The Philosophy of the Enlightenment.* Translated by Fritz C. A. Koelln and James P. Pettegrove. Princeton: Princeton University Press.

D'Alembert, Jean-Baptiste le Rond. (1751) 1995. *Preliminary Discourse to the* Encyclopédie *of Diderot.* Translated by Richard Schwab and Walter Rex. Chicago: University of Chicago Press.

Diderot, Denis. (1754) 1999. *Thoughts on the Interpretation of Nature and Other Philosophical Works.* Translated and edited by David Adams. Manchester: Clinamen Press.

Dupré, Louis. 2004. *The Enlightenment and the Intellectual Foundations of Modern Culture.* New Haven, CT: Yale University Press.

Fleischacker, Samuel. 2013. *What Is Enlightenment?* New York: Routledge.

Gay, Peter. 1970. *The Enlightenment: An Interpretation.* 2 vols. London: Weidenfeld and Nicolson.

Hankins, Thomas L. 1970. *Jean d'Alembert: Science and the Enlightenment.* Oxford: Oxford University Press.

Hume, David. (1739) 1888. *A Treatise of Human Nature: Being an Attempt to Introduce the Experimental Method of Reasoning into Moral Subjects.* Oxford: Clarendon Press.

Israel, Jonathan I. 2006. *Enlightenment Contested: Philosophy, Modernity, and the Emancipation of Man 1670–1752*. Oxford: Oxford University Press.

Matthews, Michael R. 2015. *Science Teaching: The Contribution of History and Philosophy of Science, 20th Anniversary Revised and Enlarged Edition*. New York: Routledge.

Pagden, Anthony. 2013. *The Enlightenment and Why It Still Matters*. Oxford: Oxford University Press.

Porter, Roy. 2000. *The Enlightenment: Britain and the Creation of the Modern World*. London: Penguin Books.

Preliminary Discourse to the *Encyclopédie* of Diderot (1751)

Part I

We can divide all our knowledge into direct and reflective knowledge. We receive direct knowledge immediately, without any operation of our will; it is the knowledge which finds all the doors of our souls open, so to speak, and enters without resistance and without effort. The mind acquires reflective knowledge by making use of direct knowledge, unifying and combining it.

. . .

In our study of Nature, which we make partly by necessity and partly for amusement, we note that bodies have a large number of properties. However, in most cases they are so closely united in the same subject that, in order to study each of them more thoroughly, we are obliged to consider them separately. Through this operation of our intelligence we soon discover properties which seem to belong to all bodies, such as the faculty of movement or of remaining at rest, and the faculty of communicating movement, which are the sources of the principal changes we observe in Nature. By examining these properties—above all the last one—with the aid of our own senses, we soon discover another property upon which all of these depend: impenetrability, which is to say, that specific force by virtue of which each body excludes all others from the place it occupies, so that when two bodies are put together as closely as possible, they can never occupy a space smaller than the one they filled separately.

Impenetrability is the principal property by which we make a distinction between the bodies themselves and the indefinite portions of space in which we conceive them as being placed—at least the evidence of our senses tells us such is the case. Even if they are deceptive on this point, it is an error so metaphysical that our existence and the preservation of our lives have nothing to fear from it, and it continually crops up in our mind almost involuntarily, as part of our ordinary way of thinking. Everything induces us to conceive of space as the place (if not real, at least supposed) occupied by bodies. And indeed, it is by conceiving of sections of that space as being penetrable and immobile that our idea of movement achieves the greatest clarity it can have for us. We are therefore almost naturally impelled to differentiate, at least mentally, between two sorts of extension, one being impenetrable and the other constituting the place occupied by bodies. And thus, although impenetrability belongs of necessity to our conception of the parts of matter, nevertheless, since it is a relative property (that is, we get an idea of it only by examining two bodies together), we soon accustom ourselves to thinking of it as distinct from extension and to considering the latter separately from it.

. . .

The only resource that remains to us in an investigation so difficult, although so necessary and even pleasant, is to collect as many facts as we can, to arrange them in the most natural order, and to relate them to a certain number of principal facts of which the others are only the consequences. If we presume sometimes to raise ourselves higher, let it be with that wise circumspection which befits so feeble an understanding as ours.

Such is the plan we must follow in that vast part of physics called General and Experimental Physics. It differs from the physico-mathematical sciences in that it is properly only a systematic collection of experiments and observations. On the other hand, the physico-mathematical sciences, by applying mathematical calculations to experiment, sometimes deduce from a single and unique observation a large number of inferences that remain close to geometrical truths by virtue of their certitude. Thus, a single experiment on the reflection of light produces all of Catoptrics, or the science of the properties of mirrors. A single experiment on the refraction of light produces the mathematical explanation of the rainbow, the theory of colors, and all of Dioptrics, or the science of concave and convex lenses. From a single experiment on the pressure of fluids, we derive all the laws of their equilibrium and their movement. Finally, a single experiment on the acceleration of falling bodies opens up the laws of their descent down inclined planes and the laws of the movements of pendulums.

. . .

Thus, nothing is more necessary than a revealed Religion, which may instruct us concerning so many diverse objects. Designed to serve as a supplement to natural knowledge, it shows us part of what was hidden, but it restricts itself to the things which are absolutely necessary for us to know. The rest is closed for us and apparently will be forever. A few truths to be believed, a small number of precepts to be practiced: such are the essentials to which revealed Religion is reduced. Nevertheless, thanks to the enlightenment it has communicated to the world, the common people themselves are more solidly grounded and confident on a large number of questions of interest than the sects of the philosophers have been.

. . .

This most valuable art of assigning a suitable connection to ideas, and consequently of facilitating the passage from one to the other, furnishes the means of effecting at least a partial reconciliation among men who seem to differ the most. Indeed, all our knowledge is ultimately reduced to sensations that are approximately the same in all men. And the art of combining and relating direct ideas in reality adds nothing to them except a more or less exact arrangement and an enumeration which can be rendered more or less intelligible to others. The difference between the man who combines ideas easily and the one who combines them with difficulty is scarcely greater than that between the man who judges a picture at one glance and the one who needs to have all the parts pointed out to him one after another in order to appreciate it. Both have experienced the same sensations in their first glance, but these sensations have only slid over the second man, so to speak. To lead him to the same point at which the other man arrived instantaneously, it would only have been necessary to stop him and make him concentrate for a longer time on each sensation. By this means, the reflective ideas of the first man would have become as much within reach of the second as the direct ideas.

Hence it is perhaps true that there is hardly a science or an art which cannot, with rigor and good logic, be taught to the most limited mind, because there are but few arts or sciences whose propositions or rules cannot be reduced to some simple notions and arranged in such a close order that their chain of connection will nowhere be interrupted. As the mind operates more or less slowly, that chain will be required in greater or less degree, and the only advantage possessed by great geniuses is that they have less need of it than others, or rather they are able to form it rapidly and almost unconsciously.

The science of communication of ideas is not confined to putting order in ideas themselves. In addition, it should teach how to express each idea in the clearest way possible, and consequently how to perfect the signs that are designed to convey it; and, indeed, this is what men have gradually done. Languages, born along with societies, doubtless began as only a rather bizarre collection of signs of all sorts, and consequently, the natural bodies which impinge upon our senses were the first objects to be designated by names. But so far as we can judge, languages in this first beginning were intended only for the most pressing use, and they must have been very imperfect and limited, and subject to very few definite principles. The arts or sciences which were of absolute necessity may have made considerable progress while the rules of diction and of style were yet to be born. The communication of ideas hardly suffered in any case from this lack of rules or even from the paucity of words; or rather it suffered only to the degree required to oblige each man to augment his own knowledge by stubborn effort, without depending too much upon others.

Too much communication can sometimes benumb the mind and prejudice the efforts of which it is capable. If one observes the prodigies of some of those born blind, or deaf and mute, one will see what the faculties of the mind can perform if they are lively and called into action by difficulties which must be overcome.

. . .

These three faculties form at the outset the three general divisions of our system of human knowledge: History, which is related to memory; Philosophy, which is the fruit of reason; and the Fine Arts, which are born of imagination.

Placing reason ahead of imagination appears to us to be a well-founded arrangement and one which is in conformity with the natural progress of the operations of the mind. Imagination is a creative faculty, and the mind, before it considers creating, begins by reasoning upon what it sees and knows. Another motive which should decide us to place reason ahead of imagination is that in the latter faculty the other two are to some extent brought together. The mind creates and imagines objects only insofar as they are similar to those which it has known by direct ideas and by sensations. The more it departs from these objects, the more bizarre and unpleasant are the beings which it forms. Thus, in the imitation of Nature, invention itself is subjected to certain rules. It is principally these rules which form the philosophical part of the Fine Arts, which is still rather imperfect because it can be the work only of genius, and genius prefers creation to discussion.

. . .

The science of Nature is simply the science of bodies. But since bodies have general properties which are common to them, such as impenetrability, mobility, and extension, the science of Nature ought therefore to begin with the study of these properties. They have, so to speak, a purely intellectual side, by which they open an immense scope to the speculations of the mind, and a material and sensible side by which we can measure them. Intellectual speculation is related to General Physics, which is, properly speaking, simply the metaphysics of bodies, and measurement is the object of Mathematics, whose divisions extend almost to infinity.

Part II

We are now going to consider this work as a *Reasoned Dictionary of the Sciences and the Arts*. This object is all the more important, since it may possibly be of greater interest to the majority of our readers [than the object of Part I], and fulfilling it has required the most care and work. But before entering upon this subject in all the detail which may legitimately be required of us, it will be worth our while to examine at some length the present state of the sciences and the arts, and to show what series of steps have led us to it. Our metaphysical analysis of the origin and connection of the sciences has been of great utility in designing the encyclopedic tree; an historical analysis of the order in which our knowledge has developed in successive steps will be no less useful in enlightening us concerning the way we ought to convey this knowledge to our readers.

Moreover, the history of the sciences is naturally bound up with that of the small number of great geniuses whose works have helped to spread enlightenment among men. And since these works have been helpful in a general way to our own, we ought to begin by speaking of them before giving account of the particular contributions and assistance that we have obtained. So as not to go back too far, let us turn our attention to the renaissance of letters.

· · ·

[In medieval times] The careful examination of Nature and the grand study of mankind were replaced by a thousand frivolous questions concerning abstract and metaphysical beings—questions whose solution, good or bad, often required much subtlety, and consequently a great abuse of intelligence. Added to this confusion were the condition of slavery into which almost all of Europe was plunged and the ravages of superstition which is born of ignorance, and which spawns it in turn. If one considers all these difficulties, it will be plain that nothing was lacking to the obstacles that for a long time delayed the return of reason and taste. For liberty of action and thought alone is capable of producing great things, and liberty requires only enlightenment to preserve itself from excess.

· · ·

While poorly instructed or badly intentioned adversaries made open war on it, philosophy sought refuge, so to speak, in the works of a few great men. They had not the dangerous ambition of removing the blindfolds from their contemporaries' eyes; yet silently in the shadows they prepared from afar the light which gradually, by imperceptible degrees, would illuminate the world.

The immortal Chancellor of England, Francis Bacon [1561–1626], ought to be placed at the head of these illustrious personages. His works, so justly esteemed (and more esteemed, indeed, than they are known), merit our reading even more than our praises. One would be tempted to regard him as the greatest, the most universal, and the most eloquent of the philosophers, considering his sound and broad views, the multitude of objects to which his mind turned itself, and the boldness of his style, which everywhere joined the most sublime images with the most rigorous precision. Born in the depths of the most profound night, Bacon was aware that philosophy did not yet exist, although many men doubtless flattered themselves that they excelled in it (for the cruder a century is, the more it believes itself to be educated in all that can be known). Therefore, he began by considering generally the various objects of all the natural sciences. He divided these sciences into different branches, of which he made the most exact enumeration that was possible for him. He examined what was already known concerning each of these objects and made the immense catalogue of what remained to be discovered. This is the aim of his admirable book *The Advancement of Learning.*

In his *Novum Organum,* he perfects the views that he had presented in the first book, carries them further, and makes known the necessity of experimental physics, of which no one was yet aware. Hostile to systems, he conceives of philosophy as being only that part of our knowledge which should contribute to making us better or happier, thus apparently confining it within the limits of the science of useful things, and everywhere he recommends the study of Nature. His other writings were produced on the same pattern. Everything, even their titles, proclaims the man of genius, the mind that sees things in the large view. He collects facts, he compares experiments and points out a large number to be made; he invites scholars to study and perfect the arts, which he regards as the most exalted and most essential part of human science; he sets forth with a noble simplicity his *Conjectures and Thoughts* on the different objects worthy of men's interest; and he would have been able to say, like that old man in Terence, that nothing which touches humanity was alien to him. Natural science, ethics, politics, economics, all seem to have been within the competence of that brilliant and profound mind. . . . However, we have not believed it necessary to follow on every point the great man whom we acknowledge here to be our master.

. . .

As a philosopher he [Descartes] was perhaps equally great, but he was not so fortunate. Geometry, which by the nature of its object always gains without losing ground, could not fail to make a progress that was most sensible and apparent for everyone when plied by so great a genius. Philosophy found itself in quite a different state. There everything remained to be done, and what do not the first steps in any branch of knowledge cost? One is excused from making larger steps by the merit of taking any at all. If Descartes, who opened the way for us, did not progress as far along it as his sectaries believe, nevertheless the sciences are far more indebted to him than his adversaries will allow; his method alone would have sufficed to render him immortal. His *Dioptrics* is the greatest and the most excellent application that has yet been made of geometry to physics. In a word, we see his inventive genius shining forth everywhere, even in those works which are least read now.

If one judges impartially those vortices which today seem almost ridiculous, it will be agreed, I daresay, that at that time nothing better could be imagined. The astronomical observations which served to destroy them were still imperfect or hardly established. Nothing was more natural than to postulate a fluid which carried the planets. Only a long sequence of phenomena, of reasonings, and of calculations, and consequently a long sequence of years, could cause such an attractive theory to be renounced.

Moreover, it had the singular advantage of explaining gravitation of bodies by the centrifugal force of the vortex itself, and I am not afraid to assert that this explanation of weight is one of the finest and most ingenious hypotheses that philosophy has ever imagined. Thus, physicists had to be carried forward almost in spite of themselves by the theory of central forces and by experiments made much later before they would abandon it.

Let us recognize, therefore, that Descartes, who was forced to create a completely new physics, could not have created it better; that it was necessary, so to speak, to pass by way of the vortices in order to arrive at the true system of the world; and that if he was mistaken concerning the laws of movement, he was the first, at least, to see that they must exist.

. . .

Newton [1642–1727], whose way had been prepared by Huygens, appeared at last, and gave philosophy a form which apparently it is to keep. That great genius saw that it was time to banish conjectures and vague hypotheses from physics, or at least to present them only for what they were worth, and that this science was uniquely susceptible to the experiments of geometry. It was perhaps with this aim that he began by inventing calculus and the method of series, whose applications are so extensive in geometry itself and still more so in explaining the complicated effects that one observes in Nature, where everything seems to take place by various kinds of infinite progressions. The experiments on weight and the observations of Kepler led the English philosopher to discover the force which holds the planets in their orbits. Simultaneously he showed how to distinguish the causes of their movements and how to calculate them with a precision such as one might reasonably expect only after several centuries of labor. Creator of an entirely new optics, he made the properties of light known to men by breaking it up into its constituent parts. Anything we could add to the praise of the great philosopher would fall far short of the universal testimonial that is given today to his almost innumerable discoveries and to his genius, which was at the same time far-reaching, exact, and profound. He has doubtless deserved all the recognition that has been given him for enriching philosophy with a large quantity of real assets.

But perhaps he has done more by teaching philosophy to be judicious and to restrict within reasonable limits the sort of audacity which Descartes had been forced by circumstances to bestow upon it. His Theory of the World (for I do not mean his System) is today so generally accepted that men are beginning to dispute the author's claim to the honor of inventing it (because at the beginning great men are accused of being mistaken, and at the end they are treated as plagiarists).

. . .

It appears that Newton had not entirely neglected metaphysics. He was too great a philosopher not to be aware that it constitutes the basis of our knowledge and that clear and exact notions about everything must be sought in metaphysics alone. Indeed, the works of this profound geometer make it apparent that he had succeeded in constructing such notions for himself concerning the principal objects that occupied him. However, he abstained almost totally from discussing his metaphysics in his best-known writings, and we can hardly learn what he thought concerning the different objects of that discipline, except in the works of his followers. This may have been because he himself was somewhat dissatisfied with the progress he had made in metaphysics, or because he believed it difficult to give mankind sufficiently satisfactory and extensive enlightenment on a discipline too often uncertain and disputed. Or finally, it may have been because he feared that in the shadow of his authority people might abuse his metaphysics as they had abused Descartes', in order to support dangerous or erroneous opinions. Therefore, since he has not caused any revolution here, we will abstain from considering him from the standpoint of this subject.

. . .

Let us end this history of the sciences by noting that the different forms of government, which have so much influence on [men's] minds and on the cultivation of letters, also determine the principal types of knowledge which are to flourish under them, each of these types having its particular merits. In general, there should be more orators, historians, and philosophers in a republic and more poets, theologians, and geometers in a monarchy. This rule is not, however, so absolute that it cannot be altered and modified by an infinite number of causes.

DIDEROT

Rationale for the *Encyclopédie* **(1755)**	Baconian rationale for the *Encyclopédie* project; expectation of effecting a change in society's "manner of thinking"

DENIS DIDEROT (1713–1784) was among the most prominent *philosophes* of the French Enlightenment. His lasting legacy was the incomparable, vaultingly ambitious, multi-volume *Encyclopédie*, which he began in 1751 with his close friend, the mathematician Jean le Rond d'Alembert (1717–1784), and which he co-edited and constantly contributed to for twenty years, until 1771. The *Encyclopédie* aimed at no less than, as he wrote, "changing the general way of thinking" of mankind. In this, it had immediate and local effect and, consequently, international impact. Its more than 71,000 entries in 28 volumes covered the widest range of intellectual and applied topics. Thirty years later an expanded version ran to 166 volumes with 2,250 contributors, among them Rousseau, Montesquieu, Turgot, and Voltaire.

The religious, theological, and political entries were written in either a neutral, historical, and social-scientific manner or else with partisan and critical advocacy. Entries routinely criticized the dogmas, functioning, and practices of the Catholic Church. Predictably, Pope Clement XIII placed the work on the Index of Prohibited Books in 1758. The following year the French government banned the work; other European monarchs and governments soon did likewise. In France and all countries, there were constant battles occasioned by political and religious censorship.

While all the Enlightenment writers were committed to science, Diderot, more than others, concerned himself with the philosophy of science. He sought to delineate just what it was about the method and processes of the new science that made it so spectacularly successful in its quest for knowledge. The methodology of the new sciences ranged from Cartesian rationalism and systematism flowing from Descartes

through to the non-systematic experimentalism following Bacon. Diderot's rumina-
tions were gathered in his brief 1754 book *Thoughts on the Interpretation of Nature*.

Diderot's philosophy of science was, as with so many others, avowedly Baconian.
In considering "the vast realm of the sciences," he writes:

> We have three approaches at our disposal: the observation of nature, reflec-
> tion and experimentation. Observation serves to assemble the data, reflection
> to synthesize them and experimentation to test the results of this synthesis. The
> observation of nature must be assiduous, just as reflection must be profound,
> and experimentation accurate. These three approaches are rarely found together,
> which explains why creative geniuses are so rare. (Diderot [1754] 1999, 42)

Earlier, he wrote that observations and experiments are like weights at either end of a
thread of reasoned argument where "Without these weights, the thread would be at
the mercy of the slightest breath of air" (Diderot [1754] 1999, 39).

The thousands of entries in the *Encyclopédie* explicitly brought together theory and practice. The English natural philosophers (scientists)—Joseph Black (1728–1799), Matthew
Boulton (1728–1809), Henry Cavendish (1731–1810), Joseph Priestley (1733–1804),
and James Watt (1736–1819)—were born within eight years of each other and twenty
years after the publication of the first volume of the *Encyclopédie*. Of more consequence,
their work was intimately connected to the Industrial Revolution, which transformed
England and, in rapid order, the rest of Europe (Crowther 1962; Uglow 2002).

Such "applied" science was not just English but occurred between natural philosophers and nascent industry, and then government, everywhere. The *Encyclopédie*
facilitated, indeed commanded, such integration. It is difficult to envisage pneumatic
chemistry apart from the technical apparatus needed to pursue it and its industrial
application in everything from making soda water to being utilized in iron foundries.
The same for the science of fertilizers, electricity, geology, thermodynamics, optics,
electromagnetism, and properties of liquids.

The whole *Encyclopédie* project is Baconian and applied science. It is a gathering of
the multitude of known facts about nature, society, and manufacturing, along with
reflections and lessons drawn from these facts. The two-decade project that Diderot
and d'Alembert pursued was not just to deepen and spread the realm of knowledge,
but also to effect a "revolution that will occur in the minds of men and in the
national character." This "Rationale" was one of scores of Diderot's own entries in
the *Encyclopédie*. An extract follows.

REFERENCE

Crowther, James G. 1962. *Scientists of the Industrial Revolution*. London: Cresset Press.
Diderot, Denis. (1754) 1999. *Thoughts on the Interpretation of Nature and Other Philosophical Works*. Translated and edited by David Adams. Manchester: Clinamen Press.

Furbank, Philip N. 1992. *Diderot: A Critical Biography*. New York: Alfred A. Knopf.

Uglow, Jenny. 2002. *The Lunar Men: Five Friends Whose Curiosity Changed the World*. London: Faber & Faber.

Wilson, Arthur M. 1957. *Diderot: The Testing Years, 1713–1759*. New York: Oxford University Press.

Rationale for the *Encyclopédie* (1755)

When one discusses the phenomena of nature, what more can one do than summarize as scrupulously as possible all their properties as they are known at the time of writing? But observation and experimental science unceasingly multiply both phenomena and data, and rational philosophy, by comparing and combining them, continually extends or narrows the range *of* our knowledge and consequently causes the meanings of accepted words to undergo change, renders their former definitions inaccurate, false, or incomplete, and even compels the introduction of new words.

But the circumstance that will give a superannuated appearance to the work and bring it the public's scorn will be above all the revolution that will occur in the minds of men and in the national character. Today, when philosophy is advancing with gigantic strides, when it is bringing under its sway all the matters that are its proper concern, when its tone is the dominant one, and when we are beginning to shake off the yoke of authority and tradition in order to hold fast to the laws of reason, there is scarcely a single elementary or dogmatic book which satisfies us entirely. We find that these works are put together out of the productions of a few men and are not founded upon the truths of nature. We dare to raise doubts about the infallibility of Aristotle and Plato, and the time has come when the works that still enjoy the highest reputation will begin to lose some of their great prestige or even fall into complete oblivion. Certain literary forms—for want of the vital realities and actual custom that once served them as models—will no longer possess an unchanging or even a reasonable poetic meaning and will be abandoned; while others that remain, and whose intrinsic value sustains them will take on an entirely new meaning. Such are the consequences of the progress of reason, an advance that will overthrow so many old idols and perhaps restore to their pedestals some statues that have been cast down, the latter will be those of the rare geniuses who were ahead of their own times. We have had, if one may thus express it, our contemporaries in the age of Louis XIV.

. . .

In a systematic, universal dictionary, as in any work intended for the general education of mankind, you must begin by contemplating your subject in its most general aspects; you must know the state of mind of your nation, foresee the direction of its future development, hasten to anticipate its progress so that the march of events will not leave your book behind but will rather overtake it along the road; you must be prepared to work solely for the good of future generations because the moment of your own existence quickly passes away, and a great enterprise is not likely to be finished before the present generation ceases to exist. But if you would have your work remain fresh and useful for a long time to come—by virtue of its being far in advance of the national spirit, which marches steadily forward—you must shorten your labors by multiplying the number of your helpers, an expedient that is not, indeed, without its disadvantages, as I shall try to make plain hereafter.

. . .

We have had occasion to learn in the course of our editorial labors that our *Encyclopedia* is a work that could only be attempted in a philosophical century; that this age has indeed dawned; and that posterity, while raising to immortality the names of those who will bring man's knowledge to perfection in the future, will perhaps not disdain to remember our own names.

. . .

Now, in our own age, we must trample mercilessly upon all these ancient puerilities, overturn the barriers that reason never erected, give back to the arts and sciences the liberty that is so precious to them. . . . The world has long awaited a reasoning age, an age when the rules would be sought no longer in the classical authors but in nature, when men would come to sense the false and the true that are mingled in so many of the arbitrary philosophies of art, whatever field one works in. (I take the term *philosophy of art* in its most general meaning, that of a system of accepted rules to which it is claimed that one must conform in order to succeed.)

But the world has waited so long for this age to dawn that I have often thought how fortunate a nation would be if it never produced a man of exceptional ability under whose aegis an art still in its infancy makes its first too-rapid and too ambitious steps forward, thereby interrupting its natural, imperceptible rhythm of development. The works of such a man must necessarily be a monstrous composite for the reason that genius and good taste are two different things. Nature bestows the first in an instant; the second is the product of centuries.

X

DU CHÂTELET

Fundamentals of Physics (1740)   Preface dedicated to her thirteen-year-old son

"Hypotheses" (1740/1765)   Entry for *Encyclopédie* (1765)

ÉMILIE DU CHÂTELET (1706–1749) was an important figure in the French Enlightenment. She had a serious education, becoming competent in Italian, German, and Euclidean geometry by age twelve. In 1725, at age nineteen, she married Marquis Du Châtelet-Lomont in the cathedral of Notre Dame and later resided in the château Cirey in Champagne, near the Lorraine border. Her home became a comfortable, well-provided, and prominent center of scholarship and a major destination for mathematicians, writers, and philosophers from throughout Europe. It was more an academy than a salon in the current pre-revolutionary Parisian style. In quick succession, Du Châtelet gave birth to a daughter (1725) and two sons (1726, 1733).[1]

After the birth of her second son, Du Châtelet was first tutored in mathematics by Pierre-Louis Moreau de Maupertuis (1698–1759), a mathematician and member of the French Académie des Sciences, who became a lifelong intellectual friend. In 1734, Alexis Claude Clairaut (1713–1765), a French mathematical prodigy, became her second tutor. Her third tutor was the Swiss mathematician Samuel König (1712–1757), who instructed her in advanced calculus as well as Leibnizian physics and metaphysics.

Having had the best of teachers, Du Châtelet's pronounced mathematical competence enabled her to have early and full mastery of Newton's science. This set her apart from her more mathematically challenged philosophical colleagues who struggled to

---

1. On the life of Du Châtelet, see Zinsser (2006); for selections of her work, see Zinsser (2009); for an overview of her place in Enlightenment debate and an extensive bibliography, see Brading (2019).

appreciate Newton's science and hence struggled to understand his philosophy. Her posthumously published translation (1759) of Newton's *Principia* has remained the standard French translation through the following 250 years; it has not yet been bettered.

Du Châtelet not only translated Newton but contributed to the early growth of Newtonianism by reconceptualizing the conservation laws, extending optics and embryonic thermodynamics. She published her own *Fundamentals [Institutes] of Physics* in 1740. This natural philosophy treatise discussed a wide range of subjects: from the basic principles of epistemology, the nature of space and time, the existence of God, and the understanding of natural phenomena—such as the shape of the earth, oscillation of pendulums, projectile motion, and free fall—all associated with gravity.

Katherine Brading, a philosopher of physics and Du Châtelet scholar, has, in a draft manuscript, written of the *Fundamentals*:

> In the *Fundamentals* Du Châtelet: identified the most pressing foundational problems in physics of the time; articulated them with clarity and perspicuity; drew on resources from all leading philosophical approaches to contemporary physics; was current with the most recent results in physics; and moved the debates forward in interesting and novel ways. In the Preface, she wrote that physics is "an immense building," and that rather than adding to its construction with a stone here or there she would "survey the plan of the building." (Brading, forthcoming)

Du Châtelet was seriously engaged by methodological and epistemological issues in natural philosophy. She recognized that the deep dispute between Newtonians and Leibnizians over putative mechanisms for the law of attraction, the *vis viva* debate, could not be solved just on the evidence. No amount of measurement or more accurate observation was going to settle the dispute. A proper and correct methodology had to be utilized in interpretation of the evidence. The debate was not just empirical; it was conceptual. Following Leibniz, she argued that the force transmitted to, or received by, a body be measured by its mass times the square of its velocity, mv^2, or as now written, $\frac{1}{2} mv^2$. The property was labeled *force vive*. On this topic, she clashed with Jean-Jacques Dortous de Mairan, the secretary of the Académie des Sciences in Paris.[2] This published exchange was commented upon by Immanuel Kant in *Living Forces* (1747), his first publication in natural philosophy.

In 1733 Voltaire took up residence at Cirey to escape arrest after the French publication of his too-liberal *Letters Concerning the English Nation* (Voltaire [1733] 2007). Du Châtelet tutored him in Newton's science, an intellectual debt he acknowledged

---

2. On Du Châtelet's efforts to disentangle physics, metaphysics, and methodology in the Newton/Leibniz controversy, see Brading (2018), Janiak (2018), and contributions to Hagengruber (2012).

in *Elémens de la philosophie de Newton* (1738). They became deep friends, lovers, and intellectual collaborators for sixteen years until her untimely death six days after the birth of her fourth child (Zinsser 2006).

In philosophy, mathematics, and physics, she was Voltaire's equal and more. They were a "power couple" of the French Enlightenment, something recognized and undisputed by contemporaries. Subsequently, however, her light has dimmed almost to extinction in the Anglo-American world.

Du Châtelet published or circulated studies on fire (1738), optics (Gessell 2019), diverse biblical texts, education, issues relating to freedom of will, and much else (Zinsser 2009). Her work had a significant influence on European philosophy and science in the 1730s and 1740s. The works were published and republished in Paris, London, and Amsterdam; they were translated into German and Italian and discussed in the most important learned journals of the era, including the *Memoirs des Trévoux*, the *Journal des Sçavans*, and others. She maintained correspondence with Johann II Bernoulli, Leonhard Euler, Julien Offray de La Mettrie, Frederick the Great, and numerous other Enlightenment figures.[3]

D'Alembert's *Encyclopédie* entry on "Newtonianism or Newtonian Philosophy" fully recognized her work, giving it wide publicity. Many of her ideas were presented in different entries of the *Encyclopédie*. One study identifies twelve entries as coming directly from her *Fundamentals of Physics*, but six of them without attribution.

In the Preface below from the *Fundamentals*, Du Châtelet explains to her thirteen-year-old son why it is important to study the methods and results of physics, to understand the centrality of physics in the philosophical life of a nation, and to appreciate our debt to clear thinking physicists (natural philosophers) on whose shoulders they stood.

The second selection, on hypothesis (theory), is one of the six *Encyclopédie* entries written by Du Châtelet but published without attribution to her.[4] The "Hypothesis" entry is condensed from chapter 4 of her 1740 *Fundamentals* and can be found in vol. 8, 417–418 of the 1765 edition of the *Encyclopédie* published in Paris. The logic of hypotheses (or theories) was a central and disputed topic of the period. Newton, in the General Scholium of the second edition of the *Principia* (1713), famously said, "I frame no hypotheses" (see selection from Newton in Chapter 7). Newton left hypothesizing to his "misguided" Cartesian opponents. Nevertheless, here was Du Châtelet, his French champion and translator, correcting him; saying that hypotheses were essential to the conduct of science.

The *Fundamentals* chapter has four thousand words; the encyclopedia entry has one thousand words. Both range over basic methodological matters concerning

---

3. Extensive materials on Du Châtelet can be found on the Duke University Project Vox website.
4. For English translations of *Encyclopédie* entries, see the University of Michigan translation site.

theory, observation, experiment, confirmation, proof, probable knowledge, meta-physics, and ontology; these issues are still the currency of philosophy of science texts today.

In chapter 4 of the *Fundamentals*, after introductory comments about hypothesis, observation, and probability, Du Châtelet writes:

> The example of astronomers can further serve marvellously well to clarify this matter; for the true orbits of the planets were ascertained by first supposing they made their revolutions in circles, of which the Sun occupied the center; but the variation in their speed and their apparent diameters being contradictory to this hypothesis, it was supposed they moved in eccentric circles, that is to say, in circles of which the Sun did not occupy the center. This supposition, which corresponded to the movements of the Earth well enough, deviated greatly from what is observed about the planet Mars; and to remedy this, attempts were made to make a new correction to the curve the planets describe in their annual revolution. This procedure succeeded so well that finally Kepler, going from supposition to supposition, found their true orbit, which admirably cor-responded to all the appearances of the planets, and this orbit is an ellipse, of which the Sun occupies one of the foci. (Zinsser 2009, 149)

As with most Enlightenment texts, this is written to be intelligible to both natural philosophers and the general educated public.

It was explicitly for the sake of the general public that, thirty years later, the *Encyclopédie* chapter was condensed, probably by Diderot, d'Alembert, or Voltaire; or maybe by some anonymous assisting editor. Such editing is understandable, as the *Encyclopédie* was a massive twenty-eight-volume project with seventy thousand entries. The edited version can be read in the third paragraph of the selection below.

Her account of the experimental (observational) falsification of a hypothesis (the-ory) is in the hypothetico-deductive methodological tradition of Huygens (see selec-tions in Chapter 6), whom she greatly, and deservedly, admired. Her falsificationism is refined; it is akin to Karl Popper's sophisticated version where assumptions about initial conditions, the adequacy of instruments, and so on are all taken as part of the hypothesis-testing situation and so can be independently refuted whilst the hypothe-sis is retained (Popper 1963, ch.1). She writes:

> §.66. Thus, in making a hypothesis one must deduce all the consequences that can legitimately be deduced, and next compare them with experiment; for should all these consequences be confirmed by experiments, the probabil-ity would be greatest. But if there is a single one contrary to them, either the entire hypothesis must be rejected, if this consequence follows from the entire hypothesis, or that part of the hypothesis from which it necessarily follows. (Zinsser 2009, 153)

And she recognizes that in natural philosophy (science), true hypotheses, or theories, are probably true, not absolutely true:

§.67. Hypotheses, then, are only probable propositions that have a greater or lesser degree of certainty, depending on whether they satisfy a more or less great number of circumstances attendant upon the phenomenon that one wants to explain by their means. And, as a very great degree of probability gains our assent, and has on us almost the same effect as certainty, hypotheses finally become truths when their probability increases to such a point that one can morally present them as a certainty; this is what happened with Copernicus's system of the world, and with M. Huygens's on the ring of Saturn. (Zinsser 2009, 154)

REFERENCES

Brading, Katherine. 2018. "Émilie Du Châtelet and the problem of bodies." In *Early Modern Women on Metaphysics*, edited by Emily Thomas, 150–168. Cambridge: Cambridge University Press.

———. 2019. *Émilie Du Châtelet and the Foundations of Physical Science*. New York: Routledge.

———. Forthcoming. "Emilie Du Châtelet and the philosophy of physics." In *The Routledge Handbook of Women and Early Modern European Philosophy*, edited by Karen Detlefsen and Lisa Shapiro. New York: Routledge.

The Encyclopedia of Diderot & d'Alembert Collaborative Translation Project. n.d. Michigan Publishing, University of Michigan Library. https://quod.lib.umich.edu/d/did/.

Gessell, Bryce. 2019. "'Mon petit essai': Émilie du Châtelet's *Essai dur l'optique* and Her Early Natural Philosophy." *British Journal for the History of Philosophy* 27: 860–879.

Hagengruber, Ruth, ed. 2012. *Émilie du Châtelet between Leibniz and Newton*. Dordrecht: Springer.

Huygens, Christiaan. (1690) 1945. *Treatise on Light*. Translated and edited by Silvanus P. Thompson. Chicago: University of Chicago Press.

Janiak, Andrew. 2018 "Émilie Du Châtelet: Physics, Metaphysics and the Case of Gravity." In *Early Modern Women on Metaphysics*, edited by Emily Thomas, 49–71. Cambridge: Cambridge University Press.

Popper, Karl R. 1963. *Conjectures and Refutations: The Growth of Scientific Knowledge*. London: Routledge & Kegan Paul.

Project Vox Team. 2019. "Gabrielle Émilie Le Tonnelier de Breteuil, la Marquise Du Châtelet." *Project Vox*. Duke University Libraries. https://projectvox.org/du-chatelet-1706-1749/.

Voltaire. (1733) 2007. *Philosophical Letters or Letters Regarding the English Nation*. Edited by John Leigh and translated by Prudence L. Steiner. Indianapolis: Hackett Publishing Company.

Zinsser, Judith. 2006. *Emilie Du Châtelet: Daring Genius of the Enlightenment*. New York: Penguin.

———, ed. 2009. *Emilie Du Châtelet: Selected Philosophical and Scientific Writings*. Translated by Isabelle Bour and Judith P. Zinsser. Chicago: University of Chicago Press.

Fundamentals of Physics (1740)
Preface

I have always thought that the most sacred duty of men was to give their children an education that prevented them at a more advanced age from regretting their youth, the only time when one can truly gain instruction. You are, my dear son, in this happy age when the mind begins to think, and when the heart has passions not yet lively enough to disturb it.

Now is perhaps the only time of your life that you will devote to the study of nature. Soon the passions and pleasures of your age will occupy all your moments; and when this youthful enthusiasm has passed, and you have paid to the intoxication of the world the tribute of your age and rank, ambition will take possession of your soul; and even if in this more advanced age, which often is not any more mature, you wanted to apply yourself to the study of the true Sciences, your mind then no longer having the flexibility characteristic of its best years, it would be necessary for you to purchase with painful study what you can learn today with extreme facility. So, I want you to make the most of the dawn of your reason; I want to try to protect you from the ignorance that is still only too common among those of your rank, and which is one more fault, and one less merit.

You must early on accustom your mind to think, and to be self-sufficient. You will perceive at all the times in your life what resources and what consolations one finds in study, and you will see that it can even furnish pleasure and delight.

The study of physics seems made for man, it turns upon the things that constantly surround us, and on which our pleasures and our needs depend. In this work, I will try to place this science within your reach, and to disengage it from this admirable art, called algebra, which separating things from images, eludes the senses, and speaks only to the understanding. You are not yet able to understand this language, which seems rather that of the mind than of the whole of man. It is reserved to be the study of the years of your life that will follow those of today; but the truth can take different forms, and I will try to give to it here that which suits your age, and only to speak to you of things that can be understood by resorting only to the standard geometry which you have studied.

Never cease, my son, to cultivate this science that you have learned from your very tender years. With no resort to it, one would hope in vain to make great progress in the study of nature. It is the key to all discoveries; and if there are still several inexplicable things in physics, that is because geometry has been insufficiently used to explain them, and one has perhaps not yet gone far enough in this science.

I am often surprised that so many clever people as France possesses have not preceded me in this work that I embark upon for you today. For, it must be admitted that, although we have several excellent books of physics in French, we have no complete book of physics, except the short treatise of Rohault, written eighty years ago. But this treatise, although very good for the time when it was composed, has become very insufficient because of the quantity of discoveries that have been made since it was written; and a man who had studied physics only in this book, would still have many things to learn.

As for me, who in deploring this scarcity, am very far from believing myself capable of supplying it, I only propose in this work to gather together before your eyes the discoveries scattered in so many good Latin, Italian, and English books. Most of the truths they contain are known in France by only a few readers, and I want to spare you the trouble of drawing them from sources, the depth of which would frighten and might discourage you.

Although the work I undertake requires much time and effort, I will not regret the trouble it will cost me, and I will believe it well spent if it can instill in you love of the sciences, and the desire to cultivate your reason. What trouble and what cares does one not give oneself every day in the uncertain hope of procuring honors and augmenting the fortune of one's children! Are the knowledge of the truth and the habit of looking for it and following it objects less worthy of my pains—especially in a century when a taste for physics has reached all ranks, and is beginning to become a part of the science of the world?

I will not write for you here the history of the revolutions experienced by physics, a thick book would be needed to report them all. I propose to make you acquainted *less with what has been thought than with what must be known.*

Up to the last century, the sciences were an impenetrable secret, to which only the so-called learned were initiated; it was a kind of cabal, the cipher of which consisted of barbarous words that seemed to have been invented to confuse the mind and to discourage it.

Descartes appeared in that profound night like a star come to illuminate the universe. The revolution that this great man caused in the sciences is surely more useful, and perhaps even more memorable, than that of the greatest empires, one, it can be said, that human reason owes most to Descartes. For it is very much easier to find the truth, when once one is on the track of it, than to leave those of error. The geometry of this great man, his dioptrics, his method, are masterpieces of sagacity that will make his name immortal, and if he was wrong on some points of physics, that was because he was a man, and it is not given to a single man, nor to a single century, to know all.

We rise to the knowledge of the truth, like those giants who climbed up to the skies by standing on the shoulders of one another. The Huygenses, and the Leibnizes learned from Descartes and Galileo, these great men who, so far, are known to you only by name, and with whose works I hope soon to make you acquainted. It is by making the most of the works of Kepler, and using the theorems of Huygens, that M. Newton discovered this universal force spread throughout nature, which makes the planets circle around the Sun, and that operates as gravity on Earth.

Today the systems of Descartes and Newton divide the thinking world, so you should know the one and the other; but so many learned men have taken care to expound and to correct Descartes' system that it will be easy for you to learn from their works. One of my aims in the first part of this work is to put before your eyes the other part of this great process, to make you acquainted with the system of M. Newton, to show you how far making connections and determining probability are pushed, and how the phenomena are explained by the hypothesis of attraction.

You can draw much instruction on this subject from the *Elémens de la philosophie de Newton* [*Elements of the Philosophy of Newton*], which appeared last year. And I would omit what I have to tell you about that—Newton's system—if the illustrious author had embraced a vaster terrain; but he confined himself within such narrow boundaries that he made it impossible for me to dispense with my own exposition of this matter.

Guard yourself, my son, whichever side you take in this dispute among the philosophers, against the inevitable obstinacy to which the spirit of partisanship carries one: this frame of mind is dangerous on all occasions of life; but it is ridiculous in physics. The search for truth is the only thing in which the love of your country must not prevail, and it is surely very unfortunate that the opinions of Newton and of Descartes have become a sort of national affair. About a book of physics one must ask if it is good, not if the author is English, German, or French.

It seems to me, moreover, that it would be just as unfair on the part of the Cartesians to refuse to admit attraction as a hypothesis as it is unreasonable of a few Newtonians to want to make it an inherent property of matter. It must be admitted that a few among them have gone too far in this, and it is with some reason that they are reproached for resembling a man at the opera whose bad eyesight prevents him from seeing the ropes that make flights possible, and who, for example, on seeing Bellerophon suspended in the air, said: *Bellerophon is suspended in the air because he is pulled equally on all sides from the wings.* For, in order to decide that the effects the Newtonians attribute to attraction are not produced by impulsion, it would be necessary to know all the ways in which impulsion can be used, but we are still very far from knowing that.

We are still in physics, like this man blind from birth whose sight Chiselden restored. At first this man saw nothing but a blur; it was only by feeling his way and at the end of a considerable time that he began to see well. This time has not quite come for us, and perhaps will never come entirely; there are probably some truths not made to be perceived by the eyes of our mind, just as there are objects, that those of our body will never perceive. But he who refused to learn because of this limitation would resemble a lame person who, having a fever, would not take the remedies which can cure it, because these remedies would not stop him from limping.

One of the mistakes of some philosophers of our time is to want to banish hypotheses from physics; they are as necessary as the scaffolding in a house being built; it is true that, when the building is completed, the scaffolding becomes useless, but it could not have been erected without it. All of astronomy, for example, is founded only on hypotheses, and if they had always been avoided in physics, it seems that fewer discoveries would have been made. So nothing is more likely to delay the progress of the sciences than to want to banish them, and to persuade oneself that one has found the great mainspring that moves all of nature, for one does not search for a cause that one believes one knows. This is why the application of the geometric principles of mechanics to physical effects, which is very difficult and very necessary, remains imperfect, and why we find ourselves deprived of the work and the research of several fine geniuses who would perhaps have been able to discover the true cause of phenomena.

It is true that hypotheses become the poison of philosophy when they are made to pass for the truth, and perhaps they are then even more dangerous than was the unintelligible jargon of the Schoolmen; for this jargon being absolutely meaningless, it only required a little attention from a clear-thinking mind to perceive how ridiculous it was, and to seek the truth elsewhere. But an ingenious and bold hypothesis, which has some initial probability, leads human pride to believe it, the mind applauds itself for having found these subtle principles, and next uses all its sagacity to defend them. Most great men who have made systems provide us with examples of this failing. These are great ships carried by the currents; they make the most beautiful maneuvers in the world, but the current carries them away.

In all your studies, remember, my son, that experiment is the cane that nature gave to us blind ones, to guide us in our research; with its help we will make good progress, but, if we cease to use it, we cannot help falling. It is experiment that teaches us about the physical characteristics of things and it is for our reason to use it and to deduce from it new knowledge and new enlightenment.

If I thought it incumbent upon me to caution you against the spirit of partisanship, I believe it even more necessary to advise you not to carry respect for the greatest men to the point of idolatry, as the majority of their disciples do. Each philosopher has seen something, and none has seen all; no book is so bad that nothing can be learned from it, and no book is so good that one might not improve it. When I read Aristotle, this philosopher who has suffered fortunes so diverse and so unjust, I am astonished sometimes to find ideas so sound on several points of general physics, beside the greatest absurdities; but when I read some of the questions that M. Newton put at the end of his *Opticks*, I am struck with a very different astonishment. This example of the two greatest men of their century can but make you see that he who is endowed with reason must take nobody at his word alone, but must always make his own examination, setting aside the consideration always allotted to a famous name.

This is one of the reasons why I have not filled this book with citations, I did not want to seduce you with authorities; and more, there would have been too many. I am very far from believing myself capable of writing a book of physics without consulting any book, and I even doubt that without this help one might be able to write a good one. The greatest philosopher may well add new discoveries to those of others, but once a truth has been found, he has to follow it; for example, M. Newton had to begin by establishing Kepler's two analogies when he wanted to explain the course of the planets, without which he would never have arrived at the beautiful discovery of the gravitation of the celestial bodies.

Physics is an immense building that surpasses the powers of a single man. Some lay a stone there, while others build whole wings, but all must work on the solid foundations that have been laid for this edifice in the last century, by means of geometry and observations; still others survey the plan of the building, and I, among them.

In this work, I have not aimed at flaunting my intelligence, but at being right; and I have nurtured your reason enough to believe that you are capable of seeking the truth independently of all the alien adornments with which it is being overwhelmed in our day. I merely removed the thorns that might have wounded your delicate hands, but I did not think that I must replace them with alien flowers, and I am certain that a good mind, however weak it might still be, finds more pleasure, and a more satisfying pleasure, in clear, precise reasoning that it grasps easily, than in an ill-timed joke.

In the first chapters I explain to you the principal opinions of M. Leibniz on metaphysics; I have drawn them from the works of the celebrated Wolff, of whom you have heard me speak so much with one of his disciples, who was for some time in my household, and who sometimes made abstracts for me.

M. Leibniz's ideas on metaphysics are still little known in France, but they certainly deserve to be. Despite the discoveries of this great man, there are no doubt still many obscure things in metaphysics; but it seems to me that with the principle of sufficient reason, he has provided a compass capable of leading us in the moving sands of this science.

The obscurities in which some parts of metaphysics are still shrouded serve as pretext for the laziness of the majority of men not to study it. They persuade themselves that because not everything is known, nothing can be. Yet, there certainly are points of metaphysics susceptible to demonstrations as rigorous as geometric demonstrations, although they are of another type. We lack a system of calculation for metaphysics similar to that which has been found for mathematics, by means of which, with the aid of certain *givens*, one arrives at knowledge of *unknowns*. Perhaps some genius will one day find this system. M. Leibniz gave this much thought; he had ideas on this, which he unfortunately never communicated to anyone, but even if it could be invented, it seems that there are some unknowns for which no *equation* could ever be found. Metaphysics contains two types of things: the first, that which all people who make good use of their mind, can know; and the second, which is the most extensive, that which they will never know.

Several truths of physics, metaphysics, and geometry are obviously interconnected. Metaphysics is the summit of the edifice; this summit is so elevated that our image of it often is a little blurred. This is why I thought I should begin by bringing it closer to you, so that, no cloud obscuring your mind, you might be able to have a clear and unassailable view of the truths in which I want to instruct you.

"Hypothesis" from *Fundamentals* (1740) and *Encyclopédie* (1765)

Hypothesis. It is the supposition made about certain things to account for what is observed, although the truth of these suppositions cannot be demonstrated. When the causes of certain phenomena are not accessible by either experience or demonstration, philosophers have recourse to hypotheses. The true causes of natural effects and phenomena that we observe are often so far removed from the principles upon which we can rely and the experiments that we can make, that we are obliged to be satisfied with probable reasons to explain them. Probabilities are therefore not to be rejected in the sciences; a beginning is necessary in all research, and this beginning must almost always be a very imperfect attempt, often without success. There are unknown truths, like undiscovered countries, to which the correct road can be found only after having tried all the others; thus some people must run the risk of going astray in order to show the right way to others.

Hypotheses must therefore find a place in the sciences, since they are appropriate to the discovery of truth and to the revelation of new perspectives; for once we state a *hypothesis*, many experiments are performed to determine whether it is correct. If we find that the experiments verify it and that the *hypothesis* not only accounts for the given phenomenon but that all the inferences drawn from it are also in agreement with the observations, then the probability increases to such a point that we cannot dispute it, for it has become the equivalent of a demonstration.

The example of the astronomers can be extraordinarily useful in clarifying this matter. It is obvious that we owe to *hypotheses* that have been successively made and corrected the beautiful and sublime knowledge that now abounds in astronomy and dependent sciences. For example, it was by means of a *hypothesis* concerning the ellipticity of planetary orbits that Kepler succeeded in discovering the proportionality of areas and time and of time and distances as well as the two famous theorems called the analogies of Kepler; these discoveries permitted Newton to demonstrate that the supposition of the ellipticity of planetary orbits agrees with the laws of mechanics and to determine the proportion of forces directing the movement of celestial bodies.

In the same manner we finally know that Saturn is surrounded by a ring that reflects light and that is separated from the body of the planet and inclined to the ecliptic; for Mr. Huygens, who first discovered it, did not observe the ring in the same way as the astronomers who now describe it. But he did observe several phases of the planet which sometimes resembled nothing less than a ring; and then comparing the successive changes of these phases and all the observations he had made of them, he looked for a *hypothesis* that could satisfy them and account for these different appearances. The idea of a ring was so successful that it could not only account for these appearances but also predict the phases of this ring with precision.

There are two excesses to avoid in regard to *hypotheses*: the one of valuing them too much, the other of forbidding them entirely. Descartes, who had based a good part of his philosophy on *hypotheses*, gave the entire learned world a taste for these *hypotheses*. Before long this vogue deteriorated, and people actually preferred works of fiction. Newton and especially his disciples went to the opposite extreme. Disgusted with the conjectures and errors that filled the books of philosophy, they protested against the use of *hypotheses*, they tried to render them suspect and ridiculous by calling them the poison of reason and the plague of philosophy. Nevertheless, could not one say that they passed judgment on themselves, and will the fundamental principle of Newtonianism ever be granted with a more honorable title than that of a *hypothesis*? Only the one who would be in a position to assign and demonstrate the causes of everything we see would have the right to banish entirely all *hypotheses* from philosophy.

It is necessary that a *hypothesis* not contradict any of the first principles that serve as a foundation for our knowledge; it is even necessary to be quite certain of the facts within our reach and to know all the circumstances relating to the phenomenon we wish to explain.

The most common danger is to want to pass off a *hypothesis* for the truth itself without being able to give incontestable proof. It is very important for the progress of the sciences not to deceive oneself or others about the *hypothesis* that one has invented. Most of those who since Descartes have filled their writings with *hypotheses* to explain facts that quite often they knew only imperfectly, ran straight into this danger and wanted to pass off their conjectures for truths; this is in part the source of the disgust that people have developed for *hypotheses*. But if we distinguished between their good and their bad use, we can avoid on the one hand works of fiction and on the other we do not take away from the sciences a very necessary method in the art of invention, the only one, moreover, that can be used in difficult research, which requires the correction of several centuries and the works of several men, before attaining a certain degree of perfection.

Good *hypotheses* will always be the work of the greatest men. Copernicus, Kepler, Huygens, Descartes, Leibniz, even Newton have all conceived useful *hypotheses* to explain complicated and difficult phenomena. We would badly interpret the interests of science in wishing to condemn examples that can be justified by such brilliant success in metaphysics.

A *hypothesis* can be regarded demonstrably false if by examining the proposition that expresses it we find that the terms are devoid of meaning or have no fixed or determinate idea, if they explain nothing, if they produce as a consequence certain difficulties that are more important than those one intended to resolve, etc. There are many *hypotheses* of this kind. *See* chap. IV of the *Institution of Physics* [Du Châtelet] and especially the *Treatise on Systems* by the Abbé de Condillac.

XI

ROUSSEAU

Letter to Voltaire on	Defends the Optimism of Leibniz against the severe
Optimism (1756)	and very public criticisms of Voltaire occasioned by
	the catastrophic 1755 Lisbon earthquake

JEAN-JACQUES ROUSSEAU (1712–1778), the Swiss/French philosopher, political theorist, educator, and major Enlightenment figure, stood against the Lisbon earthquake-induced pessimism of Voltaire (1694–1778). On August 18, 1756, he wrote a long 6,300-word letter to Voltaire, who was a close friend and social/political ally, that directly engaged, almost line-by-line, with Voltaire's 180-line "Poem on the Lisbon Disaster: An Inquiry into the Maxim 'Whatever is, is right.'"

In the mid-eighteenth century, Lisbon was Europe's fourth-largest city after London, Paris, and Naples, with a population of about three hundred thousand. It was the imperial center of the Portuguese Empire, with gold, silver, jewels, spices, and much else pouring in from Brazil and other Portuguese possessions and trading posts acquired during the "Golden Age" of Portugal's maritime explorations. On November 1, All Souls Day, 1755, at 9:30 a.m., the city was shaken by a massive series of earthquakes; thirty minutes later, the riverside and low-lying areas were swamped by a tsunami, with the harbor water rising six meters and flooding 250 meters into the hilly city. Thirty-five of Lisbon's forty churches either collapsed or were severely damaged, most packed with parishioners praying for the souls of their departed loved ones; only three thousand of the city's twenty thousand houses were left habitable; commercial buildings were in ruins; numerous fine palaces were gone; the royal library, with its seventy thousand books and one thousand manuscripts, destroyed; hospitals, the opera house, and government buildings all were reduced to rubble. Thousands of citizens who escaped to the harborside were drowned in the tsunami.

In the aftermath, five days of widespread fires destroyed more property and live-lihoods and ended the lives of still more people; patients in hospitals were burnt in their wards and beds. Initial estimates were that thirty to fifty thousand people were killed, which was about 10–20 percent of the city's population. The quake was felt up and down the Portuguese, Spanish, and North African coasts, as well as in central Europe. The tsunami reached Brazil and the coasts of England, Ireland, and Scotland. In Cornwall, the sea rose three meters. The quake disturbed lakes in modern day Italy, Switzerland, and Germany.

Even in an era of rudimentary communication, the Lisbon earthquake quickly became a European event. Philosophers, theologians, natural philosophers (scientists), clergymen, artists, writers, poets, playwrights, musicians, and politicians all quickly responded to the earthquake, and many from these groups have kept responding to the present day. It is perhaps the most written about earthquake in history.[1]

Many Protestants thought the quake befell Lisbon as divine revenge. John Wesley (1703–1791), a co-founder with his brother of the Methodist Church, preached, within weeks of the quake, a famous sermon on the tragedy pointing to it as a sign of divine revenge for, among other things, the Protestant blood spilled by the Lisbon Inquisition (Wesley [1755] 1996).

Voltaire's "Poem on the Lisbon Disaster" was composed in anger within a month of the event and published in 1756. Its first stanza expressed the tortured thoughts of many:

> Oh wretched man, earth-fated to be cursed;
> Abyss of plagues and miseries the worst!
> Horrors on horrors, griefs on griefs must show,
> That man's the victim of unceasing woe,
> And lamentations which inspire my strain,
> Prove that philosophy is false and vain. (Voltaire [1756] 2000, 99)

In his *Candide*, Voltaire immortalized for his own and subsequent ages the infamous "holy" action of the Lisbon Inquisition:

> After the earthquake, which had wrecked three quarters of Lisbon, the wise men of Portugal had identified no more effective method to prevent the rest being destroyed than to hold a fine *auto-da-fé* to educate the people. It was decided by the University of Coïmbra that the spectacle of a few people being burned over a slow fire, accompanied by the most elaborate rituals, was an infallible, if little known, method for preventing earthquakes. (Voltaire [1759] 2000, 12–13)

---

1. See at least Molesky (2015), Paice (2008), and Shrady (2008).

In far-away Königsberg, Immanuel Kant had, within twelve months of the event, written a number of thoroughly naturalistic papers on the earthquake and tsunami.[2] The contrasting responses of Wesley and Kant to the earthquake well illustrate the different outlooks of, essentially, the medieval and modern worlds.

The Lisbon quake was an occasion for widespread and serious examination of the "Optimistic" philosophy of Gottfried Leibniz (1646–1716). Leibniz was a dominant figure in European scientific and philosophical thought. In his 1686 *Discourse on Metaphysics*, he provides a detailed argument from natural theology (a theology without input from Revelation) for the conclusion:

> Finally, since God is at the same time the most just and most good-natured of monarchs and since he demands only a good will, as long as it is sincere and serious, his subjects cannot wish for a better condition, and, to make them perfectly happy, he wants only for them to love him. (Leibniz [1686] 1989, 68)

For him, this deist conclusion is, happily, buttressed by Christian Revelation:

> The ancient philosophers knew very little of these important truths; Jesus Christ alone has expressed them divinely well, and in a manner so clear and familiar, that the coarsest of minds have grasped them. (Leibniz [1686] 1989, 68)

These arguments were elaborated on in his 1710 *Essays of Theodicy*.

This optimistic world picture was shaken by the Lisbon earthquake, which was so widely experienced and known about that it brought the problem of evil before everyone.[3] Some thinkers, Voltaire among them, found Optimism's solutions insufficient to explain suffering at this scale. Rousseau thought that the defenders of Optimism were able to deal with the specific arguments of Voltaire and, more generally, of those denying the Christian God's dominion over nature or Providence. Throughout his 1756 letter, he alludes to, but does not fully develop, now familiar arguments in the philosophy of science concerning the relation of hypotheses to evidence. He is content to be a relativist in physics but wanted absolutism in ethics.

REFERENCES

Leibniz, Gottfried W. (1686) 1989. *Discourse on Metaphysics*. In *Philosophical Essays*, translated by Roger Ariew and Daniel Garber, 35–68. Indianapolis: Hackett Publishing Company.

---

2. Pleasingly, these papers, largely overlooked in the Anglo-American world, have been translated. See Reinhardt and Oldroyd (1983).
3. See McBrayer and Howard-Snyder (2014).

———. (1710) 1985. *Theodicy: On the Goodness of God, the Freedom of Man and the Origin of Evil*. Translated by E. M. Huggard. *Project Guttenberg*. Release date November 24, 2005. https://www.gutenberg.org/files/17147/17147-h/17147-h.htm.

McBrayer, Justin P., and Daniel Howard-Snyder, eds. 2014. *The Blackwell Companion to the Problem of Evil*. Hoboken, NJ: Wiley-Blackwell.

Molesky, Mark. 2015. *This Gulf of Fire: The Destruction of Lisbon, or Apocalypse in the Age of Science and Reason*. New York: Knopf.

Paice, Edward. 2008. *Wrath of God: The Great Lisbon Earthquake of 1755*. London: Quercus.

Pope, Alexander. (1733) 2000. "An Essay on Man." In *Candide and Related Texts*, by Voltaire, translated and edited by David Wootton, 86–94. Indianapolis: Hackett Publishing Company.

Reinhardt, Olaf, and David R. Oldroyd. 1983. "Kant's Theory of Earthquakes and Volcanic Action." *Annals of Science* 40, no. 3: 247–272.

Shrady, Nicholas. 2008. *The Last Day: Wrath, Ruin and Reason in the Great Lisbon Earthquake of 1755*. Harmondsworth: Penguin.

Voltaire [François-Marie Arouet]. (1756) 2000. "Poem on the Lisbon Disaster: An Inquiry into the Maxim, 'Whatever is, is right.'" In *Candide and Related Texts*, translated and edited by David Wootton, 99–108. Indianapolis: Hackett Publishing Company.

———. (1759) 2000. *Candide and Related Texts*. Translated and edited by David Wootton. Indianapolis: Hackett Publishing Company.

———. (1764) 2000. "Well (All is)." From *Portable Philosophical Dictionary*. In *Candide and Related Texts*, translated and edited by David Wootton, 137–142. Indianapolis: Hackett Publishing Company.

Wesley, John. (1755) 1996. "Serious Thoughts Occasioned by the Late Earthquake at Lisbon." In *John Wesley Collected Works*, vol. 11, 12–24. Albany, OR: Books for the Ages.

Letter to Voltaire on Optimism (1756)

All my criticisms, then, are aimed at your "Poem on the Lisbon Disaster," for I expected it would have an effect on me that was worthier of the concern for the welfare of others, which seems to have inspired you to write it. You reproach Pope and Leibniz with showing contempt for the evils we suffer when they claim that all is well, and you portray such a vast extent of misery that you make us more miserable than before. In place of the consolations that I hoped to find, all you do is weigh me down; one might think that you fear that I am insufficiently aware of how unhappy I am, and it seems as though you may believe that you reassure me by proving to me that all is ill.

Don't be misled, sir. The result is exactly the opposite of what you intend. This optimism that you find so cruel consoles me while I suffer the very pains that you describe to me as being insupportable. Pope's poem[4] alleviates my sufferings and encourages me to be patient; yours increases my sufferings, incites me to complain, and, taking from me everything but a shattered hope, it reduces me to despair. In this strange conflict, which occurs between what you prove to be the case and what I experience to be the case, I beg you to calm the perplexity that agitates me and tell me which is wrong, the viewpoint of sentiment or that of reason.

"Humans, be patient," Pope and Leibniz say to me; "your ills are a necessary consequence of your nature and of the design of this universe. The eternal and benevolent Being who governs it would have wished to have protected you from them. Of all the possible economies, he chose the one that combined the least evil with the most good; or, to say the same thing even more bluntly if needs must, if he has not made a better universe it is because he could not."

Now what does your poem say to me? "Suffer without respite, unhappy human. If there is a God who has created you, then he is surely all-powerful, and could have prevented your sufferings. So, you have no ground for hoping they will ever end, for there's no conceivable reason why you exist, if it is not to suffer and to die." I can't see what would make such a doctrine more consoling than optimism, or even than fatalism. As far as I'm concerned, I confess that it seems to me even more cruel than Manicheism. If the little difficulty of the entry of evil into the world requires that you vary one of God's perfect qualities, why defend his power at the expense of his goodness? If one must choose between two untruths, I would prefer the opposite choice.

You do not want us, sir, to think of your work as a poem against Providence, and I will take care not to call it this, although you have described a work I wrote in which I defended humanity against its own accusations as a book against the human species. I know the distinction that must be drawn between an author's intentions and the consequences that can be drawn from his teaching. But my obligation to defend myself against false charges merely requires me to point out to you that in portraying the miseries of human existence, my purpose was one that can be excused and perhaps should even be praised for all that I can tell: for I showed human beings how their sufferings were of their own making, and consequently how they could avoid them.

I do not see that one can look for the origins of moral evil anywhere except in human nature: free, as far as it could be, yet corrupted. As for physical suffering, if a type of matter that feels but cannot suffer is a contradiction in terms, as it seems to me to be, then such suffering is inevitable in any universe that contains human beings; in which case the question is not why are human beings not perfectly happy, but why do they exist? Moreover, I believe I have shown that, with the exception of death, which is scarcely to be counted as an evil except for the antechambers one is made to pass through to reach it, most of the physical evils we experience are likewise of our own making. Without leaving your chosen subject of Lisbon, you must acknowledge, for

---

4. For "An Essay on Man," see Pope (1733) 2000.

example, that it was not nature that piled up there twenty thousand houses of six or seven floors each; and that if the inhabitants of this great city had been spread out more evenly and had lived in less massive buildings, the destruction would have been a lot less, and perhaps insignificant. Everyone would have run away at the first shock, and one would have found them the next day fifty miles away and just as happy as if nothing had happened. But they had to stay put, stubbornly remain on the Mazures, expose themselves to new shocks because what they would be leaving behind was worth far more than what they could carry away with them. How many poor creatures died in this disaster because one wanted to go back for his clothes, another for his papers, a third for his money? Can't you see that the physical existence of a human being has become the least important part of themselves, and that it seems to be scarcely worth saving it when one has lost all the rest?

You would have wanted the earthquake to occur in the distant reaches of some desert rather than in Lisbon. Is there any reason to think earthquakes don't occur in deserts? But we don't discuss them, because they do no harm to the city dwellers, the only human beings to whom we attribute any significance. It's true they don't do much harm to the animals and the savages who live scattered through those inaccessible zones, and who don't worry about their roofs falling in or their houses being undermined. But supposing you had your wish, what would it imply? Would it mean that the order of nature must change to suit our fancies, that nature must submit herself to our laws, and that, to forbid the occurrence of an earthquake in any particular place, all that would be necessary would be to build a town there?

. . .

Thus, sir, your examples seem to me more ingenious than convincing. I can see a thousand credible reasons why it was not without significance for Europe that on a particular day the next in line to the throne of Burgundy was well or badly dressed, nor to the destiny of Rome that Caesar turned his eyes to the left or the right and spat on one side or the other on his way to the senate the day that he met his just deserts there. In a word, in recalling the grain of sand that Pascal refers to [in *Pensées*], I am in certain respects of the same opinion as your Brahmin; and, however one looks at matters, if all events do not have effects that can be identified, still it seems to me beyond question that all of them have real effects; even if our human intelligence easily loses track of them, nature never does.

You say that it has been demonstrated that the celestial bodies travel on their orbits through a space that offers no resistance; this would be quite something to prove, but, as is normally the case with people who know very little, I have very little confidence in demonstrations I cannot follow. I would imagine that in order to construct this proof one would have to reason roughly as follows: such a force, acting according to such a law, ought to give the heavenly bodies such and such a movement in a space which offers no resistance; and the heavenly bodies have exactly the predicted movement; therefore they pass through a space that offers no resistance. But who can know if there are not, perhaps, a million other possible laws, not to mention the authentic law, according to which the same movement could be better explained as taking place within a fluid rather than by your law governing movement in a vacuum? Wasn't nature's horror of a vacuum for a long time used to explain most of the effects that are now explained by atmospheric pressure? Other experiments having later served to destroy the idea of the horror of a vacuum, wasn't it taken to follow that a vacuum was impossible? Was the idea of vacuum not then reestablished on the basis of new calculations? How can we know that a yet more powerful theory will not destroy it once again? Let us leave aside the innumerable difficulties that a natural scientist might make when it comes to the nature of light and its passage through space; but do you honestly think that Bayle, whom I agree with you in admiring for his wisdom and his grasp when it comes to matters in dispute, would have found your case so completely convincing? In general, it seems that skeptics forget their principles a bit as soon as they begin to speak at all dogmatically; they of all people ought to be careful how they use the word "demonstrate." How do you expect to be believed when you take pride in knowing nothing and assert so much?

As for the rest, you have made a very sensible corrective to Pope's system when you remark that there is no graduated proportion between the creatures and their creator, and that if the chain of created beings stops at God it is because he holds the end of it, not because he is the last link in it.

. . .

In order to think straight on this matter it seems that we have to think relatively when it comes to questions of physics, and absolutely when it comes to questions of morality. The finest idea that I can construct of Providence is that each material being is placed in the best possible relationship to the whole and each intelligent and sensitive being is placed in the best possible relationship to himself. What I mean, to put it differently, is that for any creature that is aware of its own existence it is better to exist than not to exist. But we have to apply this rule to the whole period of the life of each sensitive being, and not to some particular moment in its existence, such as its life as a human being: which shows just how closely the question of Providence is linked to that of the immortality of the soul, in which I have the good fortune to believe even though I realize that there are rational grounds for questioning it; and to that of the doctrine of eternal damnation, which neither you, nor I, nor ever any man who thought well of God would believe for a moment.

If I take these different questions back to their common origin, it seems to me that they all relate to that of the existence of God. If God exists he is perfect; if he is perfect he is wise, strong, and powerful; if he is wise and strong all is well; if he is just and powerful my soul is immortal; if my soul is immortal, thirty years on earth have no importance to me and are perhaps necessary to the functioning of the universe. If you concede the first principle then you will never unpick those that follow from it; if you deny it, then there's no point in arguing about the consequences.

Neither of us denies the key premise. At least it would seem that I had no grounds for imagining that you might deny it as I read through the volumes of your works. Most of them present me with ideas of the divinity that are exceptionally noble, sweet, reassuring, and I much prefer a Christianity like yours to that of the Sorbonne.

As for me, I will openly admit to you that in this matter neither the argument for nor the argument against seem to me demonstrated conclusively in rational terms; if the theist grounds his opinion, in the end, on probabilities, the atheist is even further from conclusive proof, and seems to me to rely on the possibility that the opposite is true. Moreover, the objections that each side makes against the other can never be refuted because they depend on matters about which human beings have no real idea. I admit all that, and yet I believe in God as strongly as I believe any other truth, because believing and not believing are, of all that is, the things over which I have least control. Moreover, being in a state of doubt is far too stressful for my spirit. When my reason floats free, my faith is incapable of remaining for long in suspense and anchors itself on its own. Finally, there are a thousand factors that induce me to adopt the opinion that is the most comforting; and the weight of experience tips the balance of reason. . . .

But, like you, I am indignant that each individual is not perfectly free to decide for themselves what they wish to believe, and outraged that there are people who dare to claim authority over our conscientious convictions, to which we alone have access, as if we had a choice as to whether to believe or not to believe with regard to questions that are not susceptible to demonstration, and as if reason could ever be enslaved by authority. Do the rulers of this world have some jurisdiction in the next? Do they have the right to torture their subjects down here in order to force them to go to paradise? No, all earthly government is by its nature restricted to our civil obligations, and, no matter what that sophist Hobbes may have claimed [*Leviathan* (1651)], as long as a person is a good servant of the state they are under no obligation to account to anyone for the manner in which they serve God.

XII

PRIESTLEY

"Restoration of Air" (1772)   (contra Aristotelian identification of different components of air; existential problem of replenishing bad air; discovery of role of green plants and daylight; photosynthesis)

JOSEPH PRIESTLEY (1733–1804) was born in Yorkshire and died in Pennsylvania. His life spanned the core years of the Enlightenment, to which he was a prominent contributor. An ordained dissenting Christian minister, Priestley is now best known for his work in chemistry and the "discovery" of oxygen. In fact, he was a polymath who made original and lasting contributions across the widest range of subjects, writing over two hundred books, pamphlets, and articles covering metaphysics (specifically a defense of materialism), the history of science (specifically the histories of electricity and of optics), political theory (defending republicanism, liberalism, and secularism), theology (arguing for Unitarianism against orthodox Trinitarianism), biblical criticism (rejecting fundamentalist interpretation in favor of Spinoza-like textural study), theory of language, philosophy of education (for liberal education), and rhetoric; as well as authoring books and pamphlets on chemistry.[1]

Priestley was not just knowledgeable across the board: all of his intellectual activity was explicitly interconnected. For Priestley, knowledge was not compartmentalized; his epistemology (sensationalism) related to his ontology (materialism), both related to his theology (Unitarianism) and to his psychology (associationism), and these all bore upon his political and social theory (liberalism). He was a consciously *synoptic* or *systematic* thinker: all components of knowledge (and life as a whole) had to relate consistently.

---

1. For the life and achievements of Priestley, see Jackson (2005), Rivers and Wykes (2008), Schofield (1997, 2004), and Schwartz and McEvoy (1990).

Contemporary appreciation of Priestley has been blighted by Thomas Kuhn's harsh and unfair judgment of him in his best-selling *The Structure of Scientific Revolutions* (1970). In a famous, but more properly infamous, passage, Kuhn writes of the irrational nature of paradigm change in science with old paradigms just dying off until "at last only a few elderly hold-outs remain." He then singularly names Priestley as an example "of the man who continues to resist after his whole profession has been converted" and adds that such a man "has *ipso facto* ceased to be a scientist" (Kuhn 1970, 159). A more generous and accurate assessment of Priestley was given by Frederic Harrison in his introduction of a nineteenth-century edition of Priestley's *Scientific Correspondence*:

> If we choose one man as a type of the intellectual energy of the eighteenth century, we could hardly find a better than Joseph Priestley, though his was not the greatest mind of the century. His versatility, eagerness, activity, and humanity; the immense range of his curiosity in all things, physical, moral, or social; his place in science, in theology, in philosophy, and in politics; his peculiar relation to the Revolution, and the pathetic story of his unmerited sufferings, may make him the hero of the eighteenth century. (Bolton 1892, introduction)

As with all Enlightenment thinkers, Priestley preached the importance of good education for individuals and society. In *The Proper Objects of Education*, he affirmed:

> All great improvements in the state of society ever have been, and ever must be . . . the result of the most peaceable but assiduous endeavours in pursuing the slowest of all processes—that of enlightening the minds of men. (Priestley 1791)

While many *philosophes* and philosophers championed education, Priestley was of the minority who practiced what they preached. In 1758 at age twenty-five, Priestley became the minister for a congregation at Nantwich in Cheshire, where he established a school with thirty boys and, in a separate room, six girls. He taught in the school for three years, six days a week, from 7:00 a.m. to 4:00 p.m., teaching Latin, Greek, English grammar, and geography. Additionally, he taught natural philosophy and purchased an air pump and an electrical machine, and instructed his pupils in their use. Thus, Priestley may well have been the first person ever to teach laboratory science to schoolchildren.

Priestley did not begin serious chemical studies until his early thirties, during his ministry at the Leeds Presbyterian Chapel (1767–1773). The physical properties of air had long been studied by, for instance, Bacon, Galileo, Torricelli, and Boyle. But all believed they were studying a single thing. Priestley, in quick succession, by utilizing a new method of collecting different airs over water and mercury, and by utilizing a new and massive twelve-inch magnifying glass as a source of heat, created, isolated, and listed properties of a dozen or more of the major "airs"; he showed everyday air to have components, to be a mixture. In so doing, he dislodged the over two-thousand-year-old Aristotelian belief that air, undifferentiated, is one of the five basic elements. This was, again, the triumph of physics over metaphysics; it fueled Enlightenment convictions about the primacy of science in acquiring knowledge of nature and society.

Priestley's experiments and investigations of airs, conducted in Leeds, were announced in a series of talks he delivered to the Royal Society in London in March 1772. The talks subsequently were published as his famous 118-page paper in the Society's *Philosophical Transactions* of the same year—"Observations on Different Kinds of Air" (Priestley 1772).[2] In this paper he wrote:

> The quantity of air which even a small flame requires to keep it burning is prodigious. It is generally said that an ordinary candle consumes, as it is called, about a gallon in a minute. Considering this amazing consumption of air, by fires of all kinds, volcanoes, etc. it becomes a great object of philosophical inquiry, to ascertain what change is made in the constitution of the air by flame, and to discover what provision there is in nature for remedying the injury which the atmosphere receives by this means. Some of the following experiments will, perhaps, be thought to throw a little light upon the subject. (Priestley 1772, 162)

Priestley's Christian worldview animated this quest: with centuries of animal and human respiration, plus volcanoes and natural fires, the atmosphere should be progressively rendered unfit for human life, but there were *theological* reasons why this could not happen. A beneficent all-powerful creator would not design such a world; God must have made some provision for the natural restoration of air. Priestley assuredly did not believe in an intervening, miracle-working deity who would periodically visit his creation to restore the quality of its air; restoration would have been in-built into the Creation. The task of natural philosophy was to ascertain how this was being done.

The 1772 paper is a tour de force and is justly known as a landmark in the history of science. It describes: Priestley's manufacture of soda water (Pyrmont water);[3] his creation, but not recognition, of oxygen by heating saltpeter (potassium nitrate); his nitric oxide test for the "goodness of air"; and last, but not least, his identification of the mechanisms, now called photosynthesis, for the restoration of "the goodness of air" (Matthews 2009).

At the November 30, 1773 meeting of the Royal Society the president, Sir John Pringle (1707–1782) presented the Society's prestigious Copley Medal to Priestley, declaring:

---

2. All Royal Society transactions papers are now available on the Society's web page.

3. In 1793, Johann J. Schweppe (1740–1821) offered to buy Priestley's soda water process. Instead, Priestley gave it to him saying, "natural philosophers only seek truth not money." The rest, as they say, is commercial history.

From these [Priestley's] discoveries we are assured, that no vegetable grows in vain, but that from the oak of the forest to the grass of the field, every individual plant is serviceable to mankind; if not always distinguished by some private virtue yet making a part of the whole which cleanses and purifies our atmosphere. In this the fragrant rose and deadly nightshade co-operate; nor is the herbage, nor the woods that flourish in the most remote and un-peopled regions unprofitable to us, nor we to them; considering how constantly the winds convey to them our vitiated air, for our relief, and for their nourishment. And if ever these salutary gales rise to storms and hurricanes, let us still trace and revere the ways of a beneficent Being; who not fortuitously but with design, not in wrath but in mercy, thus shakes the waters and the air together, to bury in the deep those putrid and pestilential *effluvia*, which the vegetables upon the face of the earth had been insufficient to consume. (McKie 1961, 9–11)

Pringle restates, as a shared English belief, Leibniz's "best of all possible worlds" picture that was painted in his 1710 *Theodicy*. Selections from Priestley's famous paper follow.

REFERENCES

Bolton, Henry Carrington, ed. 1892. *Scientific Correspondence of Joseph Priestley: Ninety-Seven Letters*. New York: privately printed.

Jackson, Joe. 2005. *A World on Fire: A Heretic, an Aristocrat, and the Race to Discover Oxygen*. New York: Penguin.

Kuhn, Thomas S. (1962) 1970. *The Structure of Scientific Revolutions*. 2nd ed. Chicago: Chicago University Press.

Matthews, Michael R. 2009. "Science and Worldviews in the Classroom: Joseph Priestley and Photosynthesis." In *Science, Worldviews and Education*, edited by Michael R. Matthews, 271–302. Dordrecht: Springer.

McKie, Douglas. 1961. "Joseph Priestley and the Copley Medal." *Ambix* 9, no. 1: 1–22.

Priestley, Joseph. 1772. "Observations on Different Kinds of Air." *Philosophical Transactions of Royal Society* 62: 147–264.

Priestley, Joseph. (1791) 1999. "The Proper Objects of Education." In *The Theological and Miscellaneous Works of Joseph Priestley*, vol. 15, edited by John Towill Rutt, 420–440. London: Thoemmes.

Rivers, Isabel, and David L Wykes, eds. 2008. *Joseph Priestley: Scientist, Philosopher, and Theologian*. Oxford: Oxford University Press.

Schofield, Robert E. 1997. *The Enlightenment of Joseph Priestley: A Study of His Life and Work from 1733 to 1773*. University Park, PA: Penn State Press.

———. 2004. *The Enlightened Joseph Priestley: A Study of His Life and Work from 1773 to 1804*. University Park, PA: Penn State Press.

Schwartz, A. Truman, and John G. McEvoy, eds. 1990. *Motion Toward Perfection: The Achievement of Joseph Priestley*. Boston: Skinner House Books.

"Restoration of Air" (1772)

The following observations on the properties of several different kinds of air, I am sensible, are very imperfect, and some of the courses of experiments are incomplete; but a considerable number of facts, which appear to me to be new and important, are sufficiently ascertained; and I am willing to hope, that when philosophers in general are apprised of them, some persons may be able to pursue them to more advantage than myself. I therefore think it my duty to give this Society an account of the progress I have been able to make; and I shall not fail to communicate any further lights that may occur to me, whenever I resume these inquiries.

In writing upon this subject, I find myself at a loss for proper terms, by which to distinguish the different kinds of air. Those which have hitherto obtained are by no means sufficiently characteristic, or distinct. The terms in common use are fixed air, mephitic, and inflammable. The last, indeed, sufficiently characterizes and distinguishes that kind of air which takes fire and explodes on the approach of flame; but it might have been termed fixed with as much propriety as that to which Dr. Black and others have given that denomination, since it is originally part of some solid substance, and exits in an inelastic state, and therefore may be also called factitious. The term mephitic is equally applicable to what is called fixed air, to that which is inflammable, and to many other kinds; since they are equally noxious, when breathed by animals. Rather, however, than to introduce new terms, or change the signification of old ones, I shall use the term fixed air, in the sense in which it is now commonly used, and distinguish the other kinds by their properties, or some other periphrasis. I shall be under a necessity, however, of giving a name to one species of air, to which no name was given before.

. . .

It is well known that flame cannot subsist long without change of air, so that the common air is necessary to it, except in the case of substances, into the composition of which nitre enters; for they will burn *in vacuo*, in fixed air, and even under water, as is evident in some rockets, which are made for this purpose. The quantity of air which even a small flame requires to keep it burning is prodigious. It is generally said that an ordinary candle consumes, as it is called, about a gallon in a minute. Considering this amazing consumption of air, by fires of all kinds, volcano's, etc. it becomes a great object of philosophical inquiry, to ascertain what change is made in the constitution of the air by flame, and to discover what provision there is in nature for remedying the injury which the atmosphere receives by this means. Some of the following experiments will, perhaps, be thought to throw a little light upon the subject.

. . .

Though this experiment failed, I flatter myself that I have accidentally hit upon a method of restoring air which has been injured by the burning of candles, and that I have discovered at least one of the restoratives which nature employs for this purpose. It is vegetation. In what manner this process in nature operates, to produce so remarkable an effect, I do not pretend to have discovered; but a number of facts declare in favour of his hypothesis. I shall introduce my account of them, by reciting some of the observations which I made on the growing of plants in confined air, which led to this discovery.

One might have imagined that, since common air is necessary to the vegetable, as well as to animal life, both plants and animals had affected it in the same manner, and I own I had that expectation, when I first put a sprig of mint into a glass-jar, standing inverted in a vessel of water; but when it had continued growing there for some months, I found that the air would neither extinguish a candle, nor was it at all inconvenient to a mouse, which I put into it.

. . .

Finding that candles burn very well in air in which plants had grown a long time, and having had some reason to think, that there was something attending vegetation, which restored air that had been injured by respiration, I thought it was possible that the same process might also restore the air that had been injured by the burning of candles.

Accordingly, on the 17th of August 1771, I put a sprig of mint into a quantity of air, in which a wax candle had burned out, and found that, on the 27th of the same month, another candle burned perfectly well in it. This experiment I repeated, without the least variation in the event, not less than eight or ten times in the remainder of the summer. Several times I divided the quantity of air in which the candle had burned out, into two parts, and putting the plant into one of them, left the other in the same exposure, contained, also, in a glass vessel immersed in water, but without any plant; and never failed to find, that a candle would burn in the former, but not in the latter. I generally found that five or six days were sufficient to restore this air, when the plant was in its vigour; whereas I have kept this kind of air in glass vessels, immersed in water many months, without being able to perceive that the least alteration had been made in it, I have also tried a great variety of experiments upon it, as by confining, rarefying, exposing to the light and heat, etc. and throwing into it the effluvia of many different substances, but without effect.

. . .

That candles will burn only a certain time, is a fact not better known, than it is that animals can live only a certain time, in a given quantity of air; but the cause of the death of the animal is not better known than that of the extinction of flame in the same circumstances; and when once any quantity of air has been rendered noxious by animals breathing it in as long as they could, I do not know that any methods have been discovered of rendering it fit for breathing again. It is evident, however, that there must be some provision in nature for this purpose, as well as for that of rendering the air fit for maintaining flame; for without it the whole mass of the atmosphere would, in time, become unfit for the purpose of animal life; and yet there is no reason to think that it is, at present, at all less fit for respiration than it has ever been. I flatter myself, however, that I have hit upon two of the methods employed by nature for this great purpose. How many others there may be, I cannot tell.

When animals die upon being put into air in which other animals have died, after breathing in it as long as they could, it is plain that the cause of their death is not the want of any *pabulum vitae*, which has been supposed to be contained in the air, but on account of the air being impregnated with something stimulating to their lungs; for they almost always die in convulsions, and are sometimes affected so suddenly, that they are irrecoverable after a single inspiration, though they be withdrawn immediately, and every method has been taken to bring them to life again. They are affected in the same manner, when they are killed in any other kind of noxious air that I have tried, viz. fixed air, inflammable air, air filled with fumes of brimstone, infected with putrid matter, in which a mixture of iron filings and brimstone has stood, or in which charcoal has been burned, or metals calcined, or in nitrous air, etc.

If a mouse (which is the animal that I have commonly made use of for the purpose of these experiments) can stand the first shock of this stimulus, or has been habituated to it by degrees, it will live a considerable time in air in which other mice will die instantaneously. I have frequently found that when a number of mice have been confined in a given quantity of air, less than half the time that they have lived in it, a fresh mouse has been instantly thrown into convulsions, and dies upon being put to them. It is evident, therefore, that if the experiment of the Black Hole were to be repeated, a man would stand the better chance of surviving it, should he enter at the first, rather than at the last hour. . . .

. . .

When air has been freshly and strongly tainted with putrefaction, so as to smell through the water, sprigs of mint have presently died, upon being put into it, their leaves turning black; but if they do not die presently, they thrive in a most surprising manner. In no other circumstances have I ever seen vegetation so vigorous as in this kind of air, which is immediately fatal to animal life. Though these plants have been crowded in jars filled with this air, every leaf has been full of life; fresh shoots have branched out in various directions, and have grown much faster than other similar plants, growing in the same exposure in common air.

This observation led me to conclude, that plants, instead of affecting the air in the same manner with animal respiration, reverse the effects of breathing, and tend to keep the atmosphere sweet and wholesome, which it is become noxious, in consequence of animals living and breathing, or dying and putrefying in it.

In order to ascertain this, I took a quantity of air, made thoroughly noxious, by mice breathing and dying in it, and divided it into two parts; one of which I put into a phial immersed in water; and to the other (which was contained in a glass jar, standing in water) I put a sprig of mint. This was about the beginning of August 1771, and after eight or nine days, I found that a mouse lived perfectly well in that part of the air, in which the sprig of mint had grown, but died the moment it was put into the other part of the same original quantity of air; and which I had kept in the very same exposure, but without any plant growing in it.

This experiment I have several times repeated; sometimes using air, in which animals had breathed and died; sometimes using air tainted with vegetable or animal putrefaction, and generally with the same success.

. . .

These proofs of a partial restoration of air by plants in a state of vegetation, though in a confined and unnatural situation, cannot but render it highly probable, that the injury which is continually done to the atmosphere by the respiration of such a number of animals, and the putrefaction of such masses of both vegetable and animal matter, is, in part at least, repaired by the vegetable creation.

. . .

Dr. Franklin, who, as I have already observed, saw some of my plants in a very flourishing state, in highly noxious air, was pleased to express very great satisfaction with the result of the experiments. In his answer to the letter in which I informed him of it, he says:

> That the vegetable creation should restore the air, which is spoiled by the animal part of it, looks like a rational system, and seems to be of a piece with the rest. . . . The strong thriving state of your mint in putrid air seems to show that the air is mended by taking something from it, and not by adding to it. . . . I hope this will give some check to the rage of destroying trees that grow near houses, which as accompanied our late improvements in gardening, from an opinion of their being unwholesome. I am certain, from long observation, that there is nothing unhealthy in the air of woods; for we Americans have everywhere our country habitations in the midst of woods, and no people on earth enjoy better health, or are more prolific.

. . .

That plants restore noxious air, by imbibing the phlogiston with which it is loaded, is very agreeable to the conjectures of Dr. Franklin, made many years ago, and expressed in the following extract from the last edition of his Letters:

> I have been inclined to think that the fluid *fire*, as well as the fluid *air*, is attracted by plants in their growth, and becomes consolidated with the other materials of which they are formed, and makes a great part of their substance; that, when they come to be digested, and to suffer in the vessels a kind of fermentation, part of the fire, as well as part of the air, recovers its fluid active

state again, and diffuses itself in the body, digesting and separating it; . . . in short, what escapes and is dissipated in the burning of bodies, besides water and earth, is generally the air, and fire, that before made parts of the solid.

. . .

I have frequently mentioned my having, at one time, exposed equal quantities of different kinds of air in jars standing in boiled water. The common air in this experiment was diminished four sevenths, and the remainder extinguished flame. This experiment demonstrates that water does not absorb air equally, but that it decomposes it, taking one part, and leaving the rest. To be quite sure of this fact, I agitated a quantity of common air in boiled water, and when I had reduced it from eleven ounces measures to seven, I found that it extinguished a candle, but a mouse lived in it very well. . . .

. . .

As I generally made use of mice in the experiments which relate to respiration, and some persons may choose to repeat them after me, and pursue them further than I have done; it may be of use to them to be informed, that I kept them without any difficulty in glass receivers, open at the top and bottom, and having a quantity of paper, or tow, in the inside, which should be changed every three or four days; when it will be most convenient also to change the vessel, and wash it. But they must be kept in a pretty exact temperature, for either much heat or much cold kills them presently. The place in which I have generally kept them is a shelf over the kitchen fireplace, where, as it is usual in Yorkshire, the fire never goes out; so that the heat varies very little; and I find it to be a medium about 70 degrees of Fahrenheit's thermometer.

Priestley's equipment

Joseph Priestley, LL.D., F.R.S.
Philosophical Transactions of the Royal Society
Read March 5, 12, 19, 26, 1772

XIII

KANT

Metaphysical Foundations of Natural Science (**1786**)	Preface (science needs laws established *a priori*, not experiential laws; natural science presupposes metaphysics of nature; absolute and relative space)
What Is Enlightenment? (**1784**)	(people need to think for themselves; public use of reason must be free and uncensored)

IMMANUEL KANT (1724–1804) was one of the most influential philosophers of the modern era. Away from his philosophy, most academics, students, and many ordinary citizens of his day knew him to be the lonely, meticulous, routinized, perambulating Prussian bachelor whose daily walks to Königsberg University were occasions for the local residents and shopkeepers to set their clocks to the correct time. Beyond this, his reputation was that of an austere person. Johann Gottfried Herder (1744–1803), a philosopher, theologian, and literary critic, provided a contemporary correction to the caricature:

> I have had the good fortune to know a philosopher. He was my teacher. In his prime he had the happy sprightliness of a youth; he continues to have it, I believe, even as a very old man. His broad forehead, built for thinking, was the seat of an imperturbable cheerfulness and joy. Speech, the richest in thought, flowed from his lips. Playfulness, wit, and humor were at his command. His lectures were the most entertaining talks. His mind, which examined Leibniz, Wolff, Baumgarten, Crusius, and Hume, and investigated the laws of nature of Newton, Kepler, and the physicists, comprehended equally the newest works of Rousseau . . . and the latest discoveries in science. He weighed them all, and always came back to the unbiased knowledge of nature and to the moral

worth of man. The history of men and peoples, natural history and science, mathematics, and observation, were the sources from which he enlivened his lectures and conversation. He was indifferent to nothing worth knowing. No cabal, no sect, no prejudice, no desire for fame could ever tempt him in the slightest away from broadening and illuminating the truth. He incited and gently forced others to think for themselves; despotism was foreign to his mind. The man, whom I name with the greatest gratitude and respect, was Immanuel Kant. (Beck 1950, xxii)

Kant's philosophy cannot be understood apart from his lifelong engagement with the science of his time.[1] More specifically, with Newton's science and his efforts to understand the fundamental concepts of natural philosophy: time, space, attraction, force, matter, and motion. Kant was a contributor to the debate between Newtonians, Cartesians, and Leibnizians about these fundamentals. He was a committed Newtonian but held that his worldview's philosophical underpinnings were not adequately addressed by either Newton or Newtonians. He wrote:

All natural philosophers who want to proceed mathematically in their work had therefore always (though unknown to themselves) made use of metaphysical principles, and had to make use of them, even though they otherwise solemnly repudiated any claim of metaphysics on their science . . . Those mathematical physicists [Newtonians] could not at all, then, dispense with metaphysical principles, and among these principles, not with such as make the concept of their own special object, namely, matter, available a priori for application to external experience (as in the cases of the concept of motion, of the filling of space, or inertia, etc). (Kant [1786] 1985, 9–10)

These claims are from his principal work in the philosophy of science, his *Metaphysical Foundations of Natural Science*, written in 1786.

Kant credited the reading of David Hume's incisive empiricist critique of causation (most probably the *Treatise of Human Nature*) with jolting him out of his "Newtonian comfort zone," so to speak. Hume, to his own satisfaction, established that causation was not in the world, but only in the mind; in the world there was just constant conjunction, the mind added the necessary connection between cause and effect.

For Kant, the relation of effect to cause was a synthetic *a priori* truth, a truth about the world (hence synthetic) known independently of experience. If this proposition can be established, it is a refutation of the whole empiricist program in epistemology. Kant and Kantians believe his *Critique of Pure Reason* (1781 and 1787) so established it. This argument, and much else, is developed by Kant in his *Metaphysical*

---

1. For the centrality of science in Kant's philosophising, see Buchdahl (1970), Friedman (1992), and Watkins (2001).

Foundations of Natural Science (Kant [1786] 1985). Selections from its Preface are included below.

The brevity of the second Kant selection is inversely matched to its near international recognition and philosophic fame. The 1784 essay—the original title was *An Answer to the Question: What Is Enlightenment?* (Kant 1784/1996)—had humble origins.

In December 1783, a progressive, "enlightened," and popular Berlin magazine, *Berlinische Monatsschrift*, published an article by Johann Friedrich Zöllner (1753–1804), a clergyman and educationalist, questioning the state's sanctioning of civil marriages, that is, marriages celebrated without a clergyman. Such legalizing was one of the consequences of the spreading eighteenth-century demand for governments to be more secular; for governments to separate sin from crime, ecclesiastical law from civil law. Zöllner complained that "under the name of enlightenment the hearts and minds of men are bewildered." He added in a footnote that has probably occasioned more literary response than any footnote ever written:[2]

> What is enlightenment (*Aufklärung*)? This question, which is almost as important as what is truth, should indeed be answered before one begins enlightening! And still I have never found it answered. (Schmidt 1996, 2)

Kant composed his answer on September 30, 1784. His essay was the second of fifteen articles Kant wrote for the magazine between the years 1784 to 1796. The essay was quickly identified as an intellectual banner or marker for the Age of Enlightenment. Kant, in the essay, optimistically states that:

> This spirit of freedom is also spreading abroad, even where it has to struggle with external obstacles of a government which misunderstands itself.

> I have put the main point of enlightenment, of people's emergence from their self-incurred minority, chiefly in matters of religion because our rulers have no interest in playing guardian over their subjects with respect to the arts and sciences and also because that minority, being the most harmful, is also the most disgraceful of all. But the frame of mind of a head of state who favors the first goes still further and sees that even with respect to his legislation there is no danger in allowing his subjects to make public use of their own reason and to publish to the world their thoughts about a better way of formulating it, even with candid criticism of that already given; we have a shining example of this, in which no monarch has yet surpassed the one whom we honor [Frederick the Great (1712–1786)]. (Kant [1784] 1996, 27)

---

2. James Schmidt (1996) has translated and edited an extensive collection of eighteenth-century German responses, including Kant's, to Zöllner's question.

The printer's ink was barely dry before this optimism was attacked as naïve, and worse, as pernicious and contrary to all social order and well-being; to say nothing of religious faith and the institution of Christendom, both its Catholic and Protestant variant. The Romantic and reactionary Counter-Enlightenment's critique of science, reason, and individualism began soon enough; and accelerated with the French Revolution that occurred five years after the publication of Kant's essay. The essay, with slight editing, follows below.

References

Beck, Lewis W. 1950. Introduction. In *Immanuel Kant: Prolegomena to Any Future Metaphysics*. New York: Liberal Arts Press.

Buchdahl, Gerd. 1970. "Gravity and Intelligibility: Newton to Kant." In *The Methodological Heritage of Newton*, edited by Robert E. Butts and John W. Davis, 74–102. Toronto: University of Toronto Press.

Friedman, Michael. 1990. "Kant and Newton: Why Gravity is Essential to Matter." In *Philosophical Perspectives on Newtonian Science*, edited by Phillip Bricker and R. I. G. Hughes, 185–202. Cambridge, MA: MIT Press.

———. 1992. *Kant and the Exact Sciences*. Cambridge, MA: Harvard University Press.

Hume, David. (1739) 1888. *A Treatise of Human Nature: Being an Attempt to Introduce the Experimental Method of Reasoning into Moral Subjects*. Oxford: Clarendon Press.

Kant, Immanuel. (1783) 1950. *Prolegomena to Any Future Metaphysics*. New York: Liberal Arts Press.

———. (1784) 1996. "An answer to the question: What is Enlightenment?" In *Practical Philosophy*, translated and edited by Mary J. Gregor. Cambridge: Cambridge University Press.

———. (1786) 1985. *Metaphysical Foundations of Natural Science*. In *Philosophy of Material Nature*, translated by James W. Ellington. Indianapolis: Hackett Publishing Company.

Schmidt, James, ed. 1996, *What Is Enlightenment? Eighteenth-Century Answers and Twentieth-Century Questions*. Berkeley: University of California Press.

Watkins, Eric, ed. 2001. *Kant and the Sciences*. Oxford: Oxford University Press.

Metaphysical Foundations of Natural Science (1786)

Preface

If the word "nature" is taken merely in its formal signification (inasmuch as the word "nature" signifies the primal, internal principle of everything that belongs to the existence of a thing), then there can be as many natural sciences as there are specifically different things, and each of these things must contain its specific internal principle of the determinations belonging to its existence. On the other hand, "nature" is also taken in a material signification to be not a quality but the sum total of all things insofar as they can be objects of our senses and hence also objects of experience, under which is therefore to be understood the whole of all appearances, i.e., the sense-world with the exclusion of all objects that are not sensible. Nature taken in this signification of the word has two main parts according to the main distinction of our senses: the one contains the objects of the external senses, the other the object of the internal sense. Therefore, a twofold doctrine of nature is possible: a *doctrine of body* and a *doctrine of soul*. The first considers extended nature, and the second, thinking nature.

Every doctrine, if it is to be a system, i.e., a whole of cognition ordered according to principles, is called science. And since principles can be either of the empirical or of the rational connection of cognitions in a whole, so natural science, be it the doctrine of body or the doctrine of soul, would have to be divided into historical and rational natural science, were it not that the word "nature" (because this word designates the derivation of the manifold belonging to the existence of things from their internal principle) necessitates a rational cognition of the coherence of things, so far as this cognition is to deserve the name of natural science. Therefore, the doctrine of nature might better be divided into the historical doctrine of nature, which contains nothing but the systematically ordered facts regarding natural things (which again would consist of the description of nature as a system of classes of natural things ordered according to similarities, and the history of nature as a systematic presentation of natural things in different times and in different places), and natural science. Now, natural science would in turn be natural science either properly or improperly so called; the first would treat its object wholly according to a priori principles, and the second, according to laws of experience.

Only that whose certainty is apodeictic can be called science proper; cognition that can contain merely empirical certainty is only improperly called science. That whole of cognition which is systematic can therefore be called science, and, when the connection of cognition in this system is a coherence of grounds and consequents, rational science. But when these grounds or principles are ultimately merely empirical, as, for example, in chemistry, and when the laws from which reason explains the given facts are merely laws of experience, then they carry with themselves no consciousness of their necessity (are not apodeictically certain), and thus the whole does not in a strict sense deserve the name of science. Therefore, chemistry should be called systematic art rather than science.

A rational doctrine of nature, then, deserves the name of natural science only when the natural laws that underlie it are cognized a priori and are not mere laws of experience. Natural cognition of the first kind is called pure, but that of the second kind is called applied rational cognition. Since the word "nature" already carries with it the concept of laws and since this concept carries with it the concept of the necessity of all the determinations of a thing which belong to its existence, it is easily seen why natural science must derive the legitimacy of its designation only from a pure part of natural science, namely, from that part which contains the a priori principles of all remaining natural explications, and why natural science is only by virtue of this pure part science proper. And so every doctrine of nature must according to the demands of reason ultimately aim at natural science and terminate in it, inasmuch as the necessity of laws attaches inseparably to the concept of nature and must therefore be thoroughly understood. Hence the most complete explication of certain phenomena by chemical principles always leaves dissatisfaction in its wake, inasmuch as through these contingent laws learned by mere experience no a priori grounds can be adduced.

Thus all natural science proper requires a pure part, upon which the apodeictic certainty sought by reason in such science can be based. And since this pure part is according to its principles completely different by comparison with that part whose principles are only empirical, there is the greatest advantage (indeed according to the nature of the case there is, as regards the method, an indispensable duty) in expounding this pure part separately and entirely unmixed with the empirical part and in expounding this pure part as far as possible in its completeness, in order that one may be able to determine exactly what reason can accomplish of itself and where its capacity begins to require the assistance of principles of experience. Pure rational cognition from mere concepts is called pure philosophy, or metaphysics; on the other hand, that pure rational cognition which is based only upon the construction of concepts by means of the presentation of the object in a priori intuition is called mathematics [*Critique of Pure Reason* B740–755].

Natural science properly so called presupposes metaphysics of nature; for laws, i.e., principles of the necessity of what belongs to the existence of a thing, are occupied with a concept which does not admit of construction, because existence cannot be presented in any a priori intuition. Therefore, natural science proper presupposes metaphysics of nature. Now, the latter must indeed always contain nothing but principles which are not empirical (for that reason it bears the name of a metaphysics). But either it can treat of the laws which make possible the concept of a nature in general even without reference to any determinate object of experience, and therefore undetermined regarding the nature of this or that thing of the sense-world—and in this case it is the transcendental part of the metaphysics of nature—or it occupies itself with the special nature of this or that kind of things, of which an empirical concept is given in such a way that besides what lies in this concept, no other empirical principle is needed for cognizing the things. For example, it lays the empirical concept of a matter or of a thinking being at its foundation and searches the range of cognition of which reason is a priori capable regarding these objects. Such a science must still be called a metaphysics of nature, namely, of corporeal or of thinking nature; however, it is then not a general but a special metaphysical natural science (physics and psychology), in which the aforementioned transcendental principles are applied to the two species of sense-objects.

I maintain, however, that in every special doctrine of nature only so much science proper can be found as there is mathematics in it. For in accordance with the foregoing considerations, science proper, especially science of nature, requires a pure part, which lies at the foundation of the empirical part and is based upon an a priori cognition of natural things.

Now, to cognize anything a priori is to cognize it from its mere possibility. But the possibility of determinate natural things cannot be cognized from their mere concepts; from these concepts the possibility of the thought (that it does not contradict itself) can indeed be cognized, but not the possibility of the object as a natural thing, which can be given (as existing) outside of the thought. Therefore, in order to cognize the possibility of determinate natural things, and hence to cognize them a priori, there is further required that the intuition corresponding to the concept be given a priori, i.e., that the concept be constructed. Now, rational cognition through the construction of concepts is mathematical. A pure philosophy of nature in general, i.e., one that only investigates what constitutes the concept of a nature in general, may indeed be possible without mathematics; but a pure doctrine of nature concerning determinate natural things (doctrine of body and doctrine of soul) is possible only by means of mathematics. And since in every doctrine of nature only so much science proper is to be found as there is a priori cognition in it, a doctrine of nature will contain only so much science proper as there is applied mathematics in it.

So long, then, as there is for the chemical actions of matters on one another no concept which admits of being constructed, i.e., no law of the approach or withdrawal of the parts of matters can be stated according to which (as, say, in proportion to their densities and suchlike) their motions together with the consequences of these can be intuited and presented a priori in space (a demand that will hardly ever be fulfilled), chemistry can become nothing more than a systematic art or experimental doctrine, but never science proper; for the principles of chemistry are merely empirical and admit of no presentation a priori in intuition. Consequently, the principles of chemical phenomena cannot make the possibility of such phenomena in the least conceivable inasmuch as they are incapable of the application of mathematics. But the empirical doctrine of the soul must always remain yet even further removed than chemistry from the rank of what may be called a natural science proper. This is because mathematics is inapplicable to the phenomena of the internal sense and their laws, unless one might want to take into consideration merely the law of continuity in the flow of this sense's internal changes. But the extension of cognition so attained would bear much the same relation to the extension of cognition which mathematics provides for the doctrine of body, as the doctrine of the properties of the straight line bears to the whole of geometry.

The reason for the limitation on this extension of cognition lies in the fact that the pure internal intuition in which the soul's phenomena are to be constructed is time, which has only one dimension. But not even as a systematic art of analysis or as an experimental doctrine can the empirical doctrine of the soul ever approach chemistry, because in it the manifold of internal observation is separated only by mere thought, but cannot be kept separate and be connected again at will; still less does another thinking subject submit to our investigations in such a way as to be conformable to our purposes, and even the observation itself alters and distorts the state of the object observed. It can, therefore, never become anything more than a historical (and as such, as much as possible) systematic natural doctrine of the internal sense, i.e., a natural description of the soul, but not a science of the soul, nor even a psychological experimental doctrine. This is the reason why in the title of this work, which, properly speaking, contains the principles of the doctrine of body, we have employed, in accordance with the usual practice, the general name of natural science; for this designation in the strict sense belongs to the doctrine of the body alone and hence causes no ambiguity.

What Is Enlightenment? (1784)

Enlightenment is the emergence of humankind from its self-imposed dependency [nonage], dependency being the inability of a person to think for himself without someone else's guidance. This dependency is self-imposed since its cause is not any failure of the mind, but the lack of courage and will to think undirected by another. *Sapere aude!* Dare to know! Have the courage to think for yourself. This is the watchword of Enlightenment.

Laziness and cowardice are the reasons why so many people, though long past the age of childhood, still willingly remain in a state of childish dependency. . . . It is so easy to depend on others. I have a book that thinks for me; a pastor who acts as my conscience; a doctor who critiques my diet, . . . so I hardly need to bestir myself at all. There is no need for me to think, so long as I can pay—others will take over that bothersome task for me right away. . . .

So it is difficult for the individual to extract himself from this by now habitual dependency. He has become so fond of it that he is for the moment actually unable to exercise his own mind, since no one ever gave him the chance. Rules and regulations, those mechanisms for the sensible use, or rather misuse, of his natural gifts, are the shackles of his stubborn dependency. . . . Only a few have been able, therefore, by their own mental exertion, to unloose themselves from this dependency and take a bolder road forward.

But that a whole community, the Public, might achieve Enlightenment is highly possible—and indeed almost inevitable, if they are only left in freedom. For there will always be some who think for themselves, . . . who, once they have unburdened themselves from the yoke of dependency, will inspire others to form a rational estimation of their own worth and of each person's calling to think for himself. . . . For nothing but freedom is needed for enlightenment to take hold; and this kind of freedom is really the least fearsome there could be, that is, the freedom to make public use of one's reason in all matters.

But now I hear the cries from all sides: "Don't think," the officer says; "don't think, just march!" The tax-collector: "Don't think, just pay!" The pastor: "Don't think, just believe!" . . . All this amounts to the constriction of freedom. But what kind of limitation of freedom is the foe of enlightenment? And which is not, but rather promotes it?—My answer: the public use of reason must forever be free, and it alone can further the enlightenment of humankind; but its private use may actually be quite narrowly limited without in consequence greatly hindering the progress of enlightenment. By public use, I mean that which anyone might make of his own reason when presenting his thoughts to the whole reading Public. By private use, I mean that which a person might make of his reason in a particular civic post or office with which he has been entrusted. . . . In this case, clearly, he is not allowed to think; he must obey. . . .

It would be highly improper, accordingly, if an officer commanded to do something by his superior argued aloud, while on duty, about the appropriateness or usefulness of the order—he must only obey. But in fairness he cannot be forbidden, as a competent spokesperson, to present for the consideration of the Public observations about problems in military management. The citizen cannot refuse to pay the taxes demanded of him. . . . Yet the same citizen does not violate his civic duty if, as a competent speaker, he openly communicates his views on the inappropriateness or even the injustice of such exactions. In the same way, a pastor is bound, in teaching his catechism class and his congregation, to conform to the doctrines of the church he serves, since it was for that purpose that he was employed. But as a scholar he has complete freedom, and is even obliged, to inform the Public of all his carefully considered and well-meant thoughts on any deficiencies in those doctrines, and suggest possible improvements of religious and church management. . . .

If then it is asked: do we now live in an enlightened age? The answer is: "*No*, but we do live in an age of *Enlightenment*"—that is to say, one that is becoming enlightened. As things now stand, we fall far short of the time when people in general are ready, or will soon be ready . . . to use their own minds assuredly and well, without the guidance of others. But there are already clear signs that the possibility will soon be open to them for their free exploration, and that the obstacles to universal enlightenment, and the emergence of humankind from its self-imposed dependency, become gradually fewer. In this sense, this age is an age of Enlightenment or the century of Fredrick the Great. . . .

LINNAEUS

The System of Nature, or the Three Kingdoms of Nature, Systematically Proposed in Classes, Orders, Genera, and Species (1735)

Introduction to First Edition (Design Argument; fixity of species; primacy of *Homo sapiens*)

CARL LINNAEUS (1707–1778), a Swedish botanist, zoologist, naturalist, collector, and physician, created in the mid-eighteenth century a system for identifying and naming all species of animals and plants (Larson 1971). His system has remained, for almost three centuries, the international norm for the disciplines of botany and zoology; it is universally used by naturalists. Linnaeus identified three kingdoms of nature, each organized hierarchically: animal, vegetable, and mineral. He wrote:

> For the purpose of naming the things of Nature, this SYSTEM utilizes five divisions of natural things: they are Class, Order, Genus, Species, Variety. . . . The first action to be taken by anyone seeking to gain knowledge of Nature is to inspect the object to be known, and according to its Genus, assign the name of its Species. The SCIENCE of Nature requires an exact knowledge of natural things and a corresponding systematic Nomenclature. (King 2019, 79)

Before Linnaeus, Aristotle was a great naturalist who had identified about five hundred animals and plants. In the ancient world, Pliny's (23–79 CE) monumental ten volumes of *Natural History* considerably expanded this number (Healy 2004).[1] Pliny

---

1. The current estimate is about nine million animal species spread across land and water and about four hundred thousand plant species.

was well aware of the naming problem and consequent limitation on the growth of botanical and zoological knowledge, writing:

> Some Greek writers . . . adopted a very attractive method of description. . . . It was their plan to delineate the various plants in colours, and then to add in writing a description of the properties which they possessed. . . . Others have contented themselves for the most part with a bare recital of their names, considering it sufficient if they pointed out their virtues and properties to such as might feel inclined to make further inquiries into the subject. (Boorstin 1983, 424)

The chaotic local naming practices remained in place for the following seventeen hundred years. Linnaeus revolutionized the system by adopting the seemingly simple system of Latinized binominal names, or nomenclature, now familiar to all: first the genus (from Latin *genus*, for "kind"), then the species or adjectival name (from Latin *specere*, for "look at" or "appearance"). So, *Homo sapiens* means, "man capable of knowledge." He controversially placed *Homo* in the class of mammals, within the order of primates along with gorilla and chimpanzees. This system brought order to confusion and facilitated international communication among naturalists. Jean-Jacques Rousseau said that Linnaeus's new language did for botanists what algebra did for mathematicians.

Linnaeus himself classified and named 8,000 species of plants and 4,500 species of animals, many collected after long treks through Lapland and the northern wilderness regions. In what was an "Age of Discovery," he arranged for each of his students to travel, literally, to the four corners of the globe finding, identifying, classifying, and naming multiple thousands more species. Pehr Kalm traveled to Russia in the 1740s, Pehr Löfling to South America in the 1750s, Daniel Solander sailed with James Cook's first Pacific voyage (1768–1771), Anders Sparrman with Cook's second voyage (1772–1775); and other students and colleagues trekked and voyaged to countless other places. They in turn trained local naturalists in the Linnaean system. Joseph Banks (1743–1820), the preeminent English naturalist and longtime president of the Royal Society, promoted the Linnaean system throughout the British Empire, overseeing the employment of Linnaeans on scientific voyages.

A significant epistemological obstacle to a well-grounded, universal classification of species was the common notion of spontaneous generation of species, or animal and insect types. Aristotle believed in such spontaneous generation of small creatures: tadpoles, frogs, tiny fish appearing in water, and so on. This was accepted for two thousand years. Jan Baptist van Helmont (1580–1644), a Flemish physician, wrote of mice "emerging" out of waste food and rags twenty-one days after both were parceled together. If spontaneous generation occurred, then the basic idea of intrinsic natural order was thwarted. Closer observations and controlled experiments by Italian physician Francesco Redi (1626–1697) dispelled the idea of spontaneous generation.

John Ray (1627–1705), the English cleric, naturalist, and author of *The Wisdom of God Manifested in the Works of the Creation* (1691), thought that the fixity of species was a part of an intrinsic natural order. If cats could transmute into dogs, or even lions into leopards, then the labels he was applying to countless species were applied to a shifting substrate. The mark of a species is that it reproduced its kind; if an individual belonged to the lion species, it gave birth to lions, not dogs or even tigers.[2] He believed in fixity but did, of course, recognize crossovers or intermediate types. Dog and cattle breeders and horticulturalists were doing this all the time. Linnaeus began with the same firm convictions about the fixity of species, but his belief was not fixed—with each new edition of his *System of Nature* (first edition 1735), the belief waned. At one point he mused:

> . . . whether all these species are the children of time, or whether the Creator from the very beginning of the world had restricted this course of development to a definite number of species.

Linnaeus was not a humble man: his own motto was *Deus creavit, Linnaeu disposuit* (God created, Linnaeus organized). The selection below is from the meager seven-page first edition of his *System*, where, at the end, he promises more to the reader. On this, he delivered. By the thirteenth and final edition (1774), the *System* had grown to multiple volumes and hundreds of pages. His classificatory system assumed and bespoke a certain order in the world, and further, an unchanging, stable order that reflected the intelligence and designs of the creator. Joseph Banks's artist and illustrator, Sydney Parkinson, in 1769 captured the zeitgeist of the era:

> The more we investigate, the more we ought to admire the power, wisdom, and goodness, the Great Superintendent of the universe; whose attributes are amply displayed throughout all his works. (Kieza 2020, frontispiece)

A century later, Darwin's *Origin of Species* (1859) would dramatically challenge this deeply entrenched, cross-cultural, deist-theist worldview. This challenge came a century after Linnaeus's central work, a selection from which follows below.

References

Boorstin, Daniel J. 1983. *The Discoverers*. New York: Random House.

Healy, John F. 2004. *Pliny the Elder: Natural History: A Selection*. Harmondsworth: Penguin.

---

2. There is substantial biological and philosophical literature on the definition of species, with much of it revolving around the longtime Aristotelian idea of essentialism: Is there anything essential about a species? If so, what is it? See contributions to Sober (1984, Part VII) and Wilson (1999).

Kieza, Grantlee. 2020. *Banks*. Sydney: HarperCollins.

King, Margaret L, trans. and ed. 2019. *Enlightenment Thought: An Anthology of Sources*. Indianapolis: Hackett Publishing Company.

Larson, James L. 1971. *Reason and Experience: The Representation of Natural Order in the Work of Carl von Linné*. Berkeley: University of California Press.

Sober, Elliot, ed. 1984. *Conceptual Issues in Evolutionary Biology: An Anthology*. Cambridge, MA: MIT Press.

Wilson, Robert A., ed. 1999. *Species: New Interdisciplinary Essays*. Cambridge, MA: MIT Press.

The System of Nature, or the Three Kingdoms of Nature, Systematically Proposed in Classes, Orders, Genera, and Species (1735)

Introduction to System of Nature

God everlasting, immense, omniscient, omnipotent—I awake, I see your presence and am astounded! I have seen your handiwork in all created things. . . . What wisdom! What imperishable perfection! I have seen the layering of Animals on Vegetables, and Vegetables on Minerals, and Minerals on the crust of the Earth . . . while Earth circles ceaselessly around the Sun, from which it takes its life; and the Sun spinning on its axis . . . , and the system of the Stars, indefinable in extent and number, held in motion and suspended in nothingness by an incomprehensible First Mover, the Being of all Beings, the Cause of all Causes, the keeper and guardian of the universe, the architect and master of the miracle of this world . . .[3]

Observations on the Three Kingdoms of Nature

1. If we observe God's works, it becomes more than sufficiently evident to everybody, that each living being is propagated from an egg and that every egg produces an offspring closely resembling the parent. Hence no new species are produced nowadays.

---

3. This hymn to God's design of nature was not included in the first 1802 English translation of *System*. Text from Margaret King (2019, 76).

2. Individuals multiply by generation. Hence at present the number of individuals in each species is greater than it was at first.

3. If we count backward this multiplication of individuals in each species, in the same way as we have multiplied forward, the series ends up in one single parent, whether that parent consists of *one single* hermaphrodite (as commonly in plants) or of a double, viz. a male and a female (as in most animals).

4. As there are no new species; as like always gives birth to like; as one in each species was at the beginning of the progeny, it is necessary to attribute this progenitorial unity to some Omnipotent and Omniscient Being, namely *God*, whose work is called *Creation*. This is confirmed by the mechanism, the laws, principles, constitutions and sensations in every living individual.

5. Individuals thus procreated, lack in their prime and tender age absolutely all knowledge, and are forced to learn everything by means of their external senses. By *touch* they first of all learn the consistency of objects; by *taste* the fluid particles; by *smell* the volatile ones; by *hearing* the vibration of remote bodies; and finally by *sight* the shape of visible bodies, which last sense, more than any of the others, gives the animals greatest delight.

6. If we observe the universe, three objects are conspicuous: viz. (*a*) the very remote *celestial* bodies; (b) the *elements* to be met anywhere; (c) the solid *natural* bodies.

7. On our earth, only two of the three mentioned above are obvious; i.e. the *elements* constituting it; and the *natural* bodies constructed out of the elements, though in a way inexplicable except by creation and by the laws of procreation.

8. Natural objects belong more to the field of the senses than all the others and are obvious to our senses anywhere. Thus I wonder why the Creator put man, who is thus provided with senses and intellect, on the earth globe, where nothing met his senses but natural objects, constructed by means of such an admirable and amazing mechanism.

Surely for no other reason than that the observer of the wonderful work might admire and praise its Maker.

9. All that is useful to man originates from these natural objects; hence the industry of mining or metallurgy; plant-industry or agriculture and horticulture; animal husbandry, hunting and fishing.

In one word, it is the foundation of every industry of building, commerce, food supply, medicine etc. By them people are kept in a healthy state, protected against illness and recover from disease, so that their selection is highly necessary. Hence the necessity of natural science is self-evident.

10. The first step in wisdom is to know the things themselves; this notion consists in having a true idea of the objects; objects are distinguished and known by classifying them methodically and giving them appropriate names. Therefore, classification and name-giving will be the foundation of our science.

11. Those of our scientists, who cannot class the variations in the right species, the species in the natural genera, the genera in families, and yet constitute themselves doctors of this science, deceive others and themselves. For all those who really laid the foundation to natural science, have had to keep this in mind.

12. He may call himself a naturalist (a natural historian), who well distinguishes the parts of natural bodies by sight and describes and names all these rightly in agreement with the threefold division. Such a man *is* a lithologist, a phytologist or a zoologist.

13. Natural science is that classification and that name-giving of the natural bodies judiciously instituted by such a naturalist.

14. Natural bodies are divided into *three kingdoms* of nature: viz. the mineral, vegetable and animal kingdoms.

15. *Minerals* grow; *Plants* grow and live; *Animals* grow, live, and have feeling. Thus the limits between these kingdoms are constituted.

16. In this science of describing and picturing many have laboured for a whole life-time; how much, however, has already been observed and how much there remains to be done, the curious on-looker will easily find out for himself.

17. I have shown here a general survey of the system of natural bodies so that the curious reader with the help of this as it were geographical table knows where to direct his journey in these vast kingdoms, for to add more descriptions, space, time and opportunity lacked.

18. A new method mainly based on my own authentic observations has been used in every single part, for I have well learnt that very few people are lightly to be trusted, as far as observations go.

19. If the Interested Reader should draw any profit from this, he should acknowledge that very famous Dutch Botanist Doctor *Job. Fred. Gronovius*, as well as Mr. *Isaac Lawson*, the very learned Scotchman; as they were the ones who caused me to communicate these very brief tables and observations to the learned world.

20. If I find this proves to be welcome to the illustrious and interested Reader, he may expect more, more special, and more detailed (publications) from me soon, above all in botany.

XV

PALEY

***Natural Theology* (1802)**   Chapters 1, 2, 3 (Design Argument; watch and watch-maker analogy; eye and telescope comparison)

WILLIAM PALEY (1743–1805) was an Anglican priest, philosopher, and biblical scholar (Clarke 1974). He is now best known for his lucid, tightly argued, and beautifully written final book, *Natural Theology*, published in 1802 (Paley [1802] 2006). The book was the foremost contributor to the Anglo-American tradition of the Design Argument in natural theology (Eddy 2013). For many it has retained this status to the present day (Manson 2003). Paley also wrote *Principles of Moral and Political Philosophy* (Paley [1785] 2002), a statement of Utilitarian philosophy, which had great influence and was one of the principal works of the English late Enlightenment and for decades was an examination text at Cambridge University. His third principal work was *A View of the Evidence of Christianity* (Paley [1794] 2009), which became a standard text in Christian apologetics throughout the British Empire, selling thousands of copies.

Paley's *Natural Theology* had near-universal use in Christian evangelism, and his Design arguments, which suggested the existence of an omniscient, benevolent, omnipotent, and monotheistic creator, established a common ground among many faiths. Paley provided scores of examples of anatomical structures whose functions and purposes so clearly bespoke an artificer. The eye, as for so many other proponents of the Design Argument, was a favorite:

> In order to exclude excess of light, when it is excessive, and to render objects visible under obscurer degrees of it, when no more can be had, the hole or aperture in the eye, through which the light enters, is so formed, as to contract

or dilate itself for the purpose of admitting a greater or less number of rays at the same time. (Paley [1802] 2006, 18)

As did all Cambridge students through to the twentieth century, Charles Darwin studied Paley. In Darwin's *Autobiography* (edited and published posthumously by his son Francis), he, as did so many others of the period, described Cambridge education as "a waste of his time" except for his final year when, in order to pass the BA exam, he had to "get up Paley's *Evidence of Christianity* and his *Moral Philosophy*." He says that these two books, along with Paley's *Natural Theology*, were the only things in the Cambridge syllabus that "were of the least [any] use in the education of my mind" (Darwin [1892] 1958, 19).

Paley's "long line of argumentation" that so charmed and convinced Darwin was a restatement of the Design Argument for God's existence (Sober 2019). A century before, it had been articulated by John Ray in *The Wisdom of God Manifested in the Works of the Creation* (1691). Thirty years before that, Robert Hooke in his *Micrographia* (Hooke [1665] 2021) wrote how the exquisite structures of fleas, gnats, flies, and other denizens of the microworld, which were so exquisitely etched in his book, demonstrated the intelligence and attention of the creator who crafted the tiniest limbs and organs to fulfill their functions and so achieve the animal's purpose.

At the same time as Hooke, Robert Boyle, a champion of the new mechanical worldview, wrote an essay against ancient atomists (such as Democritus and Epicurus) and contemporary ones, as well as mechanists such as Descartes, who implied that a mechanical world did not require final causes, teleology, or, ultimately, divine intervention (Boyle [1663] 1979). Boyle thought design and teleology could be embraced together with mechanism and the mechanical worldview (Lennox 1983; McGuire 1972). This was also Newton's conviction. They both saw God revealed in two books: the book of his Word (scripture) and the book of his Works (nature). Others, especially David Hume, were not so sure about either, especially the second (Hurlbutt 1965).

Natural theology more generally might suffice for deism, or simply for belief in God, but it did not provide a rational and convincing argument for the personal, intervening, Trinitarian, Christ-centric, redemptive God of Christianity (Manning, Brooke, and Watts 2013). For Christians, natural theology had to be followed by a theology of revelation. Paley's *Evidence* did duty here. The book argued that, given textural and historical evidence, it was more reasonable to believe in Christian revelation than other purported revelations.

Paley's work was in the tradition of John Locke, who had, a century earlier in his *Essay Concerning Human Understanding* (1690), maintained:

> *Reason* is natural *revelation*, whereby the eternal Father of light, and Fountain of all knowledge, communicates to mankind that portion of truth which he

has laid within the reach of their natural faculties. *Revelation* is natural reason enlarged by a new set of discoveries communicated by God immediately, which reason vouches the truth of, by the testimony and proofs it gives that they come from God. So that he that takes away reason to make way for revelation, puts out the light of both . . . it is no wonder that some have been very apt to pretend to revelation, and to persuade themselves that they are under the peculiar guidance of heaven in their actions and opinions, especially in those of them which they cannot account for by the ordinary methods of knowledge and principles of reason. (Locke [1690] 1924, 360)

Twenty years before Paley's influential work, the Design Argument had come under searching criticism by David Hume, in part v of his posthumously published *Dialogues Concerning Natural Religion* (Hume [1779] 1963).

Eighty years later, Darwin read this critique and other works of Hume while making his many observations, collecting his countless specimens, and theorizing about the natural world, all of which culminated in his theory of evolution by natural selection. Darwin can be understood as picking up Hume's argument and advancing Natural Selection as the immanent principle of order that governs evolution in nature. Darwin, in his posthumously published *Autobiography*, writes:

The old argument of design in nature, as given by Paley, which formerly seemed to me so conclusive, fails, now that the law of natural selection had been discovered. We can no longer argue that, for instance, the beautiful hinge of a bivalve shell must have been made by an intelligent being, like the hinge of a door by man. There seems to be no more design in the variability of organic beings and in the action of natural selection, than in the course which the wind blows. Everything in nature is the result of fixed laws. (Darwin [1892] 1958, 63)

Darwin had moved on from, but had not forgotten Paley, a selection from whose *Natural Theology* follows below.

REFERENCES

Boyle, Robert. (1663) 1979. "A Requisite Digression, Concerning Those that would Exclude the Deity from Intermeddling with Matter." In *Selected Philosophical Papers of Robert Boyle*, edited by M. A. Stewart, 155–175. Manchester: Manchester University Press.

Clarke, M. L. 1974. *Paley: Evidences for the Man*. Toronto: University of Toronto Press.

Darwin, Francis. (1892) 1958. *The Autobiography of Charles Darwin and Selected Letters*. New York: Dover Publications.

Eddy, Mathew D. 2013. "Nineteenth Century Natural Theology." In *Oxford Handbook of Natural Theology*, edited by Russell R. Manning, John H. Brooke, and Fraser Watts. Oxford: Oxford University Press.

Hooke, Robert. (1665) 2021. *Micrographia: Or, Some Physiological Descriptions of Minute Bodies Made by Magnifying Glasses*. Aberdeen: Ockham Publishing.

Hume, David. (1779) 1963. *Dialogues Concerning Natural Religion*. In *Hume on Religion*, edited by Richard Wollheim, 99–204. London: Collins.

Hurlbutt, Robert H. 1965. *Hume, Newton and the Design Argument*. Lincoln, NE: University of Nebraska Press.

Lennox, James G. 1983. "Robert Boyle's Defense of Teleological Inference in Science." *Isis* 74: 38–52.

Locke, John. (1690) 1924. *An Essay Concerning Human Understanding*. Abridged and edited by A. S. Pringle-Pattison. Oxford: Clarendon Press.

Manning, Russell R., John H. Brooke, and Fraser Watts, eds. 2013. *Oxford Handbook of Natural Theology*. Oxford: Oxford University Press.

Manson, Neil, ed. 2003. *God and Design: The Teleological Argument and Modern Science*. New York: Routledge.

McGuire, James E. 1972. "Boyle's Conception of Nature." *Journal of the History of Ideas* 33: 523–542.

Paley, William. (1785) 2002. *Principles of Moral and Political Philosophy*. Indianapolis: Liberty Fund.

———. (1794) 2009. *A View of the Evidences of Christianity*. 2 vols. Cambridge: Cambridge University Press.

———. (1802) 2006. *Natural Theology; or Evidence for the Existence and Attributes of the Deity Collected from the Appearances of Nature*. Edited by Mathew D. Eddy and David Knight. Oxford: Oxford University Press.

Sober, Elliot. 2019. *The Design Argument. Elements in the Philosophy of Religion*. Cambridge: Cambridge University Press.

Natural Theology (1802)
Chapter One: State of the Argument

In crossing a heath, suppose I pitched my foot against a *stone* and were asked how the stone came to be there, I might possibly answer that for anything I knew to the contrary it had lain there forever; nor would it, perhaps, be very easy to show the absurdity of this answer. But suppose I had found a *watch* upon the ground, and it should be inquired how the watch happened to be in that place, I should hardly think of the answer which I had before given, that for anything I knew the watch might have always been there. Yet why should not this answer serve for the watch as well as for the stone; why is it not as admissible in the second case as in the first? For this reason, and for no other, namely, that when we come to inspect the watch, we perceive—what we could not discover in the stone—that its several parts are framed and put together for a purpose, e.g., that they are so formed and adjusted as to produce motion, and that motion so regulated as to point out the hour of the day; that if the different parts had been differently shaped from what they are, or placed after any other manner or in any other order than that in which they are placed, either no motion at all would have been carried on in the machine, or none which would have answered the use that is now served by it.

To reckon up a few of the plainest of these parts and of their offices, all tending to one result: we see a cylindrical box containing a coiled elastic spring, which, by its endeavor to relax itself, turns round the box. We next observe a flexible chain—artificially wrought for the sake of flexure—communicating the action of the spring from the box to the fusee. We then find a series of wheels, the teeth of which catch in and apply to each other, conducting the motion from the fusee to the balance and from the balance to the pointer, and at the same time, by the size and shape of those wheels, so regulating that motion as to terminate in causing an index, by an equable and measured progression, to pass over a given space in a given time. We take notice that the wheels are made of brass, in order to keep them from rust; the springs of steel, no other metal being so elastic; that over the face of the watch there is placed a glass, a material employed in no other part of the work, but in the room of which, if there had been any other than a transparent substance, the hour could not be seen without opening the case.

This mechanism being observed—it requires indeed an examination of the instrument, and perhaps some previous knowledge of the subject, to perceive and understand it; but being once, as we have said, observed and understood—the inference we think is inevitable, that the watch must have had a maker—that there must have existed, at some time and at some place or other, an artificer or artificers who formed it for the purpose which we find it actually to answer, who completely comprehended its construction and designed its use.

I. Nor would it, I apprehend, weaken the conclusion, that we had never seen a watch made—that we had never known an artist capable of making one—that we were altogether incapable of executing such a piece of workmanship ourselves, or of understanding in what manner it was performed; all this being no more than what is true of some exquisite remains of ancient art, of some lost arts, and, to the generality of mankind, of the more curious productions of modern manufacture. Does one man in a million know how oval frames are turned? Ignorance of this kind exalts our opinion of the unseen and unknown artist's skill, if he be unseen and unknown, but raises no doubt in our minds of the existence and agency of such an artist, at some former time and in some place or other. Nor can I perceive that it varies at all the inference, whether the question arise concerning a human agent or concerning an agent of a different species, or an agent possessing in some respects a different nature.

II. Neither, secondly, would it invalidate our conclusion, that the watch sometimes went wrong or that it seldom went exactly right. The purpose of the machinery, the design, and the designer might be evident, and in the case supposed, would be evident, in whatever way we accounted for the irregularity of the movement, or whether we could account for it or not. It is not necessary that a machine be perfect in order to show with what design it was made: still less necessary, where the only question is whether it were made with any design at all.

III. Nor, thirdly, would it bring any uncertainty into the argument, if there were a few parts of the watch, concerning which we could not discover or had not yet discovered in what manner they conduced to the general effect; or even some parts, concerning which we could not ascertain whether they conduced to that effect in any manner whatever. For, as to the first branch of the case, if by the loss, or disorder, or decay of the parts in question, the movement of the watch were found in fact to be stopped, or disturbed, or retarded, no doubt would remain in our minds as to the utility or intention of these parts, although we should be unable to investigate the manner according to which, or the connection by which, the ultimate effect depended upon their action or assistance; and the more complex the machine, the more likely is this obscurity to arise. Then, as to the second thing supposed, namely, that there were parts which might be spared without prejudice to the movement of the watch, and that we had proved this by experiment, these superfluous parts, even if we were completely assured that they were such, would not vacate the reasoning which we had instituted concerning other parts. The indication of contrivance remained, with respect to them, nearly as it was before.

IV. Nor, fourthly, would any man in his senses think the existence of the watch with its various machinery accounted for, by being told that it was one out of possible combinations of material forms; that whatever he had found in the place where he found the watch, must have contained some internal configuration or other; and that this configuration might be the structure now exhibited, namely, of the works of a watch, as well as a different structure.

V. Nor, fifthly, would it yield his inquiry more satisfaction, to be answered that there existed in things a principle of order, which had disposed the parts of the watch into their present form and situation. He never knew a watch made by the principle of order; nor can he even form to himself an idea of what is meant by a principle of order distinct from the intelligence of the watchmaker.

VI. Sixthly, he would be surprised to hear that the mechanism of the watch was no proof of contrivance, only a motive to induce the mind to think so:

VII. And not less surprised to be informed that the watch in his hand was nothing more than the result of the laws of *metallic* nature. It is a perversion of language to assign any law as the efficient, operative cause of anything. A law presupposes an agent, for it is only the mode according to which an agent proceeds: it implies a power, for it is the order according to which that power acts. Without this agent, without this power, which are both distinct from itself, the *law* does nothing, is nothing. The expression, "the law of metallic nature, " may sound strange and harsh to a philosophic ear; but it seems quite as justifiable as some others which are more familiar to him, such as "the law of vegetable nature," "the law of animal nature," or, indeed, as "the law of nature" in general, when assigned as the cause of phenomena, in exclusion of agency and power, or when it is substituted into the place of these.

VIII. Neither, lastly, would our observer be driven out of his conclusion or from his confidence in its truth by being told that he knew nothing at all about the matter. He knows enough for his argument; he knows the utility of the end; he knows the subserviency and adaptation of the means to the end. These points being known, his ignorance of other points, his doubts concerning other points affect not the certainty of his reasoning. The consciousness of knowing little need not beget a distrust of that which he does know.

Chapter Two: State of the Argument Continued

Suppose, in the next place, that the person who found the watch should after some time discover that, in addition to all the properties which he had hitherto observed in it, it possessed the unexpected property of producing in the course of its movement another watch like itself—the thing is conceivable; that it contained within it a mechanism, a system of parts—a mold, for instance, or a complex adjustment of lathes, files, and other tools—evidently and separately calculated for this purpose; let us inquire what effect ought such a discovery to have upon his former conclusion.

I. The first effect would be to increase his admiration of the contrivance, and his conviction of the consummate skill of the contriver. Whether he regarded the object of the contrivance, the distinct apparatus, the intricate, yet in many parts intelligible mechanism by which it was carried on, he would perceive in this new observation nothing but an additional reason for doing what he had already done—for referring the construction of the watch to design and to supreme art. If that construction *without* this property, or, which is the same thing, before this property had been noticed, proved intention and art to have been employed about it, still more strong would the proof appear when he came to the knowledge of this further property, the crown and perfection of all the rest.

. . .

IV. Nor is anything gained by running the difficulty farther back, that is, by supposing the watch before us to have been produced from another watch, that from a former, and so on indefinitely. Our going back ever so far brings us no nearer to the least degree of satisfaction upon the subject. Contrivance is still unaccounted for. We still want a contriver. A designing mind is neither supplied by this supposition nor dispensed with. If the difficulty were diminished the farther we went back, by going back indefinitely we might exhaust it. And this is the only case to which this sort of reasoning applies.

Where there is a tendency, or, as we increase the number of terms, a continual approach toward a limit, *there*, by supposing the number of terms to be what is called infinite, we may conceive the limit to be attained; but where there is no such tendency or approach, nothing is effected by lengthening the series. There is no difference as to the point in question, whatever there may be as to many points, between one series and another—between a series which is finite and a series which is infinite.

A chain composed of an infinite number of links can no more support itself than a chain composed of a finite number of links. And of this we are assured, though we never *can* have tried the experiment; because, by increasing the number of links, from ten, for instance, to a hundred, from a hundred to a thousand, etc., we make not the smallest approach, we observe not the smallest tendency toward self-support. There is no difference in this respect—yet there may be a great difference in several respects—between a chain of a greater or less length, between one chain and another, between one that is finite and one that is infinite. . . .

The question is not simply, how came the first watch into existence? Such question, it may be pretended, is done away by supposing the series of watches thus produced from one another to have been infinite, and consequently to have had no such *first* for which it was necessary to provide a cause. This, perhaps, would have been nearly the state of the question, if nothing had been before us but an unorganized, unmechanized substance, without mark or indication of contrivance. It might be difficult to show that such substance could not have existed from eternity, either in succession—if it were possible, which I think it is not, for unorganized bodies to spring from one another— or by individual perpetuity. But that is not the question now. To suppose it to be so is to suppose that it made no difference whether he had found a watch or a stone.

As it is, the metaphysics of that question have no place; for, in the watch which we are examining are seen contrivance, design, an end, a purpose, means for the end, adaptation to the purpose. And the question which irresistibly presses upon our thoughts is, whence this contrivance and design? The thing required is the intending mind, the adapted hand, the intelligence by which that hand was directed. This question, this demand is not shaken off by increasing a number or succession of substances destitute of these properties; nor the more, by increasing that number to infinity. If it be said that, upon the supposition of one watch being produced from another in the course of that other's movements and by means of the mechanism within it, we have a cause for the watch in my hand, namely, the watch from which it proceeded; I deny that for the design, the contrivance, the suitableness of means to an end, the adaptation of instruments to a use, all of which we discover in the watch, we have any cause whatever. It is in vain, therefore, to assign a series of such causes or to allege that a series may be carried back to infinity; for I do not admit that we have yet any cause at all for the phenomena, still less any series of causes either finite or infinite. Here is contrivance but no contriver; proofs of design, but no designer.

V. Our observer would further also reflect that the maker of the watch before him was in truth and reality the maker of every watch produced from it: there being no difference, except that the latter manifests a more exquisite skill, between the making of another watch with his own hands, by the mediation of files, lathes, chisels, etc., and the disposing, fixing, and inserting of these instruments, or of others equivalent to them, in the body of the watch already made, in such a manner as to form a new watch in the course of the movements which he had given to the old one. It is only working by one set of tools instead of another.

The conclusion which the *first* examination of the watch, of its works, construction, and movement, suggested, was that it must have had, for cause and author of that construction, an artificer who understood its mechanism and designed its use. This conclusion is invincible. A *second* examination presents us with a new discovery. The watch is found, in the course of its movement, to produce another watch similar to itself; and not only so, but we perceive in it a system or organization separately calculated for that purpose. What effect would this discovery have or ought it to have upon our former inference? What, as has already been said, but to increase beyond measure our admiration of the skill which had been employed in the formation of such a machine? Or shall it, instead of this, all at once turn us round to an opposite conclusion, namely, that no art or skill whatever has been concerned in the business, although all other evidences of art and skill remain as they were, and this last and supreme piece of art be now added to the rest? Can this be maintained without absurdity? Yet this is atheism.

Chapter Three: Application of the Argument

This is atheism: for every indication of contrivance, every manifestation of design, which existed in the watch, exists in the works of nature; with the difference, on the side of nature, of being greater and more, and that in a degree which exceeds all computation. I mean that the contrivances of nature surpass the contrivances of art, in the complexity, subtilty, and curiosity of the mechanism; and still more, if possible, do they go beyond them in number and variety; yet, in a multitude of cases, are not less evidently mechanical, not less evidently contrivances, not less evidently accommodated to their end, or suited to their office, than are the most perfect productions of human ingenuity.

I know no better method of introducing so large a subject, than that of comparing a single thing with a single thing: an eye, for example, with a telescope. As far as the examination of the instrument goes, there is precisely the same proof that the eye was made for vision, as there is that the telescope was made for assisting it. They are made upon the same principles; both being adjusted to the laws by which the transmission and refraction of rays of light are regulated. I speak not of the origin of the laws themselves; but such laws being fixed, the construction in both cases is adapted to them. For instance, these laws require, in order to produce the same effect, that the rays of light, in passing from water into the eye, should be refracted by a more convex surface than when it passes out of air into the eye. Accordingly, we find that the eye of a fish, in that part of it called the crystalline lens, is much rounder than the eye of terrestrial animals. What plainer manifestation of design can there be than this difference? What could a mathematical instrument maker have done more to show his knowledge of his principle, his application of that knowledge, his suiting of his means to his end; I will not say to display the compass or excellence of his skill and art, for in these all comparison is indecorous, but to testify counsel, choice, consideration, purpose?

XVI

DARWIN

The Origin of Species **(1859)**	Introduction and Conclusion (*Beagle* observations; no difference between species and variants; slow modification of variants; psychology on a new foundation)
The Descent of Man **(1874)**	Introduction and Chapter 5 (evolution established; natural selection follows from struggle for existence; development of intellectual and moral faculties; modification of selection in civilized societies)

CHARLES ROBERT DARWIN (1809–1882) is one of just three individuals whose names have commonly and deservedly been given to Scientific Revolutions: the others being Galileo and Einstein.[1] There were others, of course, who prepared philosophical, conceptual, technological, and social grounds for the revolutions, contributed experimentally and theoretically to them, and consolidated and spread the gains. Most notably, Archimedes (whose name Galileo says, "should never be mentioned except in awe") and Newton for the first, and Mach and Planck for the last. No less did others prepare the intellectual ground for Darwin's nineteenth-century evolutionary theory (Lyell) and consolidate its gains (Mendel).

Darwin's grandfather was the formidable Erasmus Darwin (1731–1802), a physician and proto-evolutionary naturalist who, in 1794, published *Zoonomia; or, the Laws of Organic Life* (Darwin [1794–96] 2009). This book emphasized the common features of life-forms, their probable relatedness, and the lawful underlay of the biological realm. Charles Darwin was sent by his father to Edinburgh to graduate as a doctor, but after two years, it was clear that his interests were elsewhere. Christ

---

1. On Darwin's life, see his engaging *Autobiography*, which is included in a collection edited by his son Francis (Darwin [1892] 1958). See also Bowlby (1990) and Desmond and Moore (1992).

College Cambridge followed, with Darwin having some thought of becoming an Anglican minister. This did not eventuate, but he did become close to John Stevens Henslow, the professor of botany, and he closely read, as did all students, the works of William Paley.

From the outset, Darwin was engaged by philosophy and philosophers. Beyond Paley, he read and absorbed the philosopher John Herschel's book *Preliminary Discourse on the Study of Natural Philosophy* (Herschel [1830] 2009), which, he says, "stirred up in me a yearning zeal to add even the most humble contribution to the noble structure of Natural Science" (Darwin [1892] 1958, 24). At this early stage, he also regularly met the philosopher William Whewell and attended to his works (Whewell 1989), something he would continue doing for decades.

Close reading of England's two leading philosophers of science guided Darwin in the almost thirty years of biological observing and theorizing that lead up to his 1859 *Origin of Species*. The philosophers gave an account of what a competent biological theory should be.[2] As both Herschel and Whewell—and nearly everyone else, certainly in England—took Newton and Newtonianism as the very model of science then, naturally, Darwin also sought to craft his biological theorizing with a Newtonian template (Jacob 2000). In particular, he was conscious of finding universal, lawlike relations and mechanisms operative in the natural world.

The most significant event of Darwin's early life was Henslow arranging for him, at age twenty-two, to join the Royal Society's *Beagle* voyage, one of the many national voyages of discovery of the period (Darwin [1839] 1958). In his *Autobiography*, he relates:

> The voyage of the *Beagle* has been by far the most important event in my life and has determined my whole career; . . . I have always felt that I owe to the voyage the first real training or education of my mind; I was led to attend closely to several branches of natural history, and thus my powers of observation were improved, though they were always fairly developed. (Darwin [1892] 1958, 28)

Part of the "circumstance" provided by the voyage was the time to read all of his friend Charles Lyell's just-published *Principles of Geology* (1831–1833), the first volume of which was given to him prior to boarding, and the subsequent two volumes while on the voyage (Sulloway 1985). Lyell established that the earth was several hundred million years old and further, that the processes we currently observe have been occurring since the beginning of time; natural processes have been, forever, uniform. Lyell's uniformitarianism was in Darwin's mind as he collected materials and theorized about them. Lyell's picture of the earth literally gave the time necessary for

---

2. For the impact of philosophy on Darwin's theorizing, see Hull (1973), Ospovat (1981), and Ruse (1975).

the mutability and transformation of varieties and species that Darwin would come to assert.

Ideas of common descent and mutability of species had, to varying degrees of sophistication, been put forward before Darwin did so in 1859; but these accounts did not provide a convincing mechanism for their evolutionary pictures.[3] Darwin's mechanism of natural selection provided the universal, steady, lawlike natural mechanism that Herschel and Whewell's Newtonian exemplar of scientific theory demanded.

When the *Beagle* returned on October 2, 1836, Darwin did not have a theory of evolution; rather, he had journals, notebooks, etchings, correspondence, and trunks of specimens. He had abandoned fixity of species along with the Genesis account of creation and perhaps his own faith,[4] but had no mechanism for the sketches of mutable lineages that he drew. He had pictures of trees with limbs that in turn branched, but no mechanism for the branching. In the *Origin*, he wrote:

> The affinities of all the beings of the same class have sometimes been represented by a great tree. I believe this simile largely speaks the truth. The green and budding twigs may represent existing species; and those produced during each former year may represent the long succession of extinct species. (Darwin [1859] 1958, 129)

Darwin's alighting upon a mechanism for the branching awaited another decisive event. In his *Autobiography*, he relates:

> In October 1838, that is, fifteen months after I had begun my systematic enquiry, I happened to read for amusement Malthus on *Population*, and being well prepared to appreciate the struggle for existence which everywhere goes on from long-continued observation of the habits of animals and plants, it at once struck me that under these circumstances favourable variations would tend to be preserved and unfavourable ones to be destroyed. The result of this would be the formation of new species. *Here, then, I had at last got a theory by which to work*; but I was so anxious to avoid prejudice, that I determined not for some time to write even the briefest sketch of it. (Darwin [1892] 1958, 42–43, emphasis added)

Darwin linked the Malthusian "struggle for existence" with the everyday knowledge of plant breeding and animal husbandry, whereby more bountiful plants and vigorous

---

3. On forerunners of Darwin, see McMullin (1985) and Mayr (1982, ch.7, 8).

4. In chapter 3 of his autobiography, Darwin describes his slow transition from youthful Unitarianism and simple Anglicanism through to agnosticism, concluding: "I gradually came to disbelieve in Christianity as a divine revelation. . . . I for one must be content to remain an Agnostic." (Darwin [1892] 1958, 62, 66)

animals are artificially produced, to produce his own Theory of Evolution by Natural Selection. In this, there are random small, inherited changes in a species (varieties), and nature preserves those variations that are advantageous in a particular environmental niche or habitat; and conversely, nature eliminates original types, or variations, that are injurious in the circumstance. Darwin's own "big book" on the subject was published in 1859 as *The Origin of Species* (Darwin [1859] 1958).[5]

To Darwin's dismay, Herschel rejected the theory because he could not believe that anything so random and undirected as natural selection could result in such complicated and finely attuned living things as primates and, of course, Homo sapiens. Herschel was convinced that there must be some cosmic intelligence involved. Whewell, an Anglican priest and theologian, as well as a philosopher, thanked Darwin for sending him the book, commending all of the facts, but politely rejected the theory. So, initially, did Lyell, who said that the geologic column did not allow the sufficient millions of years required by the theory. Lord Kelvin rejected it, saying that if the sun had been burning away for Darwin's supposed millions of years, there would be no sun left. The choice was Darwin's theory or best contemporary thermodynamics. Kelvin chose the latter.

In the foregoing, and commonly, the expression "Darwin's theory" is used as a singular, but it needs to be understood as a plural. There was a range of evolution-related theories that Darwin held and an even wider range that was developed in his name. This constitutes Darwinism; at its core was Darwin, but its development was contested (Moore 1979). Ernst Mayr (1904–2005), a preeminent biologist and historian of biology, notes:

> Darwin was a great pioneer, a person with an exceptionally fertile mind, but like other fertile thinkers, he had considerable trouble sticking to a consistent "party line." On almost any subject he dealt with—and this includes almost all his own theories—he not infrequently reversed himself. (Mayr 1985, 756)

Mayr sees five different theories that, individually and in combinations, can be labeled, "Darwin's Theory": evolution as such, common descent, gradualism, multiplication of species, and natural selection.

Notwithstanding initial and continuing opposition from some scientists, philosophers, and theologians within forty years of the *Origin*'s publication and certainly after the 1900 rediscovery of Mendel's 1865 genetics work which provided a "missing link" in Darwin's account of inheritance, Darwinism—meaning Darwin's formulation trimmed here and there, and elaborated and refined in other respects—became the new normal in science and most other fields, even religion and theology (Kohn 1985). No one with any education could go back to a pre-Darwinian understanding

---

5. See contributions to Ruse and Richards (2009).

of the natural world. Among much else, the impact of Darwin on philosophy has been dramatic. After the *Origin*, most philosophers working in the fields of ontology, ethics, epistemology, philosophy of mind, metaphysics, political theory, and much else did so with full cognizance, whether supporting or rejecting of its arguments.[6]

Included below are selections from the Introduction and the Conclusion of the *Origin* (1859) and the important Introduction and Chapter 5 of *Descent and Selection* (second edition, 1874).

REFERENCES

Bowlby, John. 1990. *Charles Darwin: A New Biography*. London: Pimlico.

Darwin, Charles. (1839) 1958. *The Voyage of the Beagle [Journal of Researches]*. New York: Bantam Books.

———. (1859) 1958. *The Origin of Species*. New York: Mentor Books.

———. (1871) 1874. *The Descent of Man, and Selection in Relation to Sex*. Princeton, NJ: Princeton University Press.

Darwin, Erasmus. (1794–1796) 2009. *Zoonomia Or, the Laws of Organic Life*. Cambridge: Cambridge University Press.

Darwin, Francis. (1892) 1958. *The Autobiography of Charles Darwin and Selected Letters*. New York: Dover Publications.

Desmond, Adrian, and James Moore. 1992. *Darwin: The Life of a Tormented Evolutionist*. London: Penguin Books.

Herschel, John F. W. (1830) 2009. *A Preliminary Discourse on the Study of Natural Philosophy*. Cambridge: Cambridge University Press.

Hull, David L. 1973. "Charles Darwin and Nineteenth Century Philosophies of Science." In *Foundations of Scientific Method: The Nineteenth Century*, edited by R. N. Giere and R. S. Westfall, 115–132. Bloomington: Indiana University Press.

Jacob, Margaret C. 2000. "The Truth of Newton's Science and the Truth of Science's History: Heroic Science at Its Eighteenth-Century Formulation." In *Rethinking the Scientific Revolution*, edited by Margaret J. Osler, 315–332. Cambridge: Cambridge University Press.

Kohn, David, ed. 1985. *The Darwinian Heritage*. Princeton, NJ: Princeton University Press.

Mayr, Ernst. 1982. *The Growth of Biological Thought: Diversity, Evolution, and Inheritance*. Cambridge, MA: Harvard University Press.

———. 1985. "Darwin's Five Theories of Evolution." In *The Darwinian Heritage*, edited by David Kohn, 755–772. Princeton, NJ: Princeton University Press.

McMullin, Ernan. 1985. "Introduction: Evolution and Creation." In *Evolution and Creation*, edited by Ernan McMullin, 1–58. Notre Dame, IN: University of Notre Dame Press.

---

6. See Munz (1993) and Ruse (2006) chap.10.

Moore, James R. 1979. *The Post-Darwinian Controversies*. Cambridge: Cambridge University Press.

Munz, Peter. 1993. *Philosophical Darwinism: On the Origin of Knowledge by Means of Natural Selection*. London: Routledge.

Ospovat, Don. 1981. *The Development of Darwin's Theory: Natural History, Natural Theology and Natural Selection, 1838–1859*. Cambridge: Cambridge University Press.

Ruse, Michael. 1975. "Darwin's Debt to Philosophy: An Examination of the Influence of the Philosophical Ideas of John F. W. Herschel and William Whewell on the Development of Charles Darwin's Theory of Evolution." *Studies in History and Philosophy of Science* 6: 159–181.

———. 2006. *The Evolution-Creation Struggle*. Cambridge, MA: Harvard University Press.

Ruse, Michael, and Robert J. Richards, eds. 2009. *The Cambridge Companion to the "Origin of Species."* Cambridge: Cambridge University Press.

Schweber, Silvan S. 1985. "The Wider British Context in Darwin's Theorising." In *The Darwinian Heritage*, edited by David Kohn, 35–69. Princeton, NJ: Princeton University Press.

Sulloway, Frank J. 1985. "Darwin's Early Intellectual Development: An Overview of the *Beagle* Voyage (1831–1836)." In *The Darwinian Heritage*, edited by David Kohn, 121–154. Princeton, NJ: Princeton University Press.

Whewell, William. 1989. *Theory of Scientific Method*. Edited by Robert E. Butts. Indianapolis: Hackett Publishing Company.

The Origin of Species (1859)
Introduction

When on board H.M.S. *Beagle*, as naturalist, I was much struck with certain facts in the distribution of the inhabitants of South America, and in the geological relations of the present to the past inhabitants of that continent. These facts seemed to me to throw some light on the origin of species—that mystery of mysteries, as it has been called by one of our greatest philosophers. On my return home, it occurred to me, in 1837, that something might perhaps be made out on this question by patiently accumulating and reflecting on all sorts of facts which could possibly have any bearing on it. After five years' work I allowed myself to speculate on the subject, and drew up some short notes; these I enlarged in 1844 into a sketch of the conclusions, which then seemed to me probable: from that period to the present day I have steadily pursued the same object. I hope that I may be excused for entering on these personal details, as I give them to show that I have not been hasty in coming to a decision.

My work is now nearly finished; but as it will take me two or three more years to complete it, and as my health is far from strong, I have been urged to publish this Abstract. I have more especially been induced to do this, as Mr. Wallace, who is now studying the natural history of the Malay archipelago, has arrived at almost exactly the same general conclusions that I have on the origin of species. Last year he sent to me a memoir on this subject, with a request that I would forward it to Sir Charles Lyell, who sent it to the Linnean Society, and it is published in the third volume of the Journal of that Society. Sir C. Lyell and Dr. Hooker, who both knew of my work—the latter having read my sketch of 1844—honoured me by thinking it advisable to publish, with Mr. Wallace's excellent memoir, some brief extracts from my manuscripts.

This Abstract, which I now publish, must necessarily be imperfect. I cannot here give references and authorities for my several statements; and I must trust to the reader reposing some confidence in my accuracy. No doubt errors will have crept in, though I hope I have always been cautious in trusting to good authorities alone. I can here give only the general conclusions at which I have arrived, with a few facts in illustration, but which, I hope, in most cases will suffice. No one can feel more sensible than I do of the necessity of hereafter publishing in detail all the facts, with references, on which my conclusions have been grounded; and I hope in a future work to do this. For I am well aware that scarcely a single point is discussed in this volume on which facts cannot be adduced, often apparently leading to conclusions directly opposite to those at which I have arrived. A fair result can be obtained only by fully stating and balancing the facts and arguments on both sides of each question; and this cannot possibly be here done.

. . .

In considering the Origin of Species, it is quite conceivable that a naturalist, reflecting on the mutual affinities of organic beings, on their embryological relations, their geographical distribution, geological succession, and other such facts, might come to the conclusion that each species had not been independently created, but had descended, like varieties, from other species. Nevertheless, such a conclusion, even if well founded, would be unsatisfactory, until it could be shown how the innumerable species inhabiting this world have been modified, so as to acquire that perfection of structure and coadaptation which most justly excites our admiration. Naturalists continually refer to external conditions, such as climate, food, etc., as the only possible cause of variation. In one very limited sense, as we shall hereafter see, this may be true; but it is preposterous to attribute to mere external conditions, the structure, for instance, of the woodpecker, with its feet, tail, beak, and tongue, so admirably adapted to catch insects under the bark of trees. In the case of the mistletoe, which draws its nourishment from certain trees, which has seeds that must be transported by certain birds, and which has flowers with separate sexes absolutely requiring the agency of certain insects to bring pollen from one flower to the other, it is equally preposterous to account for the structure of this parasite, with its relations to several distinct organic beings, by the effects of external conditions, or of habit, or of the volition of the plant itself.

The author of the *Vestiges of Creation* would, I presume, say that, after a certain unknown number of generations, some bird had given birth to a woodpecker, and some plant to the mistletoe and that these had been produced perfect as we now see them; but this assumption seems to me to be no explanation, for it leaves the case of the co-adaptations of organic beings to each other and to their physical conditions of life, untouched and unexplained.

It is, therefore, of the highest importance to gain a clear insight into the means of modification and co-adaptation. At the commencement of my observations it seemed to me probable that a careful study of domesticated animals and of cultivated plants would offer the best chance of making out this obscure problem. Nor have I been disappointed; in this and in all other perplexing cases I have invariably found that our knowledge, imperfect though it be, of variation under domestication, afforded the best and safest clue. I may venture to express my conviction of the high value of such studies, although they have been very commonly neglected by naturalists.

Conclusion

When the views entertained in this volume on the origin of species, or when analogous views are generally admitted, we can dimly foresee that there will be a considerable revolution in natural history. Systematists will be able to pursue their labours as at present; but they will not be incessantly haunted by the shadowy doubt whether this or that form be in essence a species. This I feel sure, and I speak after experience, will be no slight relief. The endless disputes whether or not some fifty species of British brambles are true species will cease. Systematists will have only to decide (not that this will be easy) whether any form be sufficiently constant and distinct from other forms, to be capable of definition; and if definable, whether the differences be sufficiently important to deserve a specific name.

This latter point will become a far more essential consideration than it is at present; for differences, however slight, between any two forms, if not blended by intermediate gradations, are looked at by most naturalists as sufficient to raise both forms to the rank of species. Hereafter we shall be compelled to acknowledge that the only distinction between species and well-marked varieties is, that the latter are known, or believed, to be connected at the present day by intermediate gradations, whereas species were formerly thus connected. Hence, without quite rejecting the consideration of the present existence of intermediate gradations between any two forms, we shall be led to weigh more carefully and to value higher the actual amount of difference between them. It is quite possible that forms now generally acknowledged to be merely varieties may hereafter be thought worthy of specific names, as with the primrose and cowslip; and in this case scientific and common language will come into accordance. In short, we shall have to treat species in the same manner as those naturalists treat genera, who admit that genera are merely artificial combinations made for convenience. This may not be a cheering prospect; but we shall at least be freed from the vain search for the undiscovered and undiscoverable essence of the term species.

The other and more general departments of natural history will rise greatly in interest. The terms used by naturalists of affinity, relationship, community of type, paternity, morphology, adaptive characters, rudimentary and aborted organs, etc., will cease to be metaphorical, and will have a plain signification. When we no longer look at an organic being as a savage looks at a ship, as at something wholly beyond his comprehension; when we regard every production of nature as one which has had a history; when we contemplate every complex structure and instinct as the summing up of many contrivances, each useful to the possessor, nearly in the same way as when we look at any great mechanical invention as the summing up of the labour, the experience, the reason, and even the blunders of numerous workmen; when we thus view each organic being, how far more interesting, I speak from experience, will the study of natural history become!

A grand and almost untrodden field of inquiry will be opened, on the causes and laws of variation, on correlation of growth, on the effects of use and disuse, on the direct action of external conditions, and so forth. The study of domestic productions will rise immensely in value. A new variety raised by man will be a far more important and interesting subject for study than one more species added to the infinitude of already recorded species. Our classifications will come to be, as far as they can be so made, genealogies; and will then truly give what may be called the plan of creation. The rules for classifying will no doubt become simpler when we have a definite object in view. We possess no pedigrees or armorial bearings; and we have to discover and trace the many diverging lines of descent in our natural genealogies, by characters of any kind which have long been inherited. Rudimentary organs will speak infallibly with respect to the nature of long-lost structures. Species and groups of species, which are called aberrant, and which may fancifully be called living fossils, will aid us in forming a picture of the ancient forms of life. Embryology will reveal to us the structure, in some degree obscured, of the prototypes of each great class.

When we can feel assured that all the individuals of the same species, and all the closely allied species of most genera, have within a not very remote period descended from one parent, and have migrated from some one birthplace; and when we better know the many means of migration, then, by the light which geology now throws, and will continue to throw, on former changes of climate and of the level of the land, we shall surely be enabled to trace in an admirable manner the former migrations of the inhabitants of the whole world. Even at present, by comparing the differences of the inhabitants of the sea on the opposite sides of a continent, and the nature of the various inhabitants of that continent in relation to their apparent means of immigration, some light can be thrown on ancient geography.

The noble science of Geology loses glory from the extreme imperfection of the record. The crust of the earth with its embedded remains must not be looked at as a well-filled museum, but as a poor collection made at hazard and at rare intervals. The accumulation of each great fossiliferous formation will be recognised as having depended on an unusual concurrence of circumstances, and the blank intervals between the successive stages as having been of vast duration. But we shall be able to gauge with some security the duration of these intervals by a comparison of the preceding and succeeding organic forms.

We must be cautious in attempting to correlate as strictly contemporaneous two formations, which include few identical species, by the general succession of their forms of life. As species are produced and exterminated by slowly acting and still existing causes, and not by miraculous acts of creation and by catastrophes; and as the most important of all causes of organic change is one which is almost independent of altered and perhaps suddenly altered physical conditions, namely, the mutual relation of organism to organism,—the improvement of one being entailing the improvement or the extermination of others; it follows, that the amount of organic change in the fossils of consecutive formations probably serves as a fair measure of the lapse of actual time. A number of species, however, keeping in a body might remain for a long period unchanged, whilst within this same period, several of these species, by migrating into new countries and coming into competition with foreign associates, might become modified; so that we must not overrate the accuracy of organic change as a measure of time. During early periods of the earth's history, when the forms of life were probably fewer and simpler, the rate of change was probably slower; and at the first dawn of life, when very few forms of the simplest structure existed, the rate of change may have been slow in an extreme degree. The whole history of the world, as at present known, although of a length quite incomprehensible by us, will hereafter be recognised as a mere fragment of time, compared with the ages which have elapsed since the first creature, the progenitor of innumerable extinct and living descendants, was created.

In the distant future I see open fields for far more important researches. Psychology will be based on a new foundation, that of the necessary acquirement of each mental power and capacity by gradation. Light will be thrown on the origin of man and his history.

Authors of the highest eminence seem to be fully satisfied with the view that each species has been independently created. To my mind it accords better with what we know of the laws impressed on matter by the Creator, that the production and extinction of the past and present inhabitants of the world should have been due to secondary causes, like those determining the birth and death of the individual. When I view all beings not as special creations, but as the lineal descendants of some few beings which lived long before the first bed of the Silurian system was deposited, they seem to me to become ennobled. Judging from the past, we may safely infer that not one living species will transmit its unaltered likeness to a distant futurity. And of the species now living very few will transmit progeny of any kind to a far distant futurity; for the manner in which all organic beings are grouped, shows that the greater number of species of each genus, and all the species of many genera, have left no descendants, but have become utterly extinct.

The Descent of Man, and On Selection in Relation to Sex, Second Edition (1874)
Introduction

The nature of the following work will be best understood by a brief account of how it came to be written. During many years I collected notes on the origin or descent of man, without any intention of publishing on the subject, but rather with the determination not to publish, as I thought that I should thus only add to the prejudices against my views. It seemed to me sufficient to indicate, in the first edition of my *Origin of Species*, that by this work light would be thrown on "the origin of man and his history"; and this implies that man must be included with other organic beings in any general conclusion respecting his manner of appearance on this earth. Now the case wears a wholly different aspect. When a naturalist like Carl Vogt ventures to say in his address as President of the National Institution of Geneva (1869), *personne, en Europe au moins, n'ose plus soutenir la création indépendante et de tontes pièces des espèces*, it is manifest that at least a large number of naturalists must admit that species are the modified descendants of other species; and this especially holds good with the younger and rising naturalists. The greater number accept the agency of natural selection; though some urge, whether with justice the future must decide, that I have greatly overrated its importance. Of the older and honoured chiefs in natural science, many unfortunately are still opposed to evolution in every form.

In consequence of the views now adopted by most naturalists, and which will ultimately, as in every other case, be followed by other men, I have been led to put together my notes, so as to see how far the general conclusions arrived at in my former works were applicable to man. This seemed all the more desirable as I had never deliberately applied these views to a species taken singly. When we confine our attention to any one form, we are deprived of the weighty arguments derived from the nature of the affinities which connect together whole groups of organisms—their geographical distribution in past and present times, and their geological succession. The homological structure, embryological development, and rudimentary organs of a species, whether it be man or any other animal, to which our attention may be directed, remain to be considered; but these great classes of facts afford, as it appears to me, ample and conclusive evidence in favour of the principle of gradual evolution. The strong support derived from the other arguments should, however, always be kept before the mind.

The sole object of this work is to consider, firstly, whether man, like every other species, is descended from some pre-existing form; secondly, the manner of his development; and thirdly, the value of the differences between the so-called races of man. As I shall confine myself to these points, it will not be necessary to describe in detail the differences between the several races—an enormous subject which has been fully discussed in many valuable works. The high antiquity of man has recently been demonstrated by the labours of a host of eminent men, beginning with M. Boucher de Perthes; and this is the indispensable basis for understanding his origin. I shall, therefore, take this conclusion for granted, and may refer my readers to the admirable treatises of Sir Charles Lyell, Sir John Lubbock, and others. Nor shall I have occasion to do more than to allude to the amount of difference between man and the anthropomorphous apes; for Prof. Huxley, in the opinion of most competent judges, has conclusively shewn that in every single visible character man differs less from the higher apes than these do from the lower members of the same order of Primates.

Chapter V. On the Development of the Intellectual and Moral Faculties During Primeval and Civilised Times

The subjects to be discussed in this chapter are of the highest interest, but are treated by me in a most imperfect and fragmentary manner. Mr. Wallace, in an admirable paper before referred to, argues that man after he had partially acquired those intellectual and moral faculties which distinguish him from the lower animals, would have been but little liable to have had his bodily structure modified through natural selection or any other means. For man is enabled through his mental faculties "to keep with an unchanged body in harmony with the changing universe." He has great power of adapting his habits to new conditions of life. He invents weapons, tools and various stratagems, by which he procures food and defends himself. When he migrates into a colder climate he uses clothes, builds sheds, and makes fires; and, by the aid of fire, cooks food otherwise indigestible. He aids his fellowmen in many ways, and anticipates future events. Even at a remote period he practised some subdivision of labour.

The lower animals, on the other hand, must have their bodily structure modified in order to survive under greatly changed conditions. They must be rendered stronger, or acquire more effective teeth or claws, in order to defend themselves from new enemies; or they must be reduced in size so as to escape detection and danger. When they migrate into a colder climate they must become clothed with thicker fur, or have their constitutions altered. If they fail to be thus modified, they will cease to exist.

The case, however, is widely different, as Mr. Wallace has with justice insisted, in relation to the intellectual and moral faculties of man. These faculties are variable; and we have every reason to believe that the variations tend to be inherited. Therefore, if they were formerly of high importance to primeval man and to his ape-like progenitors, they would have been perfected or advanced through natural selection. Of the high importance of the intellectual faculties there can be no doubt, for man mainly owes to them his predominant position in the world. We can see that, in the rudest state of society, the individuals who were the most sagacious, who invented and used the best weapons or traps, and who were best able to defend themselves, would rear the greatest number of offspring. The tribes which included the largest number of men thus endowed would increase in number and supplant other tribes. Numbers depend primarily on the means of subsistence, and this, depends partly on the physical nature of the country, but in a much higher degree on the arts which are there practised. As a tribe increases and is victorious, it is often still further increased by the absorption of other tribes. The stature and strength of the men of a tribe are likewise of some importance for its success, and these depend in part on the nature and amount of the food which can be obtained. In Europe the men of the Bronze period were supplanted by a more powerful and, judging from their sword-handles, larger-handed race; but their success was probably due in a much higher degree to their superiority in the arts.

. . .

Natural Selection as affecting Civilised Nations.—In the last and present chapters I have considered the advancement of man from a former semi-human condition to his present state as a barbarian. But some remarks on the agency of natural selection on civilised nations may be here worth adding. This subject has been ably discussed by Mr. W. R. Greg, and previously by Mr. Wallace and Mr. Calton. Most of my remarks are taken from these three authors. With savages, the weak in body or mind are soon eliminated; and those that survive commonly exhibit a vigorous state of health. We civilised men, on the other hand, do our utmost to check the process of elimination; we build asylums for the imbecile, the maimed, and the sick; we institute poor laws; and our medical men exert their utmost skill to save the life of every one to the last moment. There is reason to believe that vaccination has preserved thousands, who from a weak constitution would formerly have succumbed to smallpox. Thus the weak members of civilised societies propagate their kind. No one who has attended to the breeding of domestic animals will doubt that this must be highly injurious to the race of man. It is surprising how soon a want of care, or care wrongly directed, leads to the degeneration of a domestic race; but excepting in the case of man himself, hardly any one is so ignorant as to allow his worst animals to breed.

The aid which we feel impelled to give to the helpless is mainly an incidental result of the instinct of sympathy, which was originally acquired as part of the social instincts, but subsequently rendered, in the manner previously indicated, more tender and more widely diffused. Nor could we check our sympathy, if so urged by hard reason, without deterioration in the noblest part of our nature. The surgeon may harden himself whilst performing an operation, for he knows that he is acting for the good of his patient; but if we were intentionally to neglect the weak and helpless, it could only be for a contingent benefit, with a certain and great present evil. Hence we must bear without complaining the undoubtedly bad effects of the weak surviving and propagating their kind; but there appears to be at least one check in steady action, namely the weaker and inferior members of society not marrying so freely as the sound; and this check might be indefinitely increased, though this is more to be hoped for than expected, by the weak in body or mind refraining from marriage.

In all civilised countries man accumulates property and bequeaths it to his children. So that the children in the same country do not by any means start fair in the race for success. But this is far from an unmixed evil; for without the accumulation of capital the arts could not progress; and it is chiefly through their power that the civilised races have extended, and are now everywhere extending, their range, so as to take the place of the lower races. Nor does the moderate accumulation of wealth interfere with the process of selection. When a poor man becomes moderately rich, his children enter trades or professions in which there is struggle enough, so that the able in body and mind succeed best. The presence of a body of well-instructed men, who have not to labour for their daily bread, is important to a degree which cannot be over-estimated; as all high intellectual work is carried on by them, and on such work material progress of all kinds mainly depends, not to mention other and higher advantages. No doubt wealth when very great tends to convert men into useless drones, but their number is never large; and some degree of elimination here occurs, for we daily see rich men, who happen to be fools or profligate, squandering away their wealth.

Primogeniture with entailed estates is a more direct evil, though it may formerly have been a great advantage by the creation of a dominant class, and any government is better than anarchy. The eldest sons, though they may be weak in body or mind, generally marry, whilst the younger sons, however superior in these respects, do not so generally marry. Nor can worthless eldest sons with entailed estates squander their wealth. But here, as elsewhere, the relations of civilised life are so complex that some compensatory checks intervene. The men who are rich through primogeniture are able to select generation after generation the more beautiful and charming women; and these must generally be healthy in body and active in mind. The evil consequences, such as they may be, of the continued preservation of the same line of descent, without any selection, are checked by men of rank always wishing to increase their wealth and power; and this they effect by marrying heiresses. But the daughters of parents who have produced single children, are themselves, as Mr. Galton has shewn, apt to be sterile; and thus noble families are continually cut off in the direct line, and their wealth flows into some side channel; but unfortunately this channel is not determined by superiority of any kind.

Although civilisation thus checks in many ways the action of natural selection, it apparently favours, by means of improved food and the freedom from occasional hardships, the better development of the body. This may be inferred from civilised men having been found, wherever compared, to be physically stronger than savages. They appear also to have equal powers of endurance, as has been proved in many adventurous expeditions. Even the great luxury of the rich can be but little detrimental; for the expectation of life of our aristocracy, at all ages and of both sexes, is very little inferior to that of healthy English lives in the lower classes.

We will now look to the intellectual faculties alone. If in each grade of society the members were divided into two equal bodies, the one including the intellectually superior and the other the inferior, there can be little doubt that the former would succeed best in all occupations and rear a greater number of children. Even in the lowest walks of life, skill and ability must be of some advantage, though in many occupations, owing to the great division of labour, a very small one. Hence in civilised nations there will be some tendency to an increase both in the number and in the standard of the intellectually able. But I do not wish to assert that this tendency may not be more than counterbalanced in other ways, as by the multiplication of the reckless and improvident; but even to such as these, ability must be some advantage.

It has often been objected to views like the foregoing, that the most eminent men who have ever lived have left no offspring to inherit their great intellect. Mr. Galton says, "I regret I am unable to solve the simple question whether, and how far, men and women who are prodigies of genius are infertile. I have, however, shewn that men of eminence are by no means so. Great lawgivers, the founders of beneficent religions, great philosophers and discoverers in science, aid the progress of mankind in a far higher degree by their works than by leaving a numerous progeny. In the case of corporeal structures, it is the selection of the slightly better-endowed and the elimination of the slightly less well-endowed individuals, and not the preservation of strongly marked and rare anomalies, that leads to the advancement of a species. . . .

. . .

Natural selection follows from the struggle for existence; and this from a rapid rate of increase. It is impossible not bitterly to regret, but whether wisely is another question, the rate at which man tends to increase; for this leads in barbarous tribes to infanticide and many other evils, and in civilised nations to abject poverty, celibacy, and to the late marriages of the prudent. But as man suffers from the same physical evils with the lower animals, he has no right to expect an immunity from the evils consequent on the struggle for existence. Had he not been subjected to natural selection, assuredly he would never have attained to the rank of manhood. When we see in many parts of the world enormous areas of the most fertile land peopled by a few wandering savages, but which are capable of supporting numerous happy homes, it might be argued that the struggle for existence had not been sufficiently severe to force man upwards to his highest standard. Judging from all that we know of man and the lower animals, there has always been sufficient variability in their intellectual and moral faculties, for their steady advancement through natural selection. No doubt such advance demands many favourable concurrent circumstances; but it may well be doubted whether the most favourable would have sufficed, had not the rate of increase been rapid, and the consequent struggle for existence severe to an extreme degree.

BIBLIOGRAPHY

Blumenberg, Hans. 1987. *The Genesis of the Copernican World.* Cambridge, MA: MIT Press.

Bricker, Phillip, and R. I. G. Hughes, eds. 1990. *Philosophical Perspectives on Newtonian Science.* Cambridge, MA: MIT Press.

Cohen, H. Floris. 1994. *The Scientific Revolution: A Historiographical Inquiry.* Chicago: University of Chicago Press.

Cohen, I. Bernard. 1980. *The Newtonian Revolution.* Cambridge: Cambridge University Press.

Crombie, Alistair C. 1994. *Styles of Scientific Thinking in the European Tradition.* 3 vols. London: Duckworth.

D'Espagnat, Bernard. 2006. *On Physics and Philosophy.* Princeton, NJ: Princeton University Press.

Dilworth, Craig. (1996) 2006. *The Metaphysics of Science: An Account of Modern Science in Terms of Principles, Laws and Theories.* 2nd ed. Dordrecht: Kluwer Academic Publishers.

Duhem, Pierre. (1908) 1969. *To Save the Phenomena: An Essay on the Idea of Physical Theory from Plato to Galileo.* Chicago: University of Chicago Press.

Dupré, Louis. 2004. *The Enlightenment and the Intellectual Foundations of Modern Culture.* New Haven, CT: Yale University Press.

Dyksterhuis, Eduard J. 1986. *The Mechanization of the World Picture: Pythagoras to Newton.* Princeton, NJ: Princeton University Press.

Eldredge, Niles. 1995. *Reinventing Darwin: The Great Debate at the High Table of Evolutionary Theory.* New York: John Wiley & Sons.

Gaukroger, Stephen. 2010. *The Collapse of Mechanism and the Rise of Sensibility: Science and the Shaping of Modernity, 1680–1760.* Oxford: Clarendon Press.

Holmes, Richard. 2008. *The Age of Wonder: How the Romantic Generation Discovered the Beauty and Terror of Science.* London: Harper Press.

Holton, Gerald. 1973. *Thematic Origins of Scientific Thought.* Cambridge, MA: Harvard University Press.

Israel, Jonathan I. 2006. *Enlightenment Contested: Philosophy, Modernity, and the Emancipation of Man 1670–1752.* Oxford: Oxford University Press.

King, Margaret L., trans. and ed. 2019. *Enlightenment Thought: An Anthology of Sources.* Indianapolis: Hackett Publishing Company.

Kohn, David, ed. 1985. *The Darwinian Heritage.* Princeton, NJ: Princeton University Press.

Matthews, Michael R. 2015. *Science Teaching: The Contribution of History and Philosophy of Science*. New York: Routledge.

———. 2021. *History, Philosophy and Science Teaching: A Personal Story*. Dordrecht: Springer.

McMullin, Ernan, ed. 2005. *The Church and Galileo*. Notre Dame, IN: University of Notre Dame Press.

Outram, Dorinda. (1995) 2005. *The Enlightenment*. 2nd ed., New York: Cambridge University Press.

Sober, Elliot. 2019. *The Design Argument*. Elements in the Philosophy of Religion. Cambridge: Cambridge University Press.

Weinberg, Stephen. 2015. *To Explain the World: The Discovery of Modern Science*. London: Penguin Books.

Westfall, Richard S. 1971. *The Construction of Modern Science: Mechanisms and Mechanics*. Cambridge: Cambridge University Press.

Wootton, David. 2015. *The Invention of Science: A New History of the Scientific Revolution*. London: Penguin Random House.

CHRONOLOGY

Nicolaus Copernicus (1473–1543)

De Revolutionibus (*Six Books Concerning the Revolutions of the Heavenly Spheres*) (1543)

William Gilbert (1544–1603)

On the Magnet (1600)

Tycho Brahe (1546–1601)

The Nova Stella (1573)

Francis Bacon (1561–1626)

The New Organon (1620)

William Shakespeare (1564–1616)

Hamlet (1600); *Macbeth* (1606)

Galileo Galilei (1564–1642)

The Starry Messenger (1610); *The Assayer* (1623); *Dialogues Concerning the Two Chief World Systems* (1632); *Dialogues Concerning the Two New Sciences* (1638)

Johannes Kepler (1571–1630)

Harmonices Mundi (1619)

John Donne (1572–1631)

Devotions upon Emergent Occasions (1624)

William Harvey (1578–1657)

Anatomical Account of the Motion of the Heart and Blood (1628)

Thomas Hobbes (1588–1679)

Leviathan (1651)

Pierre Gassendi (1592–1655)

Disquisition Metaphysica (1644)

René Descartes (1596–1650)

Discourse on Method (1637); *Principles of Philosophy* (1644)

Robert Boyle (1627–1691)

The Skeptical Chymist (1661); *Of the Excellency and Grounds of the Corpuscular or Mechanical Philosophy* (1674)

John Ray (1627–1705)

The Wisdom of God Manifested in the Works of the Creation (1691)

Christiaan Huygens (1629–1695)

Horologium Oscillatorium (1673); *Treatise on Light* (written in 1678; published 1690)

Baruch de Spinoza (1632–1677)

A Theologico-Political Treatise (1670)

John Locke (1632–1704)

A Letter Concerning Toleration (1689); *An Essay Concerning Human Understanding* (1690)

Robert Hooke (1635–1703)

Micrographia (1665)

Isaac Newton (1643–1727)	*Mathematical Principles of Natural Philosophy* (1687); *Opticks* (1704)
Gottfried Wilhelm Leibniz (1646–1716)	*Discourse on Metaphysics* (1686); *Theodicy* (1710)
George Berkeley (1685–1753)	*Principles of Human Knowledge* (1710); *On Motion* (1721)
Voltaire (François-Marie Arouet) (1694–1778)	*Letters Concerning the English Nation* (1733); *Candide* (1759)
Émilie Du Châtelet (1706–1749)	*Fundamentals of Physics* (1740)
Carl Linnaeus (1707–1778)	*System of Nature* (1735)
David Hume (1711–1776)	*Inquiry Concerning Human Understanding* (1748); *Dialogues Concerning Natural Religion* (1779)
Jean-Jacques Rousseau (1712–1778)	*The Social Contract* (1762)
Denis Diderot (1713–1784)	*The Encyclopédie* (1751–1772); *Thoughts on the Interpretation of Nature* (1754)
Jean le Rond d'Alembert (1717–1783)	*Treatise on Dynamics* (1743)
Immanuel Kant (1724–1804)	*Critique of Pure Reason* (1781); *What Is Enlightenment?* (1784); *Metaphysical Foundations of Natural Science* (1786)
Joseph Priestley (1733–1804)	*Experiments and Observations on Different Kinds of Air* (1774); *Doctrines of Materialism and Philosophical Necessity* (1778)
William Paley (1743–1805)	*A View of the Evidence of Christianity* (1794); *Natural Theology* (1802)
Marquis of Condorcet (1743–1794)	*A Sketch for a Historical Picture of the Progress of the Human Mind* (1795)
Jean-Baptiste de Lamarck (1744–1829)	*Zoological Philosophy* (1809)
Mary Wollstonecraft (1759–1797)	*A Vindication of the Rights of Women* (1792); *An Historical and Moral View of the Origin and Progress of the French Revolution* (1794)
Thomas Robert Malthus (1766–1834)	*An Essay on the Principle of Population* (1798)
Charles Lyell (1797–1875)	*Principles of Geology*, three volumes (1831–1833)
John Stuart Mill (1806–1873)	*A System of Logic* (1843); *On Liberty* (1859)
Charles Darwin (1809–1882)	*The Origin of Species* (1859)